Segregated Sisterhood

Segregated Sisterhood

*Racism and the Politics
of American Feminism*

Nancie Caraway

The University of Tennessee Press

KNOXVILLE

Library of Congress Cataloging in Publication Data

Caraway, Nancie, 1942–
    Segregated Sisterhood : racism and the politics of American
feminism / Nancie Caraway.—1st ed.
            p.   cm.
    Includes bibliographical references and index.
    ISBN 0–87049–719–7 (cloth:alk. paper)
    ISBN 0–87049–720–0 (pbk.:alk. paper)
1. Feminism — United States — History.
2. Racism — United States — History.
3. United States — Race relations — History.
4. Afro-American women — History.
5. Feminist theory.
I. Title.
HQ1426.C247   1991
305.42'0973 — dc20   91–2528
                                          CIP

For Neil
Onipaʻa

Contents

Acknowledgments   ix

Introduction   *Voice, Representation, and Authority:*
Fragments on Speaking Difference   1

Part 1
Feminist Theory in the Flesh

Chapter 1   *"Other" Paradigms and Postcolonial*
Connections   25

Chapter 2   *The Cultural and Political Practices*
of Afrocentric Feminism   42

Chapter 3   *Bridging the (De)Constructions:*
Black Feminism and Feminist
Postmodernism   55

Part 2
Symbolic and Historical Flashpoints
of Otherness

Chapter 4   *Gender Tyranny: Coded Bodies,*
Femininity, and Black Womanhood   75

Chapter 5   *"Now I Am Here": Black Women*
and the First Wave of Feminism   117

Part 3
Conclusion

Chapter 6 *Crossover Dreams: Toward a Multicultural*
Feminist Politics of Solidarity 171

Notes 205

References 255

Index 275

Acknowledgments

Although this book is not about Hawai'i, it would not have been possible without the unique home Hawai'i has provided me for the past twenty years. Hawaiian culture, with its appreciation for *ho'omānoa*, that which is dense and "thickening" in human relationships, has provided a nurturing environment for the development of political consciousness. I want to thank the eclectic faculty of the Political Science Department at the University of Hawai'i for their part in stimulating my rebellious imagination and love of political theory.

To those committee members who began this intellectual journey with me when parts of *Segregated Sisterhood* were a dissertation — Manfred Henningsen, Deane Neubauer, Kathy Ferguson, Peter Manicas, Bob Cahill, and Belinda Aquino — I am grateful for their belief in me and their commitment to multicultural feminist theory. I was fortunate to benefit from Manfred Henningsen's learned interpretations of the tradition of political theory from the Greeks to the postmoderns. Not only was he sensitive to the feminist critique of the agonal, masculine citizen, but also his seminars provided a challenging arena to debate those issues. Professor Henningsen's very testiness endears him; his scholarly proddings and resolute resistance to the seductions of academic trends have taught me much about critical thought. Deane Neubauer's skill in recognizing future political scientists beneath the rough edges of energetic undergraduates put me on the path. I thank Bob Cahill for many compelling conversations about the spiritual and political dimensions of life in Hawai'i and about how *haoles* like ourselves might contribute.

The financial support provided me by the Norm Meller Dissertation Fellowship and the National Women's Studies Association Dissertation Award greatly advanced the project. My visit to the University of California–Berkeley as a Bain Affiliated Scholar in 1989 provided an invaluable research opportunity.

Cornel West's African-American spirit infuses the book. The long discussions we shared about political and intellectual radicalism, postcolonial discourse, and interracial praxis have been invaluable to me in writing the book. I hope some of the subversive joy about which he speaks is in evidence. I owe large debts to many feminist scholars who generously and critically commented on various stages of the manuscript. They may not recognize much of the final result, but their support, encouragement, and commitment to dialogue about racism and feminism are reflected in every page. Kathy Ferguson shared both her friendship and her talents as a feminist political theorist with me, as have Jean Elshtain, Christine Di Stefano, Joan Tronto, Shane Phelan, Kathy Jones, Farideh Farhi, and Christine White. Carolyn Di Palma sacrificed her own reading time to pore over every draft. For her witty and ironic footnote commentary, I am ever grateful.

I especially thank Eloise Buker for her many years of encouragement and her close critical reading of the introduction. And for many hours of dialogue about feminism and difference, I am grateful to Françoise Vergès. Her extraordinary Reunionnaise creole cuisine and hospitality in Berkeley during fall 1989 provided a dream setting for intellectual work (except for the earthquake!). Judith Stacey was generous in circulating my manuscripts; her support was a great spur for a new Ph.D. I can only marvel at the time, energy, and careful reading Bettina Aptheker gave to various drafts of the book. The personal attention she devoted to the project gave me the courage to include a historical chapter. Her generous spirit and commitment to interracial feminism literally made much of the book possible for me.

Many others offered penetrating critiques of the book as well as intellectual support for my work: Lata Mani, Ruth Frankenberg, Trinh T. Minh-ha, Ann Keppel, Renate Holub, Gwen Wood, Jerry Fleiger, Marshall Berman, James Early, Joseph Schwartz, George Hudes, George and Marguerite Simson, Aihwa Ong, Sandy Sturdevant, Kareda Henningsen, Michael Slackman, Ho'oipo De Cambra, Alice Chai, Ceigh Bree Watson, Emily Friedman, Barbara Christian, Susan Manuel, Dana Mollé, Pamela Caraway, Qiyamah Rahman, Anna McAnany, Hal and Shirley Abercrombie, and Margaret Randall. The competence and sunny dispositions of Sharon Shimamoto, Carole Keala Moon, and Vivian Piilani Luning often rescued me from the university bureaucracy; all three have provided nurturing contact through the years.

And to my personal *ohana* for constantly propping me up, feeding me, arguing with me, and honoring me with their friendship, an enduring appreciation. Kathryn Waddell Takara's poetry and friendship saved me more than once; watching Bonnie Berg rediscover her talent and feminist goals was equally empowering for me; Stephen and Julie Brigidi taught me to respect and care for animals and graced my walls with their luminous photographic images; Louis Herman's hikes, swims, and reggae nights often carried me through; Connie Rae and Danielle Kanoa Fisher, and Elisa and Catherine Hoapili Johnston have joyously made me both a sister and auntie; Laurie Johnston graciously provided me both an East Coast clipping service and a second home on Jones Street in Greenwich Village; Ti and Peter Manicas have sheltered and fed me superbly in both Atlantic and Pacific venues as the most loyal of friends; that pop-culture maven Bill Chaloupka taught me how to sneak movies and rock and roll into the "text" of political theory; Kathy Ferguson and Oren Kaimana took me snorkeling at just the right moment.

The energy and political daring of three young feminists reinvigorated me during the final stages of editing the book: filmmaker Jenny Lion, Native Hawaiian scholar J. Kehaulani Kauanui and Capitol Hill professional Sonia Lugmao.

Thanks to my colleagues in the Hawaii Rainbow Coalition for excusing me from so many meetings. For sustaining my soul throughout the years, I extend my thanks to Janis Joplin, Joe Cocker, Stevie Wonder, and, especially, Jimmy Cliff for taking me across the finish line.

My editor at the University of Tennessee Press, Tana McDonald, has been a skilled and charming long-distance interlocutor. I thank her for her belief in the book and the politics behind it. The superb copy-editing of Mavis Bryant and her concern for the enhancement of my readers taught me the value of detail. Freda Hellinger was the most patient of bibliographers.

There is no way to thank Dr. Amy Agbayani for bringing me to political life; she was there from the beginning, underwriting my intellectual and personal growth. To my Hawaiian mother, Auntie Aggie Cope, *mahalo nui loa*. My deepest thanks to my mother-in-law, Vera June Abercrombie, and to my own loving mother, Ellen Caraway. Without Vera and Ellen's ability to stretch themselves to understand an often driven and irascible daughter, the book could never have been written. Their lives gave me a rich education in feminist courage, intelligence, and daily acts of healing. The pawprints of Limu and Pua, animals who so intimately share my life, are present here too. The indomitable Neil Abercrombie was my energetic partner in every phase of this book and my most enthusiastic benefactor. Through wit, reflection, and discipline, he pushed me through. Neil, himself an exemplary model of solidarity, convinced me of the power of male feminism. Even in the midst of his own demanding Congressional campaign, Neil was an exuberant force. And fun.

Introduction

Voice, Representation, and Authority: Fragments on Speaking Difference

The understanding of difference is a shared responsibility which requires a willingness to reach out to the unknown.

Trinh T. Minh-ha

If my part is to tell you who I am, your part is to tell me who you are. You have to reach out to women unlike you, women who do not speak your language, and tell them your stories too.

Yolanda Tarango

I

This is a book about white racism in feminist theory and practice; it is also a meditation on the political conditions for a transformed multicultural feminist polity. I speak as a white feminist political theorist who has attempted to center my thinking in this book around the theoretical paradigms of Black feminism. The hybrid ensemble of "who I am" and how I came to a critical consciousness about racism is a necessary exploration to which I will return in the latter part of this introduction. The explorations in the following chapters arc in many directions and draw from diverse theoretical, historical, literary, and cultural sources. I speak with at least two voices: a rather distant "academic" voice which seeks to analyze the intellectual and historical practices of Black feminist theory and link them to contemporary directions in critical social theory and multicultural feminist discourse; and the agitated, engaged, and vulnerable personal voice of an antiracist feminist activist who has been both scarred and invigorated in the trenches of those difficult dialogues about difference, cultural pluralism, and identity.

I speak initially to other white feminists in a pedagogical vein, seeking to correct some of the knowledge gaps that historically have impeded our recognition and understanding of the vital dimensions of Black feminist activism and theoretical development. In the process, I have encountered and drawn upon the narratives of feminist women of color as well; I have tried not to assimilate those closely related but distinct discourses to my reading of Black feminist thought in reductive ways. Additionally, I view the book as part of my own strategy of intervention in the troubled authority of whiteness in feminist scholarship and politics. As such, this work is a response to the dictum of Malcolm X that whites ought first labor to subvert racist exploitation in their own communities. I have, however, an equally compelling personal stake in wanting to participate in our ongoing multicultural debates, positioning many of my reflections toward the broader audience of Black and other women of color. By creating the text and articulating some of the personal struggles that freed me to write it, I am trying to share my story with women of color, to tell them who I am. These expressions bear a special intensity for me. At times my voice no doubt will betray tones of ambiguity, timidity, impatience, and even frustration — when I am aiming most earnestly for clarity, confidence, and optimism. There is evidence both of my agreement with and critical resistance to some of the texts and ideas I engage. Donna Haraway has captured well for me the contradictions of this multicultural moment: "To be a subject with a sense of self in *complex complicity* with and *resistance to* the matrix of forces that made one possible."[1]

Drenched, as we all are in these postmodern days, with attitudes of contingency and contestability, throughout this project I have attempted to think nevertheless in terms of a provisional, but immanently possible, "we"— about a space of egalitarian feminist solidarity. This commitment has been my normative and interpretive core in approaching the volatile stories of segregated sisterhood. A second facet of writing this book concerned my own stamina and ability to remain politicized and to keep my eyes on the prize of my primary goal. How could I remain in the praxis circuit, given the dizzyingly decentered social universe portrayed by much contemporary cultural and social theory? How could my coalition-friendly, process-driven, theory of crossover multicultural feminism be sustained in the arid chambers of postmodern thought?

I needed first to learn to live theoretically with the tensions of attempting to think and act politically, given the reality of constantly constructed and deconstructed cultural meanings. Black feminism provided a crucially sustaining bridge discourse in this regard. The robust and profoundly centered allegiances which I found in the narratives of Black feminists, their Afrocentric affinities, helped me speak in a language which reflected both the political struggles of historically inscribed social agents, as well as insisted on the demystification of unitary categories of identity. This discourse gave me a highly politicized, critical framework — a feminist theory in the flesh[2] — that nourished, schooled, and connected my feminism to the emancipation projects of African Americans and other people of color. It reinforced the dialectical need for both negative and affirming analytical resources by critically promoting *politics*, that is, collective work toward social transformation. The paradigm of "feminist theory in the flesh" insists, though, on being open to the shifting formations of the folks who *do* politics, recognizing the densities of "selfhood." It encouraged me to ask: Aren't we all, then, inescapably "others of invention,"[3] socially, culturally, historically, and semiotically created social beings?

The central image I employ in the title of the book, "segregated sisterhood," seems to trip understanding, to invoke a paradox, to suggest a lack of coherence. In the logic of combining these two terms, each invalidates and cancels the other, rendering suspect the animating symbol — "sisterhood" — of a profoundly transforming social movement. White racism, of course, is the unseen signifier which tells us why and how it is that American feminism, in theory and practice, is a project which has segregated Black and white feminists and silenced the former. Structures of meaning, methods of inquiry, explanatory categories, and the less abstract "tools" of theoretical understanding — such as a language of women's pain, a drama of daily resistance — arose in the minds of middle-class white women with the resources to articulate a public feminist voice. Often innocently, we described what was before us with disastrous conceit, assuming that we were speaking for all of "us" in "sisterhood." Savage exclusions and over-reaching descriptions of common differences belied the mythology, foregrounding the limitations of those scripts. This book begins, therefore, with a call for alternative symbols and political principles to define our feminist polity. The "sisterhood" mythologized by white feminists has rarely been adequate to bear its rhetorical weight. And we all must live politically with those consequences. I posit in the conclusion more formal and democratic and less "organic" political representations of solidarity. But how do we find the space to begin again?

I hope to contribute to a dialogue about multicultural feminism as well as to demonstrate the dynamic capacity of feminist critique. I want to treat this growth process as an internal self-interrogation of feminist practices and politics — as a process which draws on the resources of feminist critique to lead us to less partial, more specific readings of feminist collectivities. Black and other feminist women of color are demanding accountability from a movement which has ignored their contributions to bringing it to life. They have challenged the existing stories of white feminism by asserting the details of their own personal landscapes and experiences. We are beginning to see dead air start to move.

What feminists are living through today is our own urgent moment of decolonization, our movement away from what Bettina Aptheker calls the "whitened center" which has historically described so much of American feminism. It is an important moment, I think, when things are necessarily and productively falling apart. It is a moment in the discursive and institutional life of feminist policital theory filled with both dread and a sense of exhilarating potential. What is at stake in terms of the highly contested debates over difference and the representation of feminisms is a recovery of the symbols of our political life. Such a project requires a somewhat contradictory ethos, the effects of which draw from a construction of something that might ironically be called "fragmented holism." Multicultural feminism thinks ironically in this regard, endorsing a politics which can envision and celebrate women's diversity and specificity — as well as teach us the *realpolitik* lesson that "fragmented agents" which don't congeal into "wholes" at certain strategic barricades likely will get vaporized. Readers familiar with feminist conversations about the strategies of "home" and coalition will recognize the mood here, which I expand upon in the concluding chapter. Feminist coalition theories sympathetic to the praxis of fragmented holism struggle to enact the "text" of politics in ways similiar to literary considerations described by Michelle Cliff: "My struggle to get wholeness from fragmentation while working within fragmentation, producing work which may find its strength in its depiction of fragmentation, through form as well as content."[4]

In part 1, under the conceptualization of "feminist theory in the flesh," I look at three dimensions of Black feminist theory: its affinity with postcolonial discourses; the terms of what contemporary Black feminist scholars are theorizing as Afrocentric feminism; and the politicized postmodern tendencies of Black feminist theory. Let me elaborate a bit on this framing. I have attempted to specify what I think points to "other" paradigms in feminist thought embodied in Black feminism, innovations which demonstrate a profound shift in the contours of existing white mainstream feminism. Black feminism has deconstructed the images, identities, presumptions, and methodology of hegemonic theory — not only androcentric world views but those of white feminism as well. The positive project of Black feminism validates and articulates the formerly submerged voices of Black women, affirming a rich history of resistance and of embeddedness in African-American cultural identities. My reading of Afrocentric feminism views this as an empowering, but not unproblematic, turn.

In another vital connection, Black feminists take their places alongside other hyphenated postcolonials in creating new epistemological and theoretical frontiers for politics and social theory. In their own anticolonial practices of revealing the incoherences and racism in white feminist theory, Black feminist theory exposes white feminist culpability in perpetrating against Black and other women of color many of the same ahistorical, essentialist effects of patriarchal ideology. When Audre Lorde declares, "Black feminism is not white feminism in blackface,"[5] she is calling attention to the homogenizing tendencies which have served to erase the particularity of black women's lives in white narratives. The oppositional stance which follows from Black feminism's status in that "disorderly polyphony"[6] emerging from decolonization invites us to recast our historical narratives, expand our vision, and bracket totalizing notions of sisterhood. Through these critiques, we can see how the static logic of representation which has wrongly rendered Black women or made them invisible does violence to the idea of sisterhood. Black feminist theory affords the kind of knowledge critical to our beginning to sort out the differences which make a difference. It cautions against ethnocentric theoretical mirrors in which only a single self-reflection is cast. It sensitizes us to the need for deep context which more concretely reflects the discrete lives and overlapping axes of oppression that that theory hopes to describe.

Black feminist discourse shatters white feminist illusions of inclusion, making way for new paradigms and political alternatives which bring into being previously silenced Diasporic subjectivities. We learn that feminists speak in different voices and from multiple historical, cultural, racial, economic, and sexual locations. We learn of the shaping power of overlapping allegiances and oppressions which intersect in often conflicting modes. And through Afrocentric cultural and spiritual values, enriched by collective rather than individualistic impulses, we can see our way to new political terrain which more deeply embodies the transformative and egalitarian goals of feminism. Black feminist theory in the flesh grounds us in the materiality of theorizing "a reality that one *cannot not know*," as Cornel West tells us, "the ragged edges of the Real, of Necessity, not being able to eat, not having shelter, not having health care."[7]

As an interpretive and conceptual motif, I have employed the term "deep context" to describe my own story of racial positioning as a white self. That meaning can be shifted to the language feminist women of color have employed, "theory in the flesh." This concept is, I hope to demonstrate in the first three chapters, emblematic of a cogent theoretical catalyst which can distill and hold in tension the most critical and compelling epistemological currents in contemporary social theory. I take as my generative text on feminist theory in the flesh the following mapping from Cherríe Moraga and Gloria Anzaldúa:

> A theory in the flesh means one where the physical realities of our lives — our skin color, the land or concrete we grew up on, our sexual longings — all fuse to create a politic born out of necessity. Here, we tempt to bridge the contradictions in our experience: We are the colored in a white feminist movement. We are the feminists among the people of our culture. We are often the lesbians among the straight. We do this bridging by naming our selves and by telling our stories in our own words.[8]

This concept holds the promise of giving rise to new horizons of feminist understanding, new strategies of resistance, new visions of social transformation, and new possibilities for eclectic and dynamic political subjectivities. Against the exclusivist structures of conventional feminist theory, feminist theory in the flesh signals critical challenges. For flesh-and-blood experiences, in Moraga and Anzaldúa's phrase, will drive the explanatory realms of theory, allowing the provocative images of difference to reveal themselves.

The analytical modes of Black feminist theory introduce us to a range of critical practices which position it at the interface of two important theoretical and epistemological projects — postcolonial discourse and feminist postmodernism. I argue in chapter 1 that the radical critique and demystifying potential of Black feminism's counter discourse parallels postcolonial theories of colonized otherness. In addition, I argue that Black feminist theory and feminist postmodernism share much critical insight about the dangers of universal categories, socially and discursively constructed identities, and circuits of gendered power tactically aligned in Enlightenment visions of "freedom." Black feminist theory, then, becomes a site where these discourses find a space in which, working in relation to one another, they can confront the ethical imperatives and political affinities at Black feminism's core.

What theoretical resources are brought to bear in this scenario? The iconoclastic nature of Black feminist theory makes its methodological creativity unique. The new paradigm formations that Black feminist theory reflects allow it to give voice to new forms of social explanation in a rich theoretical language which plays with a range of genres: poetic, artistic symbols from the cultural lives of Black women; self-ethnographies and everyday ethical formulations put forth by Black women themselves as "subjects" who set their own terms for "scientific" validity; as well as the more removed conventions of empirical theory-building. (This latter method evokes not deference from Black female communities but attitudes of healthy self-interest which say "Use social science when it helps, dump it when it's idiotic and oppressive.") These coordinates reflect a sparkling crossfertilization of many intellectual and cultural meanings. The shifting, contradictory ground upon which Black and other women of color "think" and define themselves — Moraga and Anzaldúa spelled out that context — means that theory needs to address myriad structural and cultural forms and be able to locate the sources of multiple assaults and pleasures.

I have attempted to employ the analytic skills of Black feminist theory and direct critique to: structure and agency; political economy and consciousness; theory and everyday life; and what Foucault has called (what Black women's embodied knowledge has "told" them since slavery) those "micropolitics of the body" surrounding race, gender, and sexuality. Black feminist theory calls attention to the social creation, the invention, of interpretive concepts, which, when institutionalized, serve to normalize and codify flesh and blood. As Diasporic peoples, Black feminists know that subjects are called into being within racially gendered ideologies and discourses which have defined and debased their humanity. In these observations, Black feminist theory reflects the critique of discourse analysis. But theory in the flesh reflects also genealogical and materialist[9] resources, taking us beyond the horizon of language and talk about talk, to historicized Afrocentric connections reflecting the collective memory of "daughters of a struggling people."[10]

These configurations, centered on Black feminist theory, engage a possibility suggested by Donna Haraway which arises in chapter 3. That the "acid tools of post-modernist theory and the constructive tools of ontological discourse about revolutionary subjects"[11] might be viewed as ironic allies, is a seductive but anxiety-producing proposition. I want to state my conviction that the acid tools badly need Black feminism's soul to save them from deracination. But we would be well advised to worry also about those purge impulses often found lurking in pure souls. What am I saying here in this *quid-pro-quo* mode?

I want to point out that my setting up this analytic coupling between Black feminism and feminist postmodernism is based on a celebration of the political vitality that Black feminist theory returns to feminist praxis and ethics. Black feminist theory should not be seen as a rescue mission for postmodernism. Even the language shifts required in our conversations about these projects clash, telling us something. Acid, for instance, is not the kind of metaphorical nourishment that would appeal to the sensibilities of many Black feminists. My assumption about what would and would not appeal to Black feminists certainly does not stem from any lack of appreciation for theoretical sophistication on the part of Black feminist theorists. On the contrary, they articulate brilliantly the deconstructive tone of what critical race scholar Patricia Williams calls "theory-magic." But Williams, along with other Black feminists, recognizes how theory-magic "has failed to make its words and un-words tangible, *reachable* and applicable" to those most needy in this society.[12] Black feminists come from a people that has sustained itself through spiritual as well as political tenacity.[13] They speak of a legacy of struggle, of which they feel very much a part, in animating languages which call forth witnesses, "prophecy deliverance,"[14] and practices capable of washing "away the shrouds of inanimate object status, so that we may say not that we own gold, but that a luminous golden spirit owns us."[15] The legal scholar Derrick Bell writes of the empowering milestones of Blacks' freedom struggles as "transcendent events" in American political history.[16] These expressions tell us that the "un-words" of social critique are inadequate to capture fully the roots of African-American political aspirations.

But this language of transcendence makes feminist postmodernists *very* uncomfortable. And perhaps for good reason. The acid folks warn us to be wary of redemptive projects, to be on the alert for the deadly hypocrisies of those who lead crusades or colonial "civilizing" campaigns. But Black feminism's very fleshiness motivates it to resist postmodernism's antihumanist sensibilities and shows what is at stake if we abandon all of those "lists of no longer possibles (realism, representation, subjectivity, history . . .)."[17] Haraway surely teaches us something, however, in her "ironic allies" formulation. Because, as I have argued, Black feminist theory's powerful deconstructive displacements of white feminist theory are one of its most valuable strategies, the critical moment must not be abandoned. In those critical moves, Black feminism performs a vital Marxian function, it stands white feminism on its head. And, importantly, it does this headstanding in a fashion which is now being acknowledged by white practitioners of feminist theory who gain knowledge from these acrobatics. The postmodern context has, in fact, provided a stance from which white feminists have engaged the criticisms Black feminist theorists have directed at existing assumptions about "woman" and "oppression." Once white feminists have been stood on our heads by such critiques, postmodernism has provided one provisional, tentative space from which to speak about the issues Black feminists have raised. As we shall see, this conjoining of Black feminist theory and postmodernism highlights contradictions and dichotomies invisible within each's conceptual scheme.

I have attempted to explore the potential of each project to serve as a countervailing influence and power-sensor for the other. This coupling can also provide valuable feminist readings about who "we" are and what feminism can "mean" in postmodernist times. Are political intensifications enhanced or hindered by the convergence of Black feminist theory and postmodernism? Do current postmodernist debates facilitate or hinder our efforts to broaden feminist theory in the direction of postcolonial Black feminist imperatives? How does the emphasis on metatheory and epistemology serve collective action against white supremacy in feminism? Whose interests are served and which modes of speaking obtain in the often rarified forms of literacy required to engage in postmodern knowledge talk? Such questions will inform the discussions in chapter 3.

These are a few of the explorations into Black feminist theory which I wish to articulate more fully in part 1. In chapter 1 I shall be more specific about the kinds of paradigm rethinkings suggested by Black feminist theory. This discussion will more fully situate Black feminist theory in the frame of postcolonial political sensibilities, while leading us in chapter 2 to a consideration of the new Afrocentric feminist theories and epistemological challenges being formulated by contemporary Black feminist scholars. At this point, however, I want further to clarify the implications of my attempt to contextualize Black feminist theory in the debates within contemporary social theory. I wish to avoid contributing to what Anthony Appiah has called the "Naipaul fallacy"— the tendency of colonial subjects too eager to establish the legitimacy of native projects by showing its similarity with the colonizer's master discourse.[18]

I have not intended to characterize Black feminism in a defensive posture, in an attempt to "prove" its intellectual legitimacy by attaching it to "larger" philosophical issues. My aim is to concretize Black feminism's creative contributions to the emerging "network of feminist multicultural discourse."[19] The radical critique and demystifying potential of Black feminism's *counterdiscourse* subverts and obviates in highly politicized and historicized ways the contradictions and problems found in liberal humanist thought and in mainstream white feminist theory, as well as in various strands of postmodernism, including feminist postmodernism. I have tried to evaluate Black feminist theory in terms of its own logics, read across the critiques and points of similarity of postmodern attitudes. As Black feminists have demonstrated, many of the oppositional practices some white feminists now deferentially trace to European white phallocratic theories are embedded in the oppositional strategies of ordinary Black women. These groundings embody opportunities for alternative conceptualizations of what "theoretical knowledge" might be, as well as provide ways to rethink the workings of agency, consciousness, and political activism. In aligning themselves with Diasporic others emerging from the residues of colonialism, Black feminists know that they live in a world, as do we all, which often demands the bracketing of fragmented selves, demands the deliberate political fictions of "whole" identities mobilized in a united front. They cannot, nor can any of us, afford to jettison those attributes of humanist discourse which give life to revolutionary subjects and radical actions. The theoretical analyses in part 1 elaborate on the potential for a positive "post-humanist conception of human agency."[20]

Part 2 focuses on certain symbolic and historical flashpoints of otherness between white and Black women. Chapter 4 interprets the symbolic construction of ideologies of gender, femininity, and beauty as they have differently subordinated Black and white women. I attempt to highlight those symbolic practices rooted in white ideals of beauty which have served to create in the minds of Black women a sense of inferiority and a psychology of shame. I inquire into those scenarios and rituals in the relationships of Black and white women which have contributed to the infantilization of bourgeois white women and intensified Black women's sense of personal degradation. The realm of household domestic labor placed Black women as menials and servants in positions of subordination to white mistresses. And I also consider the sexual violation of the Black female's body during slavery. The explication of gender tyrannies leads to a consideration of emerging feminist aesthetics within multicultural feminism around the politics of appearance. What models of beauty, desire, and cultural identity are being played with? What "politically correct" judgments are deployed around these alternative images? The force of this chapter is an appreciation of the empowering affirmation of diverse conceptions of "beauty" and racial pride voiced by Black feminists.

Chapter 5 is a historical snapshot which traces the brutal referents of segregated sisterhood in the nineteenth-century first wave of feminism. I look first at the breakdown of alliances between Black and white women in the white-dominated suffrage movement, highlighting the racist betrayals and exclusions of white feminist pioneers. I criticize the white solipsism of certain white feminist histories of this founding period, histories which ignored the theoretical and practical contributions of nineteenth-century Black women to feminist radicalism. My historical rereading displaces the comforting image of an originary "sisterhood." It was in the first wave of feminism that the battle for hegemony over feminist discourse itself arose. Which women and which practices would be defined as "feminist" in this historical configuration? What priorities and strategies were enacted to contest the race and gender barriers which arose to prevent democratization in this expectant period of the American republic? What broad coalitions for human rights were advanced during Reconstruction, and what caused their breakdowns? And, importantly, how do contemporary feminists assess the contested examples of early feminist practice? I argue that the legacy of solidarity embedded in the texts and actions of first-wave Black feminists provides a vital recovery of meaning. Passionately theorizing a politics which upheld women's collective efforts toward "justice, simple justice," in Frances Harper's phrase, despite the systematic betrayals of organized white suffragists, Black feminist intellectuals provide us the legacy to construct a new feminist public memory. This discussion emphasizes the necessity for white feminists to acknowledge and learn from the historical failures. We bear the burden of reconciling both emancipation and shame in this first-wave experiment. Absent such accountability, our efforts to build affinities will continue to be haunted by ghosts we cannot name.

I conclude in chapter 6 by engaging a playful and politically valuable metaphor which I hope can contribute to a more egalitarian feminist polity: crossover multicultural feminism. Some of the postmodern themes about difference and the constitution of subjectivity resurface in the context of a critique of identity politics. Through an alchemical reading of Bernice Johnson Reagon and Sweet Honey in the Rock, I put some tension into notions that oppressed women of color are bearers of coherent "identities," by problematizing the analytical grid of margins and centers. I point to the coercive potential of certain exclusionary practices and assumptions within the "oppositional identities" of women of color. This is an especially power-sensitive discussion, in which I contest modes of thought which offer stereotypical portraits of both women of color and white feminists. The assumption of an all-knowing generic "average Third-World woman of color" is a Manichean reversal which simply flips the errors of the generic "privileged racist white woman." I foreground some texts which demonstrate evidence of ethnocentrism in attitudes and acts of women of color.

By emphasizing the power dimensions of oppression within oppression, I do not mean to minimize white racism or white feminist accountability, but rather to insist on intellectual and political practices which are critically self-reflexive. Only when we admit to and reflect upon both the exclusionary and inclusionary actions of both women of color and white feminists, can we begin creatively to build trust and new collectivities. Audre Lorde here provides the requisite text when she asks, "What woman here is so enamored of her own oppression that she cannot see her heelprint upon another woman's face. What woman's terms of oppression have become precious and necessary to her as a ticket into the fold of the righteous, away from the cold winds of self-scrutiny."[21]

My "assessment of the damage" in the concluding discussion sets, I hope, an agenda appropriate to the lively coalition debates within multicultural feminism. (I should make the point here that white feminists, of course, are both "multi" and "multicultural," just as are those infinitely diverse women included in the term "women of color.") Crossover feminists, never pure in genre and always hyphenated, come together strategically, building upon solidarity, not sisterhood; they can, however, retreat to more affectively congenial "homes" for repair and empowerment. Mindful of the conformity demanded by organicist communities, such feminists, when they do cross over, opt for more socially modest, mediated, but immanently democratic structures for doing politics. Process-freaks and justice-driven, crossover feminists are committed to acts of translation, assuring that one another's stories and struggles be shared and advocated as democratic equivalences.

These scenarios are played as political theory seminars where the "we" gets defined, contextualized, and acted upon. Crossover feminist coalitions encourage experimentation and radical pluralism. The "unassimiliated others"[22] congregated there need to be long on patience, stamina, generosity. Not impossible, surely. But as Bernice Reagon has convivially warned us, it's *very* rough going. But crossover multicultural feminists are, if anything, loquacious to a high degree, *and political*. Their high-spirited commitment to the raggedness of doing politics can be contagious, however, stimulating the rest of us to take the risk of seeing the other "as a bridge toward syncretic possibility."[23]

II

As an interpreter, critic, and analyst of the work of Black feminists, I locate myself on precarious ground. What authority, what experiences, or what consciousness has brought me to speak? My voice is, after all, a white voice—a fact which implicates me in the racist history of segregated sisterhood. Throughout the process of writing the book, I have been aware of and tried to avoid three traps: the role of cipher in appropriating and "building my resume" on the words and experiences of Black feminists; the hubris which comes from any practice of representation; and the tendency to romanticize or simply to validate the discourse and practices of Black feminists. I worried about the climate for white feminist critique. Had the accumulated weight of racist history and *ressentiment* foreclosed honest interracial dialogue? Would tolerance for my white cultural blunders be forthcoming from women of color? These were some of the questions I asked myself. My apprehensions existed in the shadow of bell hooks' words, which haunted me:

> Black people often look at ourselves, through eyes that are unable to recognize us. We are not represented as ourselves but seen through the lens of the oppressor, or the radicalized rebel who has broken ideologically from the oppressor but still envisions the colonized through stereotypes not yet understood or relinquished.[24]

I was not sure that I did not inadvertently shelter such stereotypes. I also knew that the option of silence was not available; that, as Audre

Lorde has taught us, silence would not protect us. But how could I avoid the colonizing tendencies to which the interpreter role tends? What "voice" could I use? No reassurances, of course, were available. There was always the chance, too, that my words would be viewed as racist, arrogant, illegitimate. The fears remained, forcing me to examine both my scholarly motives to help educate myself and other white feminists, as well as my own visceral reactions and anger over the interracial tensions erupting around me. I think it's important to spell out some of the intellectual and emotional artifacts which moved me.

I began to think about the possibility of writing the book, the kernel of which began as a dissertation I was writing at the University of Hawai'i, by focusing not so much on the political outlines of the grievous chasms of difference which separated me from women of color — that was too daunting — but in terms of story sharing and "talk story." Talk story is a rich Native Hawaiian practice of community-building and speech taught me by the women of the Waianae Women's Support Group in rural O'ahu.[25] Feminism always has tried to posit the possibility that women could communicate their life-worlds and that the force of such stories could diminish some of the many differences between us. Few of us today can evoke that ethos with much certainty; in fact, poor and women of color have always known the fallacy of this feminist hope. I kept on, however, building on the story idea.

Trinh T. Minh-ha's feminist cultural critiques carried me in this direction. She opens her text *Woman Native Other* with a notion of "our" story. It "circulates like a gift," she writes, "an empty gift which anybody can lay claim to by filling it to taste, yet can never truly possess. A gift built on multiplicity."[26] I liked the open-ended implications of Trinh's formulation, the notion that no woman's "experience" reflected an ontological privilege or was more "politically correct" than any other's. I had seen how the cachet of "some oppressions are more authentic than others" enabled divisive hierarchies. I thought the chances for principled affinities between differently located women would be enhanced if we acknowledged the arbitrariness of our "selves" and "experience," acknowledged that, as Trinh writes,

Whether I accept it or not, the natures of I, i, you, s/he, We, we, they and wo/man constantly overlap. They all display a necessary ambivalence, for the line dividing I and Not-I, us and them, or him and her is not (cannot) always (be) as clear as we would like it to be. Despite our desperate, eternal attempt to separate, contain and mend, categories always leak.[27]

Trinh's framing of the protean mosaic of women's "stories," with no one "identity" claiming megastatus, opened up space. But if I were to honor the reciprocal challenge to tell my story, I needed to start with the paralysis I often felt and the rage I imagined would be directed at me — as the repository of "white racism"— by women of color. I felt urges toward self-erasure. The metaphors given by the South African poet and novelist Breyten Breytenbach in his 1985 essay, "The South African Wasteland," felt very familiar to me. His words helped me to understand why I was blocked, unable to "tell my story." He wrote about the ambivalent status of the white writer:

The situation being extraordinarily complex, the writer if he [sic] really wants to write . . . must face the splitting of the mind, the supping with the devil, the writing in dribbles from the corner of the mouth, but also the exhilarating challenge of rising to the need. But how? We don't even speak the same meanings . . . yet we all speak the same words seen through different prisms of ache. . . . As for the whites, despite the fact that some of them, some of us, are passionate observers. . . . we are alienated, marginalized, depoliticized, irrelevant.[28]

Breytenbach invites other whites to participate (even in their split, dribbling condition) in his probings about apartheid, to speak about their own racist miasma. Fear sometimes made me see myself in his description of the white writer, alienated, irrelevant, thinking that I would not be able to "exhilaratingly," as he says, rise to the challenge of being accountable for a racist feminist history. I had not then fully understood nor comprehended the *social construction* of "whiteness" as I had of Blackness. I had reified and entrapped myself within a rigid "white" identity, which is one of the ways guilt depoliticizes us by instilling a sense of fatalism. The work of Michael Omi and Howard Winant came as a theoretical gift to me during the research for the book. They taught me that "race" overflows the boundaries of skin color and that we ought to recognize the racial dimensions in *every* identity. White identities included. Especially white identities. The knowledge that "whiteness" functioned at a structural level (beyond individual intentionality) as an ideology which I might, albeit "white," contest, speak about, and struggle against was vital to me. "To challenge the position of Blacks in society," Omi and Winant write, "is to challenge the position of whites."[29]

Such an awareness motivated me to know that I could subvert what Fanon called "the all-white truth" of my life. This milestone, plus my encounter with Minnie Bruce Pratt's extraordinary essay, "Identity: Skin Blood Heart," further compelled me.[30] I shared similar geographical roots with Pratt; we were both white, Christian-born southern women struggling with the crucible of white racism, although my working-class origins meant that we grew up in different material worlds. Pratt recreated for me a sense of my own trauma of homelessness and gave me a framework for beginning to transcend the engulfment I was feeling. The integrity with which she framed her project validated the need for my own explorations.

I began to think through the screen of memory about growing up in Alabama. I could not seem to reconcile the extremes of personality I found in family members whom I loved very much. Where did the racist streak of mean-spirited intolerance and sullen hatred come from in such otherwise fun-loving, generous, and caring people? Old scenarios kept recurring in my mind: instances of territorial prerogatives about who really "belonged" in our small home town. Not the Black citizens or their children. Vicious asides were directed at me from family members about how repulsive they found the sight of Black skin. I read these as deliberate goadings intended to start arguments with me; branding whites who were supportive of and sympathetic to Black personhood with the vile epithet "nigger-lover" was standard southern practice.

I began also to think about my aunt's high-spirited, loving, and always-ready-to-serve-me Black maid and about how my childhood visits during summer vacation had posed an added burden of ironing, cooking, and cleaning on her. Of course, she never complained to me. From my point of view, we had a special bond, an emotional closeness. In all my childhood dreams she is there, as are our attempts at birthday-cake making, fishing trips to the lake, butter-bean shelling. Masks, I didn't know of as a child; nor did I know the resentment that must have coexisted alongside her affection for me. I had never, could never have, "compensated" her for that care. Had I "thanked" her, I kept asking myself? A recent financial gift to her didn't take away my anxiety.

I am not exactly sure how or when I concluded that I could, or should, write the book; perhaps it was due to the provocative anti-racist feminist conferences I had been attending on the U.S. mainland, or the encounters and debates on racism I observed and participated in with my students in Hawai'i, or the personal questioning. I became aware of certain debilitating patterns which I saw developing in myself and other white feminists as we attempted to frame responses to racism. I wrote in my journal after reading Pratt, warning myself against unproductive and pathological compensations for the loss of self and animus toward my own culture:

> Avoid purely therapeutic guilt "feelings" which displace political action. Avoid the white woman's need for absolution which becomes yet another burden for the oppressed to alleviate. Avoid the rejection of one's tainted "self" which leads to desires of becoming "the pure other" through acts of cultural impersonation. Avoid the sense of dread that no positive politics could come of such fragmentation, ambivalence, guilt.

At some point, though, I began to be uncomfortable with the stereotype of "white woman's privilege" and began to resist my image as a *de facto* bearer of benefits, as that pampered icon, the Middle-Class White Feminist. Hadn't I myself always felt marginal, an outsider, in the world of the academy in which I had fought so hard to "pass"? I came from what social workers now classify as a "dysfunctional" working-class southern family, one which as child and adult I often experienced as coarse and brutal. I was the first in my extended family to graduate from college. That latter goal had been underwritten by financial-aid loans, not family largesse, and these now demanded to be paid. I still burn with anger and regret that my high school counselor in Houston, Texas, never suggested that I apply for a scholarship "to a good school," never encouraged me to stretch my academic horizons. I envied "the popular girls" in high school whose parents were able to participate in PTA meetings and school activities, who were picked up in cars after school to be taken to dance class and private swim clubs. They were so "respectable" and "normal."

Riding the bus home at night from my dead-end secretarial job in Houston, where my parents and I had moved, I thought of others in my class who had "gone away" to college. I resented having had to drop out after one semester to work; I resented losing the decade I spent working as a secretary instead of attending college. I was not the kind of woman then for whom it came "naturally" to read *The New York Times*, the intellectual kind of white woman about whom Truman, Alice Walker's Black male protagonist in *Meridian*, fantasized.

After marriage and a move to Hawai'i, I finally was able to return to college, but with great anxiety. Without the intellectual security and confidence derived from growing up in a family which takes educational success as its natural entitlement, I always feared the moment when "they," my professors and fellow graduate students in Hawai'i, would "find me out." They would realize that a woman in her forties like me, from an Alabama "hick town," really didn't "belong there." For a long time I agreed. I felt at times like a mass of liabilities struggling to "catch up," an identity which the books and "stolen knowledge" only partially salved.[31] I abhor whining and self-pity, and even now I can work through the hostility these remembrances evoke only to establish what I argue in this book is essential to multicultural feminist theory: the need to specify *the deep context of our lives.*

Don't misunderstand my point here. That white feminists have mis-spoken, mis-represented, and ignored the deep context of the lives of women of color is only half the logic I'm getting at. I'm thinking about the reverse practice of creating false images of white women as well. When I think back over my hard-won feminist politicization, I dare anyone to shut me in the bloodless, airless tomb of "privileged white woman." Yet I see behaviors and discourses which attempt to do just that. In arguing this, my aim is not to minimize the theoretical and political urgency of struggling against white supremacy in feminism and the world. I am not attempting naively to "wish away" the discomfort which comes from conflict and confrontation. What I wanted to say to women of color is that stereotyping works both ways: What you see as "me" often is not what is "really" there, or at least not *all* that is there. I wanted to insist that the phrase "privileged women" or "women of the dominant classes" can in many cases be applied to women of color.

If Luce Irigaray's project engages in a powerful "jamming" of the patriarchal discursive machinery, can't we engage in our own jamming of feminist certainties about identities and privileges and learn to circulate, even celebrate, one another's stories?[32] Would a prerequisite for such a scenario of story-sharing mean everyone telling their story to everyone else? Would that then free me, and us, to make coalitions in which we *all* would have to deal with each other's baggage, as Bernice Reagon says? Why can't all of us declare in some vital way, "I am a whole circus by myself. . . . We know different things."[33]

Jamming hegemonic identities of Americanness is precisely the project Maxine Hong Kingston set for herself in her ribald and fiercely angry novel, *Tripmaster Monkey*. I found in her story a congenial echo of themes I develop in my concluding chapter about crossover coalition politics and the working out of democratic equivalences to understand one another's otherness. When I read *Tripmaster Monkey*, I, in my white skin, connected so powerfully with her protagonist Wittman Ah Sing's jeremiad against white supremacist America, that the pronouns of "his" discourse dissolved and became mine (speaking to the classist patriarchy).

This line of analysis is not without problems. Given that Black and other feminist women of color have insisted on defining and articulating their own subjectivity ("I"), would I then be short-circuiting or twisting Hong Kingston's archly detailed portrayal of Chinese-American autonomy and subjectivity if "I" also owned it? I don't think so. The novelist doesn't trade in imaginative private property. On the contrary, the novelist invites us all into the story. To the extent that the reader feels estranged rather than absorbed by the story, we would say that the novelist has not succeeded. That approach freed me to simply blend, as an alter-ego, into Ah Sing's wild consciousness.

In the last chapter of Hong Kingston's book, he wrests his American identity and subjectivity from white America. He invents his own Chinese-American "I" in a brilliant political performance which enacts chiseled, uniquely drawn, unmistakably-his-own *American* identity. Much as feminists of color are demanding recognition of their specificity, Ah Sing the playwright explodes hoary Orientalisms by demanding that his theatrical pieces be symbolized as *totally* American. "There is no East here. West is meeting West. This was all West. All you saw was West. This is the Journey *In* the West."[34]

Ah Sing's message is about a *new* America, one I thought great for feminism: multicolored, multicultural, multilinguistic — *tolerant and liking it* — peopled by folks possessing a militant sense of self-definition and the ability to cross over boundaries and see and be committed to new plural political subjects. "When I speak my mind," Wittman says:

> I spill my guts, I want to be understood, I want to be answered . . . [they] are cutting off our balls linguistically. . . . They depict us with an inability to say 'I.' They're taking the 'I' away from us. 'Me'— that's the fucked over, the fuckee. 'I'— that's the mean-ass motherfucker first-person pronoun of the active voice, and they don't want us to have it.[35]

Hong Kingston closes the book by putting in Wittman's mouth a gloriously sparse but profound aria.

> I. I. I.
> I. I. I.
> I. I. I.[36]

Can you think of a better paradigm for not taking racism, sexism, classism, homophobia, regionalism, ageism, normally-abledism? Hong Kingston's kind of in-your-face militance is a manifesto for all of us who fight for our voices, culture, presence. "We" can read her story of Ah Sing's "Chinese American coming to voice," appreciate it, *and* translate it into our own equivalent "I." Use its power for ourselves. Hong Kingston's story rubs our noses in those hidden injuries of race/region/ class felt by Chinese-Americans, thrusts us into a world in which we may never have been before. As was her design, every *Chinese American* detail was carefully constructed, a huge head projected on a big screen so that we could scrutinize each *Chinese American* detail — as Ah Sing goads his audience to do with his own profile. Look at my Chinese face, eyes, body, hair, he says. It is a "perfect American face," he insists. If we feminists can't do that in our own stories without fear of appropriation, then, as Barbara Christian asks, "Why read?" All of this, of course, is clouded by the always already ambiguous act of translation. Perhaps when our interpretive skills falter in translating one another's stories, as they surely will, we can fall back on other practices from the discourse of justice — a potential to which I return in chapter 6.

III

My scholarly voice in the book does assume a privileged analytical stance with respect to the politics, history, and cultural practices of the Black feminists whose texts I have considered. They, for the most part, have been my teachers. I defend this privilege as a knowledge project to be modified, criticized, and clarified by vigorous others. To bell hooks, I do seek to situate myself and my politics within the rubric of the "radicalized rebel." And I have chosen to speak without resolving the contradictions of my whiteness. From women of color I have learned that my culture, my whiteness, has exploited them; and I have tried to teach myself to intervene in that process, to be an ally. I also have learned that I will not, cannot, erase myself or my whiteness. What I can do is attempt to subvert the "culture of whiteness" which feeds on a supremacist ideology. I have attempted to view my speaking — not as a "white alienated other,"[37] not as a silent apprentice,[38] not as a "spook who sits by the door"[39] — but as a specifically and complexly situated antiracist white feminist — that is, from a position of strength. If I position myself as a silent recipient of Black feminist rage, I cannot be the dependable ally *and* equal needed to work through the knots of our troubled history. The role of being an ally is a reciprocal one which I ask for *on my behalf* in return. I like the tone of Alice Walker's strategy of working with nonsexist Black men against oppression. We will work with you, Walker has said, but we come with our minds and our mouths.

In the process of joining the din of multicultural feminists "talking back," in bell hooks' welcome phrase, I have been able to see myself as a political person in new ways. I have no assurance that I have avoided mis-representations, nor can I be sure that my admonition to Black feminists and other women of color not to substitute their own pious stance for the hegemonic white one we are attempting to neutralize, will be warmly received. I am sure, however, that I disagree with the assertion, voiced by some multicultural folks concerned with purity, that no-one may speak about "the other." Where would this kind of paranoid isolation leave the project of feminist theory itself? I worry a lot in the concluding chapter about this kind of assumption, the notion that "we" are the only ones who know what "we" are about.[40] The invitation to engagement — urgently to "come discharge cargo," as Johnella Butler has insisted — has never been more timely.[41]

Part 1

Feminist Theory in the Flesh

Chapter 1

"Other" Paradigms and
Postcolonial Connections

*We are the hyphenated people of the Diaspora whose self-defined
identities are no longer shameful secrets in the countries of our
origin, but rather declarations of strength and solidarity. We are an
increasingly united front from which the world has not yet heard.*

Audre Lorde

Both Audre Lorde and bell hooks have provided important guidelines
for new feminist paradigms in which to conceptualize difference and
otherness. They have challenged white feminism's grand narratives of
"woman," "oppression," and "experience," revealing these categories as
conditional, not transparent. They, along with other Third World
women of color, have recast the primal dialogue of feminist theory.
Feminists no longer are directing their conversations wholly to men
or against patriarchal ideology, but now are talking to one another
about domination within oppression and about the dangers of over-
reaching commonalities in theories that codify the other in hierarchical
terms.[1] In 1985, Lorde spoke to a group of white women about the
consequences of feminism's "borrowed sameness":

> We were never meant to speak together at all. I have struggled for
> many weeks to find your part in me, to see what we could share that
> would have meaning for us all. When language becomes most
> similar, it becomes most dangerous, for then differences may pass
> unremarked. As women of good faith we can only become familar
> with the language of difference within a determined commitment to

use it within our lives, without romanticism and without
guilt . . . our words frequently sound the same. But it is an error to
believe that we mean the same experience, the same commitment,
the same future, unless we agree to examine the history and particular passions that lie beneath each other's words.[2]

This brief exemplifies the kind of deep context which Lorde's "language of difference" demands of a multidimensional feminist theory.
It evokes those situated knowledges, partial and fractured identities,
and local histories which we are now beginning to acknowledge and
describe.[3] Lorde's words encourage us to think deeply about histories,
in the plural; to speak of feminisms, in the plural, and of feminist
movement, not "the" feminist movement. It suggests that one of the
ways we ought to read history is as a text, "dialogically, to be re-
written in a form other than that of a monologue," as Satya Mohanty
has argued.[4] Importantly, Lorde does not foreclose the possibility of
seeking and sharing common experiences, but reminds us that those
dense spaces cannot be taken for granted but must be negotiated in
a relationship of good faith.

Bell hooks, in her recent text, *Talking Back*, sets up other conditions for theorizing around the questions of voice and audience, demonstrating her own Black woman-centeredness. In her writings on feminism, hooks is sensitive to the way "the language we choose to use
declares who it is we place at the center of our discourse." She attempts
to rectify the exclusions of feminist theory, to privilege Black women
by putting herself and other Black women at the speaking center of
her texts. Her action, she explains, "was not an action to exclude others,
but rather an invitation, a challenge to those who whould hear us
speak, to shift paradigms rather than appropriate, to have all readers
listen to the voice of a black woman as a speaking subject and not as
underprivileged other."[5] Here hooks is providing an important decen-
tering of the white speaking subject of feminist theory, to allow for
the heterogeneous new chorus of Black women's voices.

Taken together, Lorde and hooks, in addition to foregrounding the
omissions of existing feminist analyses, suggest a series of methodological approaches with which to examine Black feminist theory. They
suggest, also, a point of convergence which I want to emphasize. I
would like to structure my inquiries into Black feminism's reconfiguration of existing feminist paradigms with readings of two postcolonial

texts. First and foremost, a global linkage is integral to Black women's thinking about justice and freedom, one which has been validated in every period of Black female activism in America.[6] As I have noted, the descriptions of postcolonial sensibilities of marginality and the struggle for self-definition involved in decolonialization strategies parallel the hybrid self-understandings defined by Black feminists in their relationship to a "colonizing" white feminism. Connecting Black feminist theory with postcolonial discourse also clarifies the crosscultural and historical affinities with people of the Diaspora which Black feminists are claiming so emphatically today. The proliferation of theoretical, literary, and historical work by Black feminists around Afrocentric themes, to which we shall turn in the next chapter, is a powerful symbol of the political significance of this postcolonial moment.

As Black feminism deconstructs the discourse of white feminism and challenges parochial canons of acceptable knowledge and institutions, it joins a global configuration of important theoretical and practical argument. Edward Said describes this scenario: "The address is a part of the revisionist postcolonial effort to reclaim traditions, histories, and cultures from imperialism, and it is also a way of entering the various world discourses on an equal footing."[7] A vital part of the revisionist project that Said identifies is the transformation of Eurocentric canons as repositories of "civilized" knowledge. The guardians of canonical power have seen fit to exclude the cultural artifacts of a majority of the globe's people, thus denying those "minorities" the symbolic expression of indigenous realities. Cornel West views the politicization of canonicity by Third World as well as Western people of color as part of a

> world-historical process [of decolonization] that has fundamentally changed not only our conceptions of ourselves and those constituted as 'others' (non-Europeans, women, gays, lesbians), but more important, our understanding of how we have constructed and do construct conceptions of ourselves and others as selves, subjects, and peoples.[8]

We can thus fruitfully situate Black feminism's transformative moves within this global anti-imperial dynamic.

Decolonizing Traveling Theory

Albert Memmi's *The Colonizer and the Colonized* provides the first postcolonial text with which to address the project of Black feminist theory. When Memmi, a Tunisian Jew exiled in Algeria, published the American edition of his phenomenology of the colonial encounter in 1965, he dedicated it "to the American Negro, also colonized."⁹ Memmi resisted the impulse to provide a programmatic blueprint for other victims of colonial domination, but his layered rendering of the drama of "implacable dependence" (ix) which rots both colonizer and colonized, offers a nuanced portrait of the contradictions involved in the struggle for national identity in postcolonial milieu. "They don't have to recognize themselves in my mirror to discover all by themselves the most useful course of action in their lives of misery" (xvii), Memmi declares, creating a space for other exploited subjects to inscribe their particularities. Memmi's text charts the sporadic movement of the colonized person in her struggle to break free of the hegemonic culture's magic power and "superiority," the trajectory of consciousness as it shifts between total assimiliation by the mother country and self negation, and an embrace of the "extraordinary places of communion" (133) of the native world.

This latter awakening begins the moment of revolt, a move nonetheless rife with contradiction, when "we witness a reversal of terms. Assimilation being abandoned, the colonized's liberation must be carried out through a recovery of self and of autonomous dignity" (128). But, as Memmi shows, part of the psyche continues to exist through the symbols, laws, and identities of the colonizer. This is the inescapably ambiguous moment when absolutism and dogma can step in to purge the foreign residue, rejecting all language, dress, and political principles that came before, "even if all the locks of the country turn with that key" (137). Memmi shows the debilitations of such a reactionary turn. He demonstrates how extremist reversals serve further to stabilize the colonizer, whose power to control the debate no longer is primary but remains, reconfigured as antithesis, a standard on the other end which still keeps the colonized in thrall. Only when she "ceases defining [herself] through the categories of the colonizers," skilfully appropriating those political principles of emancipation which can work for her people's own collective independence, does the subject emerge "to become something else"(153).

Memmi's narrative allows us to see, in a sort of psychopolitical evolutionary frame, the terrian of Black feminist theory as it deconstructs the "borrowed sameness," in Lorde's term, and validates its own African-American gendered specificity. Black feminist discourse reflects a commitment to the "necessity of self-renewal," in Memmi's language, and is empowered by "first taking up the challenge of exclusion" and embracing "being separate and different"(136). This dynamic of empowered otherness is evident in the force of contemporary Black feminist scholar Deborah King's iteration of Black feminist ideology. King grounds her theory in the "multiple oppressions and multiple consciousness" of Black women's life worlds. Her words clearly sound the decolonialization impulse that Memmi recounts:

> A black feminist ideology, first and foremost, thus declares the visibility of black women. It acknowledges the fact that two innate and inerasable traits, being both black and female, constitute our special status in American society. Second, black feminism asserts self-determination as essential. Black women are empowered with the right to interpret our reality and define our objectives. While drawing on a rich tradition of struggle as blacks and as women, we continually establish and reestablish our own priorities. As black women, we decide for ourselves the relative salience of any and all identities and oppressions, and how and the extent to which those features inform our politics.[10]

This declaration of empowerment defines a politics of otherness which, as a demonstration of theory in the flesh, points out which dynamics give rise to the differences which do make a difference, those reweavings of experience and oppression which are no longer invisible. It tells us that gender cannot hold a place of theoretical primacy for women whose very being denies the restrictions of "monist" analyses. Foreshadowing an epistemological challenge to which we shall turn shortly, King asserts the autonomy of new criteria and interpretive grounds for describing Black women's reality. Her declaration of self-determination displaces white feminism's conceptual and political authority.

The second voice to provide postcolonial resources for contextualizing current Black feminist theory comes from Zairean philosopher V. Y. Mudimbe and his 1988 text, *The Invention of Africa*. Mudimbe utilizes discourse analysis and Michel Foucault's strategy of focusing on the conditions of possibility for philosophizing. Their stance asks social theory to prove and question its "rules" for the categories and systems of European definitions and knowledge of "Africanism." Mudimbe's work illustrates the productive use postcolonial writers have made of postmodernist insights about dismantling colonial signifying systems. Rejecting the classical Western scholarly accounts on Africa developed by anthropology and history, with their empirical claims to demonstrate reality, Mudimbe wishes to locate and unmask the ideological practices embedded in those disciplines, "upstream" of the results. He describes his project: "I shall be dealing with discourses on African societies, cultures, and peoples as signs of something else. I would like to interrogate their modalities, significance, or strategies as a means of understanding the type of knowledge which is being produced."[11]

In addition to focusing on European constructions of Africa, Mudimbe reflects as well on the project of second-generation postcolonial African intellectuals, as they "reinvent" a positive African identity. He provides a sort of epistemological riposte to Western conceptual systems by pointing to the negative ideologies of the West's "invented" Africa of inferior beings and culture. Mudimbe shows how contemporary Africanist discourses in turn are now "inventing" their own "foreign traditions" of the Western epistemological order through liberatory critical readings.[12] In Mudimbe's commentary on this empowerment project for African-based knowledge systems, we can see the outlines of the demystifying effects of Black feminist theory's decolonizing impulse:

> African worlds have been established as realities for knowledge. And today Africans themselves read, challenge, rewrite these discourses as a way of explicating and defining their culture, history, and being . . . while systematically promoting a *gnosis*. From this *gnosis* ultimately arose both African discourses on otherness and ideologies of alterity.[13]

As Deborah King's declaration above indicates, many Black feminist scholars/artists/home girls are "inventing" their own worlds as "realities for knowledge," as Mudimbe says. They contest both white feminist and Eurocentric frames of knowledge as ideologically "invented" as well. But their reconstructions take on the immediacy of lives lived beyond discourse; we see not only the "invention" of the signifying systems of Western phallocratic and white feminist theory, but the resulting material consequences to the Black women who have been (literally and symbolically) "subject/ed" by its codes.

The work of Black feminist theorist Patricia Hill Collins represents such an embodied project of reconstructed or reinvented otherness and alterity. In her important 1989 article, "The Social Construction of Black Feminist Thought," Collins delivers a powerful critique of the "Eurocentric masculinist knowledge-validation process." In this essay Collins outlines the dimensions of an Afrocentric feminist episte-mology. Using richly detailed narratives from the lives of ordinary Black women—those "thick" symbolic manifestations of life: words, images, institutions, and behaviors[14]—Collins develops portraits of Black women's "distinctive interpretations" of their own oppression and the alternative knowledge criteria which lend internal integrity and understanding to their life worlds. I shall discuss the substance of Collins's Afrocentric feminism in the following chapter, but I wish to emphasize here, in the context of postcolonial imperatives to re-store practical and epistemological coherence to "indigenous" lives, the boldness with which Black feminist theorists such as Collins have embraced this task:

> Rather than trying to uncover universal knowledge claims that can withstand the translation from one epistemology to another, time might be better spent rearticulating a Black women's standpoint in order to give African-American women the tools to resist their own subordination. The goal here is not one of integrating Black female "folk culture" into the substantiated body of academic knowledge, for that substantiated knowledge is, in many ways, antithetical to the best interests of Black women. Rather the process is one of rear-ticulating a preexisting Black women's standpoint and recentering the language of existing academic discourse to accommodate these knowledge claims.[15]

Collins' reframing recuperates, *in Black women's own terms*, the au-thority of Black women themselves, to evaluate the interlocking con-tradictions of their lives. As a central premise for arguing a unique Black feminist epistemology, Collins shows how the biased assumptions of prevailing social theories require a Black feminist standpoint. Through an analysis of Black women's "everyday acts of resistance," Collins refutes the claims that subordinate groups passively identify with the powerful, and that, being less powerful, they are "less human" and less capable of articulating their own standpoint.[16] Black women's history of political activism (rarely not visible in white-centered modes of analysis) and their political and economic status, Collins argues, provide them with a keen critical facility and a "different view of material reality than that available to other groups." "The unpaid and paid work that Black women perform," Collins argues, "the types of communities in which they live, and the kinds of relationships they have with others" reflect a world view different from that of people who are not Black and female.[17]

In utilizing the standpoint analytic from Marxist theory, Collins joins previous white feminist appropriations of this methodology. This is a theoretical vehicle that is both compelling and problematical.[18] Collins is aware of the tendency to discount the class differences between Black women in positing "a" standpoint, as well as the metaphysics of projecting a static notion of Black women's activities. The standpoint, here, speaks to a description of social practices, not a theory of innate faculties. Her analysis maintains the social construction of Black women's critical practices, and she historicizes the material and ideological origins of their ways of knowing and being. Pointing to the hegemonic ideological barriers which prevent the development and articulation of Black women's consciousness, Collins suggests that the achievement of critical consciousness derives from certain experiences of struggle which she seeks to describe, rather than from any ahistorical vision of "reality." While acknowledging the problematical aspects of standpoint claims, Collins's arguments clearly demonstrate the inadequacy of existing male (and by implication, exclusivist white feminist) paradigms, which are often at odds with Black women's liberatory interests.

Collins clarifies the political agenda which underlies her standpoint inquiry, the implications of which go beyond her demonstration of Black women's ability to comprehend and produce specialized knowledge. "Such thought," she notes, "can encourage collective identities by offering Black women a different view of themselves and their world than that offered by the established social order."[19] On this view, African-American women may validate their own "subjective knowledge base," by taking elements and themes from their own culture and traditions and "infusing them with new meaning." This project of deriving knowledge of the dominated, she asserts, requires "more ingenuity" and alternative techniques than those afforded by masculinist systems. In these formulations, Collins follows longstanding feminist critiques of positivist epistemologies and the liberal political thought from which scientific reasoning flows.[20]

Collins's account of Black feminism's epistemological concerns points to a host of theoretical inquiries which, when coupled with postcolonial understandings, signal provocative new directions.[21] How might we begin to shift paradigms in the manner suggested by hooks, Lorde, King, and Collins? What are the political and epistemological moves necessary to displace the authority and misnaming of much white feminism? Reflecting on the dimensions of contemporary Black feminist theory can usefully set in dialogue many of these concerns. I concur with Patricia Hills Collins's insight that Black feminist scholars serve an important mediating role in theorizing;[22] they are adept at boundary-hopping, seeing in the dark, making their way through haze, and bringing light, wit, and spirit to campfires. The discussion will flow from Black feminism as my center, first teasing out further some of the implications for changes in the way we think about knowledge and theory.

I want to discuss two dimensions of Black feminist theory which move us toward new epistemological and political spaces for maneuvering through our emerging feminist theories in the flesh: first, the clusters of renegade new "genres" which impart theoretical knowledge; and, second, the norms of Afrocentric feminism in relation to individualist conceptions of feminism. As contemporary Black feminist theorists interpret their theoretical innovations, concepts and methods are described as interactive, mutualistic, holistic, and dialectical — as kinds of efficacious "traveling theories,"[23] in Edward Said's term, attuned to nuances of diversity. Black feminist historian Elsa Barkley Brown characterizes this attention to multidimensional forms of oppression "holistic consciousness," against the dichotomous thinking of gender-focused white feminism. The single focus on gender has disadvantaged reflection on class, and attention to the ways that race, for instance, is constructed for white women. So, while the theories of Black feminism are marked by the site and specificity of their production, they also can "travel" to expand white women's understanding of the grafting and interlocking of their own social constructions. Brown thus urges white feminists to appreciate the scope of holistic consciousness for their own richer understandings. Given this penetrating and more comprehensive effect of Black feminism, Brown projects it as a theoretical model for all women.[24]

Theoretical Genres and New Knowledge

First I turn to questions about the possible expansions of theory itself. In their rearticulation[25] of existing feminist discourse, Black feminists have delivered powerful interpretive challenges to the conditions, terms, and premises of the practice and content of theorizing. The scope of Black feminist theory, and the new spaces to which it looks for knowledge about the world and for validation of that knowledge, enlarge our assumptions about the very nature and function of theory. "We examined our own lives," says Black feminist critic Barbara Smith, "and found that everything out there was kicking our behinds — race, class, sex, and homophobia."[26] Smith's "our own lives" is the crucial existential marker which validates the need for autonomous readings, from the inside out, not the outside in, of imposed theories, in formulations about Black women. Black feminists are asserting, as *theory*, horizons of experience, from the arcs of cultures and social locales which are constantly on the verge of dissolution. A 1962 statement from Black feminist playwright Lorraine Hansberry captures a sense of the eclectic resources Blacks have needed to survive: "Negroes must concern themselves with every single means of struggle: legal, illegal, passive, active, violent and nonviolent. They must harass, debate, petition, give money to court struggles, sit-in, lie-down, strike, boycott, sing hymns, pray on steps — and shoot from their windows when the racists come cruising through their communities."[27]

This scenario, which Hansberry-as-playwright constructs, reminds us of the sense of urgency Black feminist theory brings to its politics of genre.[28] And the feminist principle, "the personal is political," takes on a new dimension of interpretive clarity when we consider the challenges to notions of "authoritative discourse" which Black feminism entails. Knowledge, for a community struggling to survive, cannot be contained within the bounds of academia nor restricted to its practitioners. And it is within this material context of vulnerability that Black feminist scholarship is produced. The politicization of the criteria for theoretical knowledge becomes one of the most significant achievements of Black feminist discourse. The questions of who is "authorized" to create theory, in what voice and from what spaces of life, become powerful interventions enabling Black feminists to reject the policing authority of both the feminist and the phallocratic establishments. Through strategies which both appropriate modes of abstract intellectual analysis and shatter their boundaries, Black feminist theory redefines the variegated forms in which "knowledge" is conveyed. Patricia Bell Collins tells us that the rich tradition of Black feminist thought often was orally transmitted, that the theorists spoke out of the dailiness[29] of Black women's lives and in idioms that arose out of the culture: "Traditionally, such women were blues singers, poets, autobiographers, storytellers, and orators validated by the large community of Black women as experts on a Black women's standpoint."[30] Ordinary Black women, in their roles as mothers, preachers, teachers, storytellers, and "metaphorical conjure women" (critic Marjorie Pryse's term),[31] provided essential reservoirs of spiritual and political wisdom to generations of Black women. This is not to say that highly articulate and influential Black female intellectuals have not, and do not today, contribute to the knowledge enterprise. Their work represents one dimension of a larger domain of struggle connected to "commonsense," artistic, and folk modes of understanding. In chapter 5 we shall see how the legacy of nineteenth-century Black female intellectuals was crucial to the politicization and survival of their communities. But here I want to stress the crucial role of creative expression in imparting theoretical knowledge in Black feminism.[32]

In African-American women's culture, the figure of the blues singer holds a highly vaunted position of authority on "specifying" about life, woman's pain, and resistance. Alice Walker's high-spirited, sensual blues singer Shug in *The Color Purple* represents the feminist mark of resistance in the text who imparts autonomy and woman-centered survival to her community of newly liberated women. Shug reappears in Walker's latest novel, *The Temple of My Familiar*, as a more mature impresario of music, dance, and poetry in the crowded-with-eccentric-artistic-Black-folk home she shares with Celie. Shug, no longer singing in public, devotes her time with Celie to "living some odd new way they'd found," organizing her female-run church, or band (as the musical metaphor identified women's churches), and refining her redemptive "Gosple According to Shug."[33]

Michele Russell's much-referenced essay, "Slave Codes and Liner Notes," powerfully articulates the liberatory tradition of Black women's blues "in helping black women own their past, present and future." Russell reads the Black women's blues as a site where the development of consciousness is played out "in our own language. They are the expression of a particular social process by which poor Black women have commented on all the major theoretical, practical, and political questions facing us." As theory, the blues are the "bearers of the self-determination tradition. . . . Unsentimental. Historical Materialist." Bessie Smith, Bessie Jackson, Billie Holiday, Nina Simone, and Esther Philips have recreated for each Black woman a different past but a past which travels the road "from rape to revolution."[34]

In addition to the blues genre as a theory-producing site of feminist consciousness, Black scholars and artists have acknowledged the powerful effects of storytelling, patterns of idiosyncratic Black woman's speech, oppositional practices of reading against the grain the white world's language.[35] Novelist Paule Marshall has written about the feminist education she received by listening to the speech of "mother poets," immigrant Black women from Barbados among whom she grew up in Brooklyn. For these not-formally-educated, pidgin-speaking women, "Words were weapons they possessed to strike out against the injustices they were subject to as black people." Their discursive activism was manifested through the "mouth gun" poetry of everyday speech which took on all the systems which oppressed them: "They were always giving *someone, something*, a tongue-lashing. The white housewives [they worked for] out in Flatbush. . . . The government, the system, the presidents. They would say to each other 'Talk your talk, souly girl. In this white man world, you got to take your mouth and make a *gun*.'"[36]

Creative artists like Marshall, Ntozake Shange, Vertamae Smart-Grosvenor, Augusta Baker—all devoted feminist *griots* (the canny African trickster-storytellers)—identify storytelling as the symbolic yeast of African-American militancy and political awareness. "Storytelling, the power of language, was like money, it was legal tender, a symbol of wealth," according to Smart-Grosvenor. And the self-articulated political project for these women is keeping the word alive. Shange: "You must believe that what we say is possible and that there's nothing that can impede a black person. . . . You *must* believe in the storyteller."[37]

But contemporary Black feminist intellectuals struggle for their voice against the embedded rhetorics of white supremacy which proliferate in the "disciplines" of academia. Feminist Ruby Sales found her experience in the white classrooms of Princeton one of confrontation with racist discourses and indifferent white students and faculty:

> The classroom wasn't a free space. It was an arena designed to aggrandize the positon of white men and women and to minimize the reality of people of color and working-class people. . . . Being Black and being female, I found myself minimized on two levels. In order to talk about myself I had to use words that had already been created by white scholars, even though the words carried implications that murdered me in my own eyes.[38]

Sales, as a teacher of working-class women of color in night-school literacy class, exploded the annihilating white canons to provide her students readings around the works of Black women writers, gospel songs, and oral histories. These submerged idioms provided her students access not only to the technical skills of literacy, but also to political traditions and modes of expression invisible in academia. Sales notes how her use of Black spirituals redefined and unmasked the ideologial biases of "normal" academic frameworks—with new *philosophical* knowledge:

> Talking about songs in the context of history. We might look at a song that says, "My soul looks back in wonder, how I got over." Historically we would be told that's a song about escapism. And a song about religion. But in the class we understood that's a philosophical statement of a people who rely on the oral tradition to talk about what it means to be in the world, and how it was that one marshaled one's resources to be in the world. It's also a statement about transitioning and moving from one step in life to the next and feeling very good about being in that place. It came from the very heart of how Black people perceive life.[39]

One of the most creative and iconoclastic attacks on conventional modes of scholarship, genre, and epistemology today come from scholars of color in the critical legal field. Rejecting traditional jurisprudential canons of "rational," "objective" modes of thought, critical legal scholars are projecting a discourse radically new in both form and content. African-American Harvard law professor Derrick Bell notes, "The traditional way of doing legal scholarship doesn't do justice to our experience. We need new ways of addressing a situation many of us feel is abominable. But minorities who are trying to blaze new trails in legal academia are meeting opposition and silencing."[40] Mari Matsuda, a Japanese-American feminist, has excoriated existing legal paradigms for excluding issues of race, class, ethnicity, and gender, as deeply felt oppressions not comprehended by "the same universal authoritative voice" of conventional legal discourse. These scholars employ poetry, fantasy, personal memoirs, and autobiography to create theory which will end the "apartheid in legal knowledge."[41]

The work of feminist legal scholar Patricia Williams is exemplary in this regard. In her moving pieces, Williams brings to her material a feeling for the silences and rage that being a Black woman in American racist patriarchy elicits: "I borrow devices from fiction," Williams says, "but I don't fictionalize. I use my own dreams, hallucinations and fantasies, as a way of empowering less authoritative ways of speaking."[42] Her essay, "On Being the Object of Property," published in the feminist journal *Signs*, is a tangle of personal reflections and memories about her grandmother, who was an ex-slave, and Williams's own attempt to connect with her African-American heritage. Williams aims to "pin myself down in history, place myself in the stream of time as significant, evolved, present in the past, continuing into the future." Part of her struggle to reappropriate the fragments of her family history is an act of political survival for herself, to inscribe a subjectivity and an agency against "those who would rewrite not merely the past but my future as well." Struggling with Euroamerican definitions of humanity, Williams finds no space in the grids of bourgeois law. This is the way she describes her efforts to resist external definitions of her "identity": "As precedent to anything I do as a lawyer, the greatest challenge is to allow the full truth of partializing social constructions to be felt for their overwhelming reality — reality that I might rationally try to avoid facing."[43]

This project of re-casting, re-membering histories, agency, and the ground for one's own personhood is a compelling part of the paradigm shift Black feminism involves. The political imperative is not only to pluralize the dominant modes of thought (meaning more than the liberal code of "toleration" to be dismissed under the rubric of free expression), but also to challenge the relative asymmetries of power between the oppositional voices and establishment truths. Critical legal scholar Richard Delgado argues that the debate is crucially about the prerogatives of a single hegemonic voice: "About making everybody speak one language. Certain cries of pain lose a lot in the translation. The whole idea of the dominant legal discourse is to limit the range of what you can express."[44]

Expressive modes of speech and theorizing are held in high esteem by African-Americans. It was often in the media of oratory, Biblical storytelling, and spirituals that social cohesion was achieved, and political knowledge communicated, to a community under seige. The milieu for discussing such expressive languages — those which seek to interpret "meaning" in cultural artifacts — is drastically curtailed by what literary critic Barbara Christian has called the "ugly" prose of academic postmodernism. The "race for theory," argues Christian, has drained the metaphoric and spiritual intensity from sustaining genres of African-American life:

> For people of color have always theorized — but in forms quite
> different from the Western form of abstract logic. And I am inclined
> to say that our theorizing . . . is often in narrative forms, in the play
> with language . . . How else have we managed to survive with such
> spiritedness the assault on our bodies, social institutions, countries,
> our very humanity? And women, at least the women I grew up
> around, continuously speculated about the nature of life through
> pithy language that unmasked the power relations of their world.[45]

Contemporary Black feminist practices continue this legacy of creating knowledge and resisting power in polyvalent forms. But if Black feminists' genre play does not replicate in style and tone that of official feminist discourse, it is often ignored, exoticized as a "funky" or "gutsy" backdrop to the "real" project of theorizing. That Black feminist scholars today wish to build upon and certify enriching modes from their heritage, gives the rest of us important pedagogical opportunities. But in academic practice, some white feminists have exhibited a tendency to ghettoize the creative and expressive writings of Black women as "empirical" supplements to the "formal" theory texts of white feminists. Bell hooks has argued this point, objecting to the dismissal of abstract theory by Black feminists, as well as to the false dichotomies assigned by white scholars to theoretical versus experiential works.

> In many feminist theory classes, this problem is addressed by including work that is taken to represent "real life" experience or fictional portrayals of concrete reality along with work that is deemed highly theoretical. Often such attempts reinforce racism and elitism by identifying writing by working-class women and women of color as "experiential" while the writing of white women represents "theory." . . . Often novels or autobiographical writings are used to mediate the tension between academic writing, theory, and the experiential.[46]

It seems precisely the point that Black feminism is pointing to the artificiality of such restrictive categorizations for obtaining theoretical insight. Hooks herself is a theorist, and rightly encourages theoretical analyses employing abstract interpretive frames as well as literary modes. She has, however, been denied the status of "theorist" and prevented from teaching feminist theory classes. Why do so many Black feminist writers and critics feel driven out of the realms of academic acceptance while their rich literature is flourishing among students and the reading public? This reflects a condescending attitude on the part of those white academic feminist guardians who, it seems, are doing the work of the patriarchal establishment by their hierarchical ranking of the work of feminists of color. And worse, as hooks argues, this practice sets up a divisive privileging mechanism. Michelle Cliff's insistence on the very *density* and scope of Black women's writing is a testament that theory and knowledge often, and should, rupture existing genres to show us fresh "realities." "Black women's writing embraces everything," Cliff asserts, "it is visual, sonic, multilingual, percussive, explosive, Hollideist, Jamisonian, Hurstonian, Ida-B-Wellesian, Hamerian, Bambaran—you get the drift."[47] We need to demystify and democratize "theory," being alert to new feminist genres and paradigms which overflow the official tombs. As Cliff insists, Black women's writing must be understood in its own terms; those works which don't fit into the latest exegesis, do not accommodate the jargon, "still matter, no matter what."[48] To incorporate such radical new scholarship and overcome the academic dismissals to which Black feminists are pointing, we need a new vision of theorizing. We ought to see theory as a dynamic vehicle, a practice which can effectively blur the boundaries of "acceptable" knowledge. Feminist theory, in this reconception, need no longer get "straight to the point, but consist [of] thoughtful wandering through the shadows of experience, not in order to bring them into light, but to reveal the ambiguous edges of things."[49]

Chapter 2

The Cultural and Political Practices
of Afrocentric Feminism

*To be without documentation is too unsustaining, too spontaneously
ahistorical, too dangerously malleable in the hands of those who
would rewrite not merely the past but my future as well.*

Patricia Williams

Perhaps the profoundest gap between interpretations of feminist praxis
offered by white and by Black feminists results from the intense legacy
of connection that Black feminists express with a broader community
of alliance and historical collectivity. Completely texturing the dynamics of Black feminism is the dual consciousness of living symbolically
in that hybrid space identified by W.E.B. Du Bois in his 1903 book,
The Souls of Black Folk: "One ever feels his twoness — An American,
A Negro, two thoughts, two unreconciled strivings, two warring ideals
in one dark body."[1] The project of historical recovery, of enacting contemporary political lives and theories which remain accountable to
Diasporic ancestors and diverse emancipation projects, is the symbolic ground upon which Black feminism today resides.[2] The circle
of culture, in Sterling Stuckey's phrase, incubated for African Americans in the slave ships of the nineteenth century an ethos that has
informed Black feminist expressions from the slave narratives to contemporary theoretical writings. These understandings have enormous
implications for the construction of feminist theory and politics, and
are shattering that segment of feminist discourse which continues to
view oppression around the single cause of gender.[3]

A commitment to exploring the meaning of Afrocentric identity has been a recurring theme in the poetic, creative writings and personal narratives of Black feminists, but increasingly its formulations are being articulated in academic feminist journals. The issues of rearticulating and redefining Black culture, Black communities, African legacies — those postcolonial projects Memmi and Mudimbe remind us of — are intensely visible today. This evolution is particularly demonstrated by the publication of previously ignored literary works by Black females, histories of American Black women, and provocative Black-centered film projects.[4] The exhilaration of this explosive cultural reawakening carries over to and coincides with the scholarly production of Afrocentric feminist formulations. Such intellectual and artistic foment contains great anticipatory potential. A welcome assault that is "ripping the lid off our neat and tidy preconceptions" should excite us all.[5]

But before I turn to the development of Black feminist Afrocentrism, I want to give a brief genealogical reading of expressions from Black feminist cultural discourses. As symbolic cultural currency, what are the dynamics of this African-connected politics and what are its implications for Black feminist theory? Albert Memmi recognized the cultural intensity attendant upon the decolonization struggle, the need for recovery of the colonized's past. "To this self-discovery movement of an entire people," he wrote, "must be returned the most appropriate tool; that which finds the shortest path to its soul, because it comes directly from it." That path, Memmi noted, is "words of love and tenderness, anger and indignation, words which the potter uses when talking to [her] pots, and the shoemaker to [her] soles. . . . Is it certain that this language which stammers today is unable to develop and become rich?"[6] For Blacks, throughout their historical trajectory to become "Americans," this path to the soul has been embodied in the spirituality of remembering and recovering an African and slave past. This commitment is emblematic in Blacks' collective understandings as a people. In the arresting and powerful prelude to their song about Fannie Lou Hamer, the African American women's vocal ensemble Sweet Honey in the Rock, delivers the following statement: "We acknowledge that we are here today because of something someone did before we came."[7] That deeply felt expression reminds us of the sense of continuity and bonding embodied in the meaning of African-American sisterhood. It concretizes and directs attention to those earlier shoulders on which Black feminists now stand.

Novelists such as Alice Walker and Toni Morrison, among many other Black female writers, have made the African living memory central to their work. Walker's most recent novel, *The Temple of My Familiar*, takes us to the Africa of the dawn of humanity to fashion a fable of recovered human origins through the redemptive vision of the African Goddess. Her central character Lissie—"the one who remembers"—is the embodiment of African matriarchal values, an eco-feminist persona who teaches an ethic of harmonious interdependence between human and nonhuman inhabitors of the planet. Walker's revisionist mythopoetics trace "the fall" through the creation of patriarchy, warfare and violence, private property, animal exploitation, and the Middle Passage of the slave trade. In the alternative historiography she creates, oppressive hierarchies are inverted: human over animal/nature, men over women, white over Black, Europe over Africa. The joyful communal spirit of the novel is reflected in the greeting of southern African-American folk:

> There was a greeting that habitues of our house used on encountering each other: "All those at the banquet!" they'd say, and shake hands or hug. Sometimes they said this laughing, sometimes they said it in tears. But that they were still at the banquet of life was always affirmed.[8]

Commenting on the book, Walker insisted it was not a novel of "research" but "a novel of memory." Walker's prerogative to invent a history for herself and her characters obtains from the need to deconstruct the fictive negatives of colonial "history." "I do not believe most of what has been written about me in the history books," Walker told an interviewer, "and I figured I could do a better job if I just remembered myself."[9]

Toni Morrison's *Beloved* represents another reading of memory—the supression of the slave memory in the psyches of contemporary African Americans, the dimming of connection to that epochal event, and the consequences for survival of forgetting. Taking her story from the historical event of Margaret Garner, a Kentucky runaway slave who in 1855 killed her daughter rather than have her submit to a life of bondage, Morrison creates a ghost story of reconciliation.[10] "People who die bad," one character muses, "don't stay in the ground"; toward the novel's end, we read this provocative declaration: "This is not a story to pass on."[11] But it is precisely this story of horror which Morrison wishes to sear into her reader's minds. *Beloved*'s dedication, "Sixty million and more," is her reinscription of those who were sacrificed to the Middle Passage, against the pull of America's forgetfulness. As Morrison has said, "[The book] is about something that the characters don't want to remember. I don't want to remember, black people don't want to remember, white people don't want to remember. I mean, it's national amnesia."[12]

One small vignette in Morrison's story speaks to the importance of mutual support networks that historically have sustained Blacks. Or rather, it is the violation of that spirit by a freed Black woman who has adopted the destructive individualism of white America that is at issue. One of Morrison's characters in *Beloved*, the gloriously named Stamp Paid, a freed Black in Ohio (a crucial point on the Underground Railroad system) who aids fugitive slaves in their efforts to escape slavery, chastises Ella for refusing to house a Black man in need:

> That don't sound like you, Ella. Me and you been pulling colored folk out the water more'n twenty years. Now you tell me you can't offer a man a bed? . . .
> He ask, I give him anything.
> Why's that necessary all of a sudden?
> I don't know him all that well.
> You know he's colored![13]

With this breach of tribal entitlement, Morrison points to the phenomenon of contemporary middle-class Black indifference to the savage forces grinding the urban poor. Morrison shows us how this principle of mutual support, so evident in Black history, born out of mutual peril, erodes when Blacks become assimilated into the dominant white society, leaving their pasts behind.[14]

In 1986, the journal *Sage: A Scholarly Journal on Black Women* published an issue devoted to "Africa and the Diaspora." Articles, photographs, reviews, and interviews with Black women detailed the many African-oriented educational programs and conferences that derived from an increasingly international orientation. The following statement, taken from the proceedings of the First African Diaspora

Studies Institute, held at Howard University in 1979, appeared in the editorial preface, entitled "Daughters of Africa." The statement defined the African Diaspora as

> the voluntary and forced dispersion of Africans at different periods in history and in several directions; the emergence of a cultural identity abroad without losing the African base, either spiritually or physically; the psychological return to the homeland, Africa.[15]

The *Sage* issue contained an interview with novelist Paule Marshall; it is an evocative record of her attention to the last of the above features, the psychological return to the homeland. Marshall frames her reflections around the imperative: "We (as people of African descent) must accept the task of 'reinventing' our own image, and the role which Africa will play in this process will be essential." Interpreting her work as the product of a sensibility where "Africa was an essential part of the emotional fabric of my world," Marshall echoes other Black feminists with this attachment:

> In order to develop a sense of our collective history, I think that it is absolutely necessary for Black people to effect this spiritual return. As the history of people of African descent in the U.S. and the diaspora is fragmented and interrupted, I consider it my task as a writer to initiate readers to the challenges this journey entails. . . . I do attempt to constantly make references to Africa through the usage of images and metaphors.[16]

Marshall presents her work as part of a reintegration of what was lost in the collective past of African Americans; she criticizes the systematic de-emphasis of African linkages in the historical constructions of white America. "Without the presence of Africa in our lives," she says, "we would not be able to feel a sense of unity while existing at the same time as a Black people with avatars in Africa, the U.S., the French-Caribbean, and the Hispanic-Caribbean."[17]

How do these powerful postcolonial evocations of histories, cultural values, and linkages translate into methodological and epistemological knowledge for feminist theory? One insight from this consciousness of the Diaspora which Black feminist scholars have stressed is the importance of employing crosscultural analyses when attempting to formulate knowledge about "women" and "women's oppression." This imperative is expressed in the research of the Sierra Leonian feminist anthropologist Filomina Chioma Steady, which has been influential in the thinking of African-American feminist scholars. In her 1981 book, *The Black Woman Cross-Culturally*, Steady brought together interdisciplinary feminist writings from women of color in various parts of the world. Although diverse in focus, the writings nevertheless were framed as a postcolonial project in dialogue with the features of African feminism as developed by Steady. By studying the Black woman crossculturally, Steady argued, we can become more aware of the complex nature of oppression.

> The experiences of the majority of black women represent multiple forms of oppression rather than simple sexual oppression. Race and class are important variables in her experience and are significantly more important barriers to the acquisition of the basic needs for survival than is sexism.
>
> Recognition of the operation of racism and class is important in preventing false polarizations between men and women. Rather than seeing men as the universal oppressor, women will also be seen as partners in oppression and as having the potential of becoming primary oppressors themselves. Above all, by studying the black woman we can avoid isolating sexism from the larger political and economic forces operating in many societies to produce internal colonialism, neocolonialism and economic dependency — all of which affect *both* men and women in Africa, the Caribbean, South America and the impoverished sections of the United States.[18]

Itself a restatement of the principles of "theory in the flesh," Steady's understanding of class allows her to demonstrate that Black women also might conceivably be in a position to oppress others. In this insight, Steady foregrounds as well an important postmodernist assumption about the configurations of power and the ability of women to embody other determinations of social privilege. The recognition that those who are oppressed on one level often exercise coercive power on another level guards against the narcissist's tendency to portray "the oppressed" in pious terms beyond the reach of critique. This penetrating observation allowed Black feminist theory itself to rupture the comforting unities of sisterhood.

Black feminist scholars in America, such as the historian Rosalyn Terborg-Penn have built upon Steady's analyses of the multiple sites of Black women's oppression within the political economy of class society. As one of the convenors of the 1983 conference on "Women in the African Diaspora," Terborg-Penn's work further expands the commonalities between American Black women and women of the Third World. Building her own theoretical models from African feminism, Terborg-Penn proposed a program of study for American historians: to examine traditional African values and their historical transformation over time in America. The preconditions for her study are based on analyses similiar to practices identified by Patricia Hill Collins in her development of a Black feminist standpoint. Terborg-Penn identified two central African values evident in Black women's culture — women's unique survival strategies, and the organizations of self-reliance in Black female networks. This combination of collective structures, she argued, "has not been present among females of Western, i.e., European origins, but can be traced among women of African descent in New World societies, as well as in Africa."[19]

At the 1983 Diaspora conference, Steady privileged African feminism as more inclusive than Western models, more dialectical in identifying the racial, sexual, class, and cultural dimensions of oppression. "An inclusive feminism," she argued, "can signal the end of all vestiges of oppression, including those glossed over by revolutions based primarily on class conflicts."[20]

The recent theoretical work of both Patricia Hill Collins and Deborah King reflects a more comprehensive and layered working out of the Afrocentric framework. As I have noted, Collins makes a phenomenal addition to feminist theory in her attempt to construct an epistemological standard which both captures the integrity of Black women's traditional mores and evaluates them within their own frame of rationality. Neither Collins nor King takes on the critiques leveled by postmodernism about the constitution of subjectivity, experience, and power, but by richly interpreting social practices of Black women, they map out feminist scenarios that have never been acknowledged in feminist theoretical writings. In this they explode normative feminist accounts of oppression and, indeed, reframe our thinking about the initiating motives leading to a feminist consciousness itself. Stressing Black women's interdependent concerns of racism, sexism, and classism, and the complex workings of these effects, King notes that "the conditions that bring black women to feminist consciousness are specific to our social and historical experiences."[21]

Collins's explication of Afrocentric feminist epistemology, then, ought to be seen as a working out of that specificity. Out of an Afrocentric consciousness and a "shared history," Collins proposes four components which constitute Black feminist criteria for knowledge: concrete experience as a criterion of meaning, the use of dialogue in assessing knowledge claims, an ethic of caring, and the ethic of personal accountability. Several of these features, as she notes, have been ascribed by white feminist scholars to a "female" consciousness.[22] Her project aims to challenge the narrow "scientific" standards of masculinist Eurocentric discourse — positivism, that is, with its presumption of detached objectivity and rationality. I do not wish to detail her entire project here, since, as I have noted, the literature of the feminist critique of science is comprehensive and complementary to Collins' analyses of the inadequacies of positivism. I do, however, want to discuss two related features of her argument which flow from Black women's specific Afrocentrism: the reciprocal nature of theorizing and the obligations that arise from the interdependence of theorist and subject; and the political and ethical practices inherent in Black cultural identification.

What are the cultural constructs, then, that give Black women's group experiences ethical and interdependent content? Consider the experiences these stories relate. Making a distinction between wisdom and knowledge, Collins argues that Black women's skepticism concerning the abstract "knowledge" which derives solely from "book learning" has led them to view as more crucial to their survival the kind of wisdom which derives from lived experience. As Collins notes, "This distinction between knowledge and wisdom is crucial . . . since knowledge without wisdom is adequate for the powerful, but wisdom is essential to the survival of the subordinate."[23] For ordinary African-American women who have to navigate the terrain of gender, race, and economic subordination, experiential wisdom is more credible than that provided by reading or thinking about a social situation.

As an example of a kind of experience that provides practical meaning, Collins cites biblical images which serve as symbolic vehicles for everyday life in Black communities: "Stories, narratives, and Bible principles, are selected for their applicability to the lived experiences of African Americans and become symbolic representations of a whole wealth of experience." This is a different way of reading Black reli-

gious affiliations, one which secular intellectuals easily might mis-
interpret as naive and escapist, another of the delusions with which
the unsophisticated negotiate daily life. Through their metaphoric
power, Bible tales, become, in Collins's interpretation, pedagogies for
common life: "Any biblical story contains more than characters and
a plot — it represents key ethical issues salient in African-American
life."[24] Knowledge, in this understanding, is crucially practical and
ethical only if it partakes of, and is related to, a social network. The
obligation of individuals to testify to the condition of their past and
present is central to African-American morality. From the slave narrative to biblical narratives, this kind of "knowledge" is meant to
educate the community for survival and express continuity with ancestors and generations lost to slavery. The insistence on engaged and
ethical knowledge gives rise to cultural practices which echo the African talking book, a record meant to be added to other records, building a literature of community. As Michelle Cliff has written, to know
is to share knowledge, and the transmission of knowledge, "testifying," presupposes "a community of selves, [urging] each other on."[25]

Collins spells out how the tradition of dialogue in Black culture provides key mechanisms for knowledge-validation. The participatory,
linguistically dramatic structure of the "call and response" tradition
of the Black church, with its spontaneous verbal and nonverbal interaction between speaker and listener, embodies a sense of mutuality
and empathy. Thus, for Black women, connectedness rather than
separation is crucial to knowing. "The fundamental requirement of
this interactive network," Collins argues, "is active participation of all
individuals. For ideas to be tested and validated, everyone in the group
must participate."[26]

In Collins's discussion of the final criteria for an Afrocentric feminist epistemology, the ethic of personal accountability, she presents
the most rigorous test of adequacy for feminist theory. Not only must
individuals develop knowledge claims in a democratic, accessible,
dialogic manner and present them with a core of empathy — "urging
one another on" — but also the theorist must, as Collins says, be accountable. The theorist's knowledge must serve the self-articulated interests
of her female subjects. Collins offers a powerful nineteenth-century
text, the "testifying" of Zilpha Elaw about slavery, to emphasize that

discursive constructions, forces, and structures do not "circulate" outside the flesh and blood of individual agents: "Oh! the abominations of slavery! . . . every case of slavery, however lenient its inflictions and mitigated its atrocities, indicates an oppressor, the oppressed, and oppression."[27] As Collins reads Elaw, every idea has an owner, and the owner's identity matters. In Elaw's testimony about power, slavery, and the ideologies which operationalize it, we see not solely a world in which *discourses* and *rhetorics*, rather than people, move; but one in which human subjects are seen as accountable and as agents, through struggle, of intervention.

In developing this argument, Collins sets up a scenario which derives its validity within a set of theoretical assumptions that are at odds with certain postmodernist formulations about the efficacy, or rather the futility, of political transformation. In the context of Black feminism, postmodern language about social change is often coded, fey. Phrases such as "the bringing into play" of submerged voices in "gestures" of resistance can be read as timid speech, speech that is chary of praxis and activism. Collins suggests that the theorist boldly embrace empowerment strategies and animate her community as well. Renato Rosaldo lucidly makes this point about the tone of our political discourse: "Historical necessity imposes harsh imperatives on the rhetoric of invention."[28]

Collins, in laying out the following relationships of accountability between the feminist theorist and the women whose lives give rise to thought, takes as a given the need to anchor oneself in ontological territory. Afrocentric values of solidarity and the ethical aims of inquiry—which must be historically inscribed and debated—necessitate a positive vision of political agency as more than merely a passive defense against walls of power.[29] The collaborative relationship Collins frames is one which engages those bearers of "healthy"[30] core identities whose aim is a wider freedom, not the lust of subsuming others under the signs of the oppressors' identities. This is the web of reciprocity she envisions.

> First black feminist thought must be validated by ordinary African-American women who grow to womanhood "in a world where the saner you are, the madder you are made to appear." To be credible in the eyes of this group, scholars must be personal advocates for their

material, be accountable for the consequences of their work, have
lived or experienced their material in some fashion, and be willing to
engage in dialogues about their findings with ordinary, everyday
people.[31]

Deborah King, in her account of the context of a Black feminist
ideology, seems less certain about the coherence of Black women's
"experience" and "interests" than does Collins in her development of
a Black feminist epistemology. King charts empirically how Black
women's status shifts on the grids of socioeconomic and educational
alignments, showing us those variables which render the concept "Black
woman" an interpretive puzzle in many respects. King's work suggests
that Black women's identities and interests are not given, nor easily
located. In her discussions, we sense the outlines of the "fractured identities" model of subjectivity employed by postmodernist feminist thinkers.
A black woman's survival depends, King argues, along the lines of Lorraine Hansberry, "on her ability to use all the economic, social, and cultural resources available to her from both the larger society and within
her community."[32]

An important insight derived from King's multiple-jeopardy/multiple-
consciousness framework is that Black women's social profile resides
in shifting social space, lacks the assurance of a secure "fit" in stable
communities of resistance. In Black liberation politics, the feminist
movement, and class-based Marxist and socialist organizations, Black
women have failed to find their interdependent concerns of racism,
sexism, and classism addressed. "Our history of resistance to multiple
jeopardies," King writes, "is replete with the fierce tensions, untenable ultimatums, and bitter compromises between nationalism, feminism, and class politics." Black women find themselves marked by
marginality in all of the radical discourses of liberation.

Ironically, black women are often in conflict with the very same
subordinate groups with which we share some interests. The groups
in which we find logical allies on certain issues are the groups in
which we may find opponents on others. To the extent that we have
found ourselves confronting the exclusivity of monistic politics, we
have had to manage ideologies and activities that did not address the
dialectics of our lives. We are asked to decide with whom to ally,
which interests to advance.[33]

Black culture, then, in King's reading, is not a wholly rewarding realm of positive attributes available to Black women, but a potential site of oppression and exclusion. All communities, she implies, are traversed by changeable social and political dynamics whose dichotomous tendencies even the empowering attributes of Afrocentrism can't always override. This "both/or" orientation of Black women locates them in a contradictory hybrid space where they belong and yet don't belong, where they are simultaneously a member of a group yet distinct from that same group. King theorizes an "interactive model" to capture this protean quality, whereby "the relative significance of race, sex, or class in determining the conditions of black women's lives is neither fixed nor absolute but, rather, is dependent on the socio-historical context and the social phenomenon under consideration."[34] King thus points to slippage in the project of determining a Black woman's standpoint, suggesting that the social positions we inhabit, theoretically rendered, place us all inescapably in a "centric" bind. We can "see" selectively from a vantage point that is invested with certain interests, which sometimes can work to overshadow other interests.[35] This insight — that all knowledge can be *located*, as a point of view, as perspectival — is itself a resource of postmodernist thought. It mandates that our theories be self-critical and self-referential about where (and on whom) we stand in communities and cultures.

In beginning to summarize how the concepts of postcolonial discourse and Black feminism (shaded by Afrocentric meanings) co-exist and contribute to paradigm reformation, let me draw on an understanding of culture from Edward Said. His insight can help to mediate King's and Collins's projects of spelling out the foundations of Black feminist theory. "If we no longer think of the relationship between cultures and their adherents," Said writes, "as perfectly contiguous, totally synchronous, wholly correspondent, and if we think of cultures as permeable and, on the whole, defensive boundaries between polities, a more promising situation appears." Said encourages us to see that the historical and normative ground of culture is a contestable, often contradictory arena with the potential for both affirmation and closure. To restate this paradox, Said employs the metaphor of the "cultural zone": culture may encompass "zones of control or of abandonment, of recollection and of forgetting, of force or of dependence, of exclusiveness or of sharing, all taking place in the global history that is our element."[33]

The postcolonial/Black feminist project reminds us that theory needs to reflect the radical pluralism of concretely situated, historical women; there no longer exists a homogeneous, generic Woman. By paying close attention to that unstable "multiple" terrain identified by Deborah King—the complex dynamics which impose on Black women untenable ultimatums and bitter compromises—we are reminded of the disruptions of contradiction and specificity in our attempts to capture solid theoretical unities. These qualifiers allow us to identify and to reject that "borrowed sameness" about which Audre Lorde warned. Black feminist theory helps remind us that the female subject of feminism "is one constructed across a multiplicity of discourses, positions, and meanings, which are often in conflict with one another and inherently (historically) contradictory."[37]

Chapter 3

Bridging the (De)Constructions:
Black Feminism and Feminist Postmodernism

Are they trying to legitimize us? Contain us?

Michelle Cliff

Increasingly, feminist theory is identified as a type of postmodern theory.[1] Jane Flax, for example, has written in Hegelian language of the fundamental transformation of the Western humanist paradigm, calling the latter a "shape of life" which is growing old. She identifies three types of thought as best challenging Western Enlightenment beliefs: psychoanalysis, feminist theory, and postmodern philosophy. Each of these projects, she argues, takes as its object of investigation one facet of what has become most problematical in our transitional state: "how to understand and (re)constitute the self, gender, knowledge, social relations, and culture without resorting to linear, teleological, hierarchal, holistic, or binary ways of thinking and being."[2]

The postmodern consciousness perceives the edifices of Western thought as increasingly fraught with uncertainty and ambivalence: transitions in geopolitical alignments; Third World resistance to Western political and intellectual hegemony; the horrendous environmental repercussions of "progress" in a nuclear age; and the continuation of structures of sexism, racism, and other imperializing prejudices of Western xenophobia. All these negative aspects of modernity, the analysis goes, throw the West's "meanings" severely into question. Critic John Barth provides an apt description of the current mood:

> [the first half of the twentieth century] did happen. Freud and Ein-
> stein and two world wars and the Russian and sexual revolutions and
> automobiles and airplanes and telephones and radios and movies and
> urbanization, and now nuclear weaponry and television and micro-
> chip technology and the new feminism and the rest, and there's no
> going back.[3]

Cultural critic Andrew Ross emphasizes how these manifestations
of a modernity-run-amuck twist in complex and often irrational attach-
ments. The complex conjuncture includes: "the vestigial personal revolutions in self-liberation and communal participation . . . just as it entails the dramatic, postwar restructuring of capitalism . . . everyday
effects of the new media . . . *as well as* the great redistribution of
power, population, and wealth that has accompanied the new structures of commodity production."[4] If we wanted to psychoanalyze the
societal unconscious, we would be tempted to distill these effects in
wholly negative terms; we might see only what critical philosophers
have called negative dialectics or, perhaps more relevant, a hermeneutics of suspicion.[5] Because our epistemic climate is so suffused with
negativity and deconstructive urges, we become anxious and forgetful
of our *desires* and abilities to *re*construct and connect in polities, however fragile. The energies required to deconstruct modernity's authoritative descriptions of our realities — to which effort feminism has contributed mightily — have in some camps turned political theory into
a demolition operation. In the rather world-weary, ironic tone appropriate to postmodernist discourse, Ross makes some startling declarations about the implications for social theory and politics inherent
in the postmodernist critique. Postmodernism's most "provocative les-
sons" include

> that terms are by no means guaranteed their meanings, and that
> these meanings can be appropriated and redefined for different pur-
> poses, different contexts, and, more important, different causes. . . .
> Everything is contestable; nothing is off-limits; and no outcomes are
> guaranteed.[6]

How has feminism, itself an emancipatory project of humanist principles, rethought its nonguarantees? How has it survived postmodernism's "epistemic mutations" (to use Foucault's biting language), as
one of humanism's "metaphors of life,"[7] without getting its oxygen cut

off? Ross's narrative about postmodern times makes clear that this assault has made room for many dissenting voices: feminists, gays, ethnics, and "nonmetropolitians" have found space to resist the totalistic definitions projected by colonial/Western/patriarchal/heterosexual/racist world views. With all the certainty afforded by a theory of uncertainty, Ross argues, "No one is able to read or interpret the *text* — social, historical, or cultural — in quite the same unmediated way, and with quite the same confidence, after the poststructuralist revolution."[8]

This challenge has been energetically taken up by certain white feminist theorists who, as I noted at the beginning of this section, have appropriated and modified postmodernism in self-critical treatments to look at the racist assumptions of feminism's own discourses. Black feminist theory's postmodern posture of unmasking "invented" identities certainly assures that the "texts" of feminism cannot be "read" in an unmediated way. To frame the theoretical practices of Black feminists as "postmodernist," however, should not signal a comfortable fit between the two projects. As I have noted, many of the political and moral commitments of Black feminists are neutralized by postmodernist anxiety-complexes. Let us look first at some images of white feminist postmodernism.

I return to Jane Flax's reinterpretation of feminist theory as constitutive of the acid terrain of postmodern philosophy. Feminist theory is postmodernist, she argues, because it "reveals and contributes to the growing uncertainty within Western intellectual circles about the appropriate grounding and methods for explaining/interpreting human experience." Feminism, she continues, like other postmodernisms, is thoroughly "deconstructive" in that it seeks to "distance us from and make us skeptical about beliefs concerning truth, knowledge, power, the self, and language that are often taken for granted within and serve as legitimation for contemporary Western culture." Feminist theory echoes postmodernist discourses in that it points to and deconstructs those categories to reveal gender inequities embedded in, but discounted by, the "neutrality" of phallocentric symbol systems.[9] But Flax does not push her analysis in a direction which would demonstrate how Black feminism itself performs those important critiques on white feminist theory to reveal the situatedness, the whiteness, of its own conceptual representations.

Theorists Sandra Harding and Donna Haraway, on the other hand, have recognized the parallel discoveries and strategies of Black and other feminists of color and postmodernist thought. Their interpretations are important because they do not conflate the orginality of Black feminists' theorizing voice into the alien vocabulary of French philosophy. Haraway's fascinatingly idiosyncratic construction of a feminist postmodernism (via a "cyborg" mythology) is one composed of potent "fractured and permanently partial" identities. These identities — which Haraway locates in the concept and praxis "women of color"— serve as a powerful antidote to the totalizing universals of both the patriarchy and white feminism: "'Women of color,' . . . as well as a historical consciousness marking systematic breakdown of all the signs of Man in 'Western' traditions, constructs a kind of postmodernist identity out of otherness and difference."[10]

What is the political content, internal to "women of color," that Haraway endorses? She adopts Chela Sandoval's political entity called "oppositional consciousness," an entity which enables a constant and deep displacing of all structures of domination "born of the skills for reading webs of power by those refused stable membership in the social categories of race, sex, or class." Drawing on the work of her graduate students, who have enlightened her about their experiences as women of color, Haraway praises their conscious appropriation of negation:

> A chicana or U.S. black woman has not been able to speak as a woman or as a black person or as a Chicano. Thus, she was at the bottom of a cascade of negative identities, left out of even the privileged oppressed authorial categories called "women and blacks," who claimed to make the important revolutions. The category "woman" negated all non-white women; "black" negated all non-black people, as well as all black women. But there was no "she," no singularity, but a sea of differences among U.S. women who have affirmed their historical identity as U.S. women of color.[11]

Opportunities for political action are diversified and enhanced by the paradigm Haraway sees in the practices of women of color. What is challenged is the hegemonic tendency of all systems of thought or politics — including feminism. The destructiveness of "unities-through-domination," as Haraway calls them, is paramount in her understanding. What women of color bring to theory is a warning against reification of the "revolutionary subjects" of previous Marxisms and feminisms.[12]

Sandra Harding's interpretations of feminism and postmodernism coincide with Haraway's positive reading of the powerful epistemological and political interrogations of Black feminism. She, too, embraces the "fractured identities" metaphor as a positive sign of diversity which precludes feminism's tendency toward wholeness and one-dimensional unities. One can use her declaration that feminists should be alert to the often "beneficial ways in which the modernist world is falling apart" to identify the new politicized subjects who are emerging from the decline of Hegel's owl of Minerva. The multiple, concrete, and overlapping political loyalties — which often transcend questions of gender — that Black feminism represents signify a kind of criterion for dominance with which white feminists may identify, not in a politics of unity, but in a politics of solidarity. "From this perspective," Harding has argued, "feminist claims are more plausible and less distorting only insofar as they are grounded in a solidarity between these modern fractured identities and between the politics they create."[13]

Kathy Ferguson's interpretation of feminist postmodernism obviates the dualistic problem of viewing postmodernism's negative deconstructive moves as *separate* and distinct from feminism's positive reconstructive projects. The feminist project of articulating women's voices or submerged identities, she argues, and postmodernism's goals of establishing an antifoundational politics of difference are *not* antagonistic effects. These two playmates rather are like contrasting themes running through the fabric of feminist theory. These need not be viewed as mutually exclusive practices but may be seen as necessary completions of feminism's self-critical imperative:

> Sometimes the two projects meet head on in debate, but more often they are both present within a particular flow of argument, encountering and evading one another in subterranean fashion. Advocates of each often speak as though they were totally separate and antagonistic endeavors, but within the general fabric of feminist thought they appear more often as connected, while contrasting, themes. While the relationship between them is not harmonious, nonetheless there are conversations possible between them. They are contrasting voices which create different, albeit related, possibilities for knowledge and politics.[14]

Ferguson's analysis helps me to argue, as I did above, that post-modernism and Black feminist theory might serve a countervailing function. Here we might want to insist, too, on down-shifting the speed of postmodernism, to think of "it" as a tendency, a critical moment, an attitude necessary to feminist theory — one, however, which lacks the quality of *soulfulness* which full-fledged political theories of recovery require and which Black feminist theory has in abundance.

How might the self-critical stance of feminist postmodernism productively be applied to Black feminist theory? We might want to emphasize the mediated quality of Patricia Hill Collins's narrative of Afrocentric feminism. While her construction of a common Afrocentric heritage and her positive reading of Black culture are symbolically meaningful rhetorics which serve important ideological and political aims of guiding Black feminist politics, she risks what Black feminist critic Hazel Carby has called "romanticization of the fold."[15] The tendency of white feminists to project the essence of "woman" was, after all, an incitement to Black feminist protest against such generalizations and universals. For Black feminist theory to ignore the many contradictory tendencies in Black culture and to remove that realm from critical scrutiny is to create yet another essentialized countermythology. The debate over the dimensions of a Black aesthetic, literary, spiritual, cultural tradition is longstanding and intense,[16] and I do not wish to reprise it here, except to caution against the notion of *any* ahistorical, unitary "culture."

Albert Memmi was cognizant of this danger when he nevertheless advocated the colonized's project of national and cultural reproduction. His cautions about this process are instructive: "Must the just cause of a people include its deceptions and errors? . . . While I was virtuously busy debunking the myths of colonization, could I complacently approve of the counter-myths fabricated by the colonized?"[17] Further in presenting his own hyphenated identity story, Memmi continually stressed the importance, the richness, of personal experience in its "initial particularity." "If in the end I have consented to a general tone," Memmi argued, "it is because I know that I could, at every line, every word, produce inummerable concrete facts."[18] Memmi thus does not take us away from cultural and political reconstruction; he cautions against the manufacture of equally repressive illusions.

An example from Audre Lorde further illustrates the understanding of culture as a permeable, contradictory zone. Lorde is cognizant of the strategic importance of a politics of otherness — or, as Mudimbe phrased it, an ideology of alterity. Lorde recognizes the potency of defining "black" as a geographical fact of culture and heritage emanating from the continent of Africa, and she sees the utility of such naming as an emblem of solidarity among peoples of the Diaspora. But she problematizes the political implications of a unified Black identity if it is viewed as an acknowledgment "that color is the bottom line the world over, no matter how many other issues exist alongside it." Lord, too, cautions against assigning a fixity to "otherness":

> Black becomes a codeword, a rallying identity for all oppressed
> people of Color. And this position reflects the empowerment and the
> world-wide militant legacy of our Black Revolution of the 1960s. . . .
> I see certain pitfalls in defining Black as a political position. It takes
> the cultural identity of a widespread but definite group and makes it
> a generic identity for many culturally diverse peoples, all on the basis
> of a shared oppression. This runs the risk of providing a convenient
> blanket of apparent similarity under which our actual and unac-
> cepted differences can be distorted or misused. This blanket would
> diminish our chances of forming genuine working coalitions built
> upon the recognition and creative use of acknowledged differences,
> rather than upon the shaky foundations of a false sense of similarity.[19]

Both Lorde's and Memmi's statements act as urgent, one could certainly say, postmodernist antidotes to our urges to "celestialize" innocent pasts of wholeness.[20] But noting this essentialist potential need not drive us to eliminate nourishing symbols from the traditions, histories, and values of Afrocentrism. Where we err is in ontologizing those "other" counterdiscourses and histories in fixed, ahistorical terms beyond critical scrutiny. This point should not be read as an argument for making anti-essentialism into a theoretical absolute.[21] We need visionary models of egalitarian feminist futures, and Black feminist Afrocentric models help turn feminist theory and politics in such a direction. Feminist political theorists have emphasized how certain "private" alternative modes of group life can lend moral and ethical bearing to public life, challenging the antidemocratic inequalities of the status quo. Iris Young's analyses of citizenship and civic culture suggest such a three-phase model in this context. First, the norms of democratic, alternative communities can serve to relativize the dominant culture, foregrounding its partiality. Alternative practices, she notes, unmask "normal" hegemonic culture, revealing it as in fact specific: Anglo, European, Protestant, masculine, straight. Second, such strategies promote a notion of group solidarity against the individualism of liberal society. And, third, the critiques of progressive "others" offer a standpoint from which to criticize prevailing institutions and norms.

> Black Americans find in their traditional communities, which refer to their members as "brother" and "sister," a sense of solidarity absent from the calculating individualism of white professional capitalist society. Feminists find in the traditional female values of nurturing a challenge to a militarist world view, and lesbians find their relationships a confrontation with the assumption of complementary gender roles in sexual relationships. From their experience of a culture tied to the land, Native Americans formulate a critique of the instrumental rationality of European culture that results in pollution and ecological destruction.[22]

This is a useful way to think about the Black feminist celebration of Afrocentric traditions. Afrocentric collective values provide an important standard from which to critique both masculinist culture and mainstream feminist practices. The generative aspects of Black, African-based spiritual and cultural resources undeniably empower Black women and black men. Suggesting the potential for "Black culture" as a construct, to embody closed logics of its own, only points to the dangers of reifying any "organic" cultural metaphors. Too often, membership in the counterdiscourses demands "other" silences and acquiescences. But I would argue against the crude postmodernist pessimism that the "fascism in our heads,"[23] as Foucault puts it, simply reproduces *de facto* in our alternatives the domination we aim to escape. Patricia Hill Collins's development of a Black feminist standpoint and Elsa Barkley Brown's notion of holistic consciousness, for instance, need not have negative connotations. Black feminist theory is holistic, not in the conceit of establishing itself as the universal agent of knowledge for the rest of us, erasing what might be "other" liberatory standpoints and identities, but in the sense of being alert to a *whole* world of potentially violent assaults and entanglements. The Black feminist standpoint *does* represent a history of solidarity and struggle which ought not be lost to feminist theory. As Sandra

Harding has argued, the standpoint tendency attempts to move us toward that "ideal world" by legitimating progressive "subjugated knowledges." The danger in standpoint strategies, however, derives from its tendency not to challenge sufficiently both "the modernist intimacies between knowledge and power" and the assumption of "a single, feminist story of reality."[24] Postmodernism, here, can be an important corrective. Our quest for firm foundations, to know "the" truth of history, brings into play the problem of how we "read" and act upon the historical record.[25]

Yet these observations linking Black feminist theory and postmodernism do not quite capture all of the political stakes involved. Some feminist theorists have recognized the fatalistic tendencies in some modes of postmodernist thought — the "everything is contestable, power accretions abound, no guarantees" kinds of paralyzing readings that Ross laid out. The imperative constantly to "decenter" the subject in a strategy guided by "indeterminacy" or "undecidability" (whether in textual or political practices) is, for feminist activists, an annihilating, impotent prospect.[26] It is certainly an unthinkable strategy for Black women and men, whose crucible as a people has been their collective survival against the "paradox of non-being," in Hortense Spillers's phrase.

Postmodernism reiterates the stance of Black feminism in its warnings about the dangers of reifying subjectivities, identities, and experience — those code-words and blankets of similarity, none of which are innocent, as Audre Lorde's reservations about "blackness" clearly show. Within the logic of Deborah King's reading of black women's multiple jeopardies, we see the "fractured" way the world's forces push and pull Black women. The hubris of Western masculinist as well as white feminist images of the "universal" subject has shown us that all-defining categories warrant skepticism. But Black feminism then forces us to ask, "So?" The fractured metaphors and ambiguous "subjecthood" to which postmodernism seems to assign us have limited viability, given that assaults on human bodies demand unambiguous collective responses. In Black feminist theory, we meet those bodies and faces head on, in the most personal landscapes. They make their claims to propel our political energies in contexts which require that, for strategic moments, we hold certain identities and histories as unproblematic. The politics of otherness, which springs from the postcolonial motivations outlined here, means that often a suspension of *dis*belief must supersede our skepticism.

Leslie Wahl Rabine's reworking of postmodernism tackles the identity/subjectivity problem within the imperative of feminist praxis. In a discussion entitled "A Feminist Politics of Non-Identity," she remarks on the incompatability between "philosophers" and "members of a social movement" dedicated to eradicating oppression through collective political action. Rabine rejects the quietism that comes from postmodernism's determination to avoid "metaphysical complicity" (Derrida) — the awareness that all resistance is suspect because of its articulation from within the very symbol systems it seeks to displace. Feminist activists, she argues, must not only write but also act within the "metaphysical logic of patriarchy" in order to dismantle it. In this understanding, we must live the paradox of knowing that we may be complicitous with patriarchal structures, possessed of a "subjectivity" which is fragmented and constructed, *and* at the same time engage in concrete action for social change. For instance, as Rabine notes, we will be called upon "to oppose lies with truth in political situations."[27] And, I would add, anticipating the voices of Black feminism, we also must be able to see ourselves as justice-seeking changers (not just victims) of those grids of history and power.

Rabine's interpretation allows us to salvage postmodernism's deconstructive critique for feminism by insisting on the status of a subjectivity, but one which is partial and provisional. As survivors and creators and dissidents in an America which has smashed their faces in "marginality" and "ambiguity," Black women have considerable experiential familiarity with the role of provisional beings. Their battles, always adversarial with the larger society, have been won from moment to moment in an "ever evolving, constantly shifting, but relentless war" for autonomy and economic liberation.[28] Do we think that such women, who in 1920 formed the Virginia *Lily-Black* Republican Party and ran the formidable feminist militant Maggie Lena Walker for state superintendent of public education, have no taste for the ironies and ambivalences of political life?[29] We can and must, then, meet the activist and ethical requirements of Black feminism in concrete scenarios, but we do so with the knowledge that every stance must be analyzed, in Rabine's words, as "lacking a full truth or a fully correct politics." We have "no choice but to take yes-or-no positions on specific issues and to communicate them as unambiguously as possible."[30]

This latter requirement of communication highlights one of the most daunting problems of postmodernist theory. We need to return to Barbara Christian's "race for theory" argument to see the depth of alienation this issue engenders:

> The race for theory—with its linguistic jargon; its emphasis on quoting its prophets; its tendency toward "biblical" exegesis; its refusal even to mention specific works of creative writers, far less contemporary ones; its preoccupations with mechanical analyses . . . has silenced many of us to the extent that some of us feel we can no longer discuss our own literature . . . we are puzzled by the incomprehensibility of the language set adrift in literary circles. . . . That language surfaced, interestingly enough, just when the literature of peoples of color, black women, Latin Americans, and Africans began to move to "the center."[31]

Michelle Cliff, too, resists the appropriation—perversion, actually—of the writings of Black women by some academic theorists. She powerfully crystalizes the spirit of Black feminism with respect to a kind of cultural vitality often not understood by nonfeminist postmodernism. She and other Black women read the works of other Black women—African, African-American, Afro-Caribbean, Afro-European—using those texts, she says, "as evidence of our survival, testimony that our voices resonate, that literature can be made from our lives."[32] Cliff vilifies theorists who cannibalize Black women's literature; it is not the act of appropriating which angers, but the instrumental distortions which deny its spirit.

Bell hooks's criticisms join those of Cliff and Christian about the language of theory. Her commitment to a liberatory pedagogy—education as the practice of freedom, she calls it—is evident in all her writings, teaching, and presence at academic conferences. Hook's insistence that theory address the concrete lives of the women and men most affected by sexist oppression ought to be taken seriously. The tyranny of much postmodernist language, and the effort of many of its practitioners to trivialize and discount other modes of thought, make us aware of the hypocrisy of theories putatively committed to "difference" and radical pluralism:

> Increasingly, only one type of theory is seen as valuable — that which
> is Euro-centric, linguistically convoluted, and rooted in Western
> white male sexist and racially biased philosophical frameworks. Here
> I want to be clear that my criticism is not that feminist theorists focus
> on such work but that such work is increasingly seen as the only
> theory that has meaning and significance. . . . Academics who pro-
> duce theory along these lines often see themselves as superior to those
> who do not. Feminist theory is rapidly becoming another sphere of
> academic elitism. . . . Each time this happens, the radical, subversive
> potential of feminist scholarship and feminist theory in particular is
> undermined.[33]

Hooks's concern about a potential anti-intellectual backlash in feminism is well founded; the problem has been commented upon by
other feminists committed to multicultural, multiracial diversity in
feminism. Bettina Aptheker's work represents a productive grappling
with the limits of existing theoretical and linguistic practices in feminism. In her text, *Tapestries of Life*, Aptheker employs poetry, storytelling, art, and dance as repositories of knowledge by and about
women. She rejects the assumption that theory is the only method of
gaining interpretive insight into the meaning of women's lives. Echoing hooks, Aptheker argues that the inaccessibility of theory to her
women students reflects not so much a problem of abstraction as a
problem of *reference* to the everyday lives of women: "Ultimately it
seemed to me that a preoccupation with fitting women into theories
that subordinated them at their core was crippling."[34] Many of us, as
well as our students, have felt suffocated by the sterility and abstraction of theoretical, particularly postmodernist, language; and I am all
too aware that my own discussions often become clotted with the
technical speech of postmodernism. Given the critiques of Black feminists, how can feminist theory hope to meet the criteria of accountability established by Patricia Hill Collins unless it finds its "everyday
voice"?[35] That relationship which Collins praised in Black feminism —
the reciprocity and accountability between theorist and those persons
for whom she ostensibly advocates, the willingness to engage in dialogues with ordinary, everyday people — demands a more humane
and democratic discourse.

Is this linguistic problem, though, an obfuscatory conspiracy by white feminist theorists? Many academics would be tempted to dismiss the criticisms of Black feminists about the elitist language of theory as anti-intellectual, illegitimate. Couldn't the problem be written off as simply one of the residual alienations arising from the necessity (and abstract thought *is* essential to the life of the mind) for speculative knowledge? Aren't we wrestling with an instance of the tensions between *phronesis*, practical knowledge of the goals of human conduct, and *sophia*, that more "exhalted" theoretical knowledge dichotomized by Aristotle?[36] This line of defense or rationalization is tempting but not justified.

Something else, I think, is evident in the rhetorics of postmodernism. The linguistic arrogance of some postmodernist writers cannot be attributed solely to the careerist diseases of academia. There is too often in postmodernism a tone of mockery, a callousness toward the domestic struggles of everyday life, a fascination with the endless "play" of life which parodies any collective action against injustice as naive. Those academics who monopolize — and do not translate — the French discourses, those "anti-fad-fads" from the "holy land of theory,"[37] will always be rewarded. But should feminists contribute to this state of affairs?

Cornel West relates these issues specifically to the context of Black life. He criticizes Continental postmodernist discourse for its ignorance and neglect of Black culture, values, and issues of race. Despite its putative aim of promoting inclusivity and heterogeneity, West asks, "Could it be that this debate that highlights ideas of difference, marginality, and otherness actually marginalizes people of difference and otherness?" West eschews the strain of French postmodernism which "highlights a world of fragments bereft of human will — a world of flashing images, quick information, and consumer activities that promotes historical amnesia and fosters political apathy."[38] Racial parochialism, according to West, circumscribes postmodernist debate, particularly in the area of Black modes of resistance manifest in popular culture. If the possibility of cultural resistance is foreclosed by a fatalistic postmodernism, the dimension which West wishes to stress has no place in its formulations and remains abstracted from political resolution.

> Black cultural practices emerge out of acknowledging the ragged
> edges of necessity constructed by white supremacist practices in
> North America during the age of Europe. These ragged edges of not
> being able to eat, not to have shelter, not to have health care, are in-
> fused into the strategies of Black cultural practice. Of course, all
> people have undergone social misery, yet people of African descent in
> the U.S. have done so in the most prosperous country in the world.[39]

West, himself a sophisticated interlocutor in politicized postmodern-
ist/postcolonialist circles, is cognizant of the potential for co-optation
of cultural practices. Yet, in agreement with the Black feminists whose
writings I have considered here, he sees the importance of Black cultural artifacts — literature, music, and art — in fostering knowledge,
opposition, and resistance. Black music, he argues, "helps keep alive
some sense of the agency and creativity of oppressed people," despite
its commodification by U.S. record companies who have colonized the
leisure time of eager consumers. West reinforces a Marcusean faith in
the space of mass culture as a potential site of freedom. If Barbara
Christian and Michelle Cliff can view the literature of Black women
as a symbol of "nourishment" for their people — a naive and unwelcome sentiment in much postmodernist thinking — West also continues
to look for the possible momentum of "common Black people who
suffer, work, and long for social freedom."[40]

West's argument resonates as a reminder that Black emancipatory
projects will always have one foot in humanist discourse, as does every
strain of feminism. The potency of Christian religious narratives, a
belief in the idea of transcendent redemption — "living by the word,"
in Alice Walker's phrase — and, indeed, the concepts of justice and
freedom themselves are, and have been, empowering narratives in
African-American life. Postmodern theories often ridicule such resources for survival, are silent about feelings of despair. Black feminist
theory here joins West in teaching the rest of us the necessity of adopting many theoretical voices to validate "other" ways of knowing about
the world. We need the skills of a "heteroglossia," the ability to communicate with both academic and nonacademic audiences, in the
manner of West — "speaking a number of English languages in radically different contexts." With fluctuating boundary-positions, Black
feminist theory allows us to root ourselves in these institutions, so that
we can "speak to a black constituency, while maintaining a conversa-

tion with the most engaging political and postmodernist debates on the outside so that the insights they provide can be brought in."[41]

My aim is not to posit a simple "take it or leave it" posture which feminists ought to adopt with regard to aspects of liberal humanism. Humanism, along with its antagonist, postmodernism, is one of the effects of contemporary life, whose legacy, ideals, and formulations must be articulated, debated, and critiqued. To recognize, with Foucault, that power can, in fact, "annex" the counterdiscourses need not consign us to the iron cage of political quietism or to a belief in power's "evanescence," to borrow Nancy Hartsock's metaphor.[42] That is, we need to utilize the resources of humanism, as we do those of postmodernism — critically and with constant reflexivity about the interpretive and theoretical apparatuses which "identify" us.[43] Iris Young adopts the kind of posture I am advocating when she spells out the exclusionary limits of the liberal humanist ideal. She describes its claims to equality and freedom in the fictive format of a civic fairy tale, with "much truth" to its story, and "many limits."[44] But in our absolutist rejection of humanism, we give too much away. If postmodern cynicism allows us to forget those emancipation projects — feminism itself — which were waged in the name of generalized liberties, then postmodernism will be of little relevance to the paradigm shifts occasioned by Black feminist theory.[45]

Although those feminists whose work employs postmodernism may take exception to this recycling of the language of humanism, certain postcolonial writers have turned their critical faculties toward redefining, but retaining, certain of humanism's categories. These writers insist that without acknowledging the force of political consciousness and human agency, interpretations of, for instance, how African-American women have changed the structures of their lives would be impossible to fathom. The historical projects of Black feminism, which subsequent chapters bring to light, pulse with stories of women who constantly remade their worlds. Few women in this tradition, as Mary Helen Washington has demonstrated so vividly, have hibernated "in dark holes contemplating their invisibility."[46]

The literary-cultural critic Satya P. Mohanty has argued powerfully that oppositional practices and emancipatory politics require some notion of agency, reason, and cross-cultural commonality. His strategies can help us to see how Black feminist theory helps to elab-

orate "post-humanist conceptions of the human." Mohanty argues
that our commitments to diversity, otherness, and difference nevertheless oblige us to think some minimal commonality between "us
and them": "The capacity to act purposefully, to be capable of agency
and the basic rationality that the human agent must in principle
possess."[47] Grounds for collective political action require a degree of
consensus that we share at least *some* liberatory political goals in common. The project of understanding the interests and political visions
of different social groups begins, Mohanty notes, with historical speci-
fication and the acceptance of human agency and coherence. He lucidly spells out what is at stake for politics in the postmodernist debates:

> For despite the mystifications of the numerous ideologies of the Sub-
> ject it would be a little too soon to conclude that humans have not
> acted, believed, and attempted to make and remake their worlds.
> This has happened in the Third World as much as in the First. To the
> extent that we specify the common terms on the level of human prac-
> tice, and seek to articulate and understand our contexts, goals and
> possibilities, we consider human history potentially intelligible, and
> the individual and collective actions of humans open to rational
> analysis. Notwithstanding our contemporary slogans of otherness,
> and our fervent denunciations of Reason and the Subject, there is an
> unavoidable conception of rational action, inquiry and dialogue in-
> herent in this political-critical project, and if we deny or obscure it
> we ought at least to know at what cost.[48]

Black feminist theory reflects clearly what would be lost if we abandon the liberatory aspirations at the core of its theoretical initiatives.
As a critical theory of the present moment, to use Seyla Benhabib's
elegant term, Black feminist theory returns feminist theory to the
discourse *and* enactment of revitalized democratic values. It recognizes, with postmodernism, that abstract "thinking about thinking" is
an important resource to the extent that such metatheories help radi-
calize feminism's own struggles against privilege and can recruit other
oppositional allies to that cause. But Black feminism provides what
epistemologies cannot — a politics built on a genre of critical theorizing that blends normative argument and empirical historical analysis.[49] Black feminist theory is neither foundationalist nor antifounda-
tionalist, but extra-foundationalist, in the sense that its abstractions
are in response to the concrete priorities of "sane people in a conquest

environment [who] are necessarily preoccupied with the realities of social existence."[50]

I have structured the postmodern contrast not as a grafting operation in which Black feminism's spiritual, cultural resonances no doubt would be drowned in acid, but because I, following Haraway, would like to see black feminism and postmodernism as allies. Black feminist theory's status as a spirited catalytic agent represents a working out of the most critical tendencies of both postcolonial discourse and feminist postmodernism: both are mechanisms for demystifying socially constructed categories, displacing hegemonic power in the face of differences, and validating a plurality of ways of being. Black feminist theory, *as* feminist theory, gives us the contours of women's lives as a means of grounding political action in the practices of real agents pinned down in history. Postmodernism's genealogical interest in historical inquiry is a powerful asset for telling us how we have been constructed historically and through which ideological codes; but, as Nancy Love has argued, genealogy cannot tell us "who stands with us or what we should *do* together."[51]

For this image of lived human *gravitas* and ethical direction, we need to return to Patricia Williams's meditative narrative. Her journey to recapture the legacy of her African-American roots, which had escaped historical scrutiny, aligned her with those who "came before," "in the stream of time as significant, evolved, present in the past, continuing into the future."[52] Black feminist theory allows us conceptions of agency and praxis with solidity, with the potential for "rootedness" in the consort of those never-totally-dependable referents of self and place. Black feminism teaches us that often we are both simultaneously rooted, grounded, solid — and not solid. Williams speaks of this trajectory as a "bizarre sort of yin-yang" culled from the "dross of an oppressive schizophrenia." Yet a politics of "truly total" relationships (as opposed to totalistic) is fashioned out of this space, calling up images of "whole people dependent on whole people; an interdependence that is both providing and laissez-faire at the same time."[53]

I think we can "testify" here about Black feminist theory's contributions to solving those tensions over praxis outlined by Haraway:

> I think my problem, and "our" problem, is how to have *simultaneously* an account of radical historical contingency for all knowl-

edge claims and knowing subjects, a critical practice for recognizing our own "semiotic technologies" for making meanings, and a no-nonsense commitment to faithful accounts of a "real" world, one that can be partially shared and that is friendly to earthwide projects of finite freedom, adequate material abundance, modest meaning in suffering, and limited happiness.[54]

But we have before us the continuing task of elaborating and debating our common terms out of the diverse practices and strategies attendant to "in the flesh" politics. I have attempted to show, in this discussion, how Black feminist theory's normative Afrocentric commitments direct us to broader, more egalitarian paradigms for judging our theories and politics. In this regard, Black feminism makes important political demands on the project of theorizing: focus intellectual resources *not* wholly on the crises of modernity or on achieving philosophical rigor, but also focus on the concrete, vulnerable lives of real women who have a tendency to disappear in the power debates over method; begin to reformulate new feminist meanings and analyses around the multifaceted conjunctions of multiple oppressions; contribute to the creation of potent, empowering language practices which can democratize conversations; and, perhaps the most important contextual precondition for moving forward, be accountable for and knowledgeable of feminism's racist histories.

This rearticulation of feminist theory ought not signal the domestication of those fractured, partial, mediated "subjects" whose guerrilla instincts against co-optation both irritate and keep us honest. They are invited to sit down at the table, to connect with Alice Walker's community, to join "all those at the banquet." Bridging the (de)constructions is simply the first course. For we need to bring out of the shadows, endow with our strongest public voices, those histories in which our segregated abandonments began. First, the symbolic.

Part 2

Symbolic and Historical Flashpoints
of Otherness

Chapter 4

Gender Tyranny: Coded Bodies, Femininity, and Black Womanhood

They said to us: That flesh, darker or lighter than your own, encloses a foreign country. You cannot know it. It speaks another language, it is alien territory: otherness.

Adrienne Rich

And again, in rebuttal, there are the works of art, skill, and craft created by us in bondage that give the lie to myths of our primitive savagery and sloth.

Michele Russell

Since slavery, Black women in America have lived their lives on the frontiers of gender definition, in an ideological world which has provided only the most brutal markers. Were we to take a stream-of-consciousness accounting of these markers, these data from the Black female's sexual and symbolic North American history, we would be compressing linear time, psychic space, generational cycles, and seemingly eternal returns of symbols and ideologies familiar to contemporary Black feminists. So generative to their collective self-identities has been this question of gender, this struggle for "womanhood." To achieve an ontological and political balance of personhood is to fathom a formation of self capable of uniting sexuality, intellect, and spirit — a synthesis denied Black women by a white world skilled in conceptual contradictions and violent atrocities.

Our cataloguing would be eclectic; it would bring together events, documents, venues, customs, labor extracted, local histories, and criminal acts, all coalescing around the notion of Black womanhood.

Documents: "Bills for Sale for cargo received. Agricultural production figures for tobacco, cotton, and sugar, and rice in ten million-pound units. The diaries of white women on the subject of concubinage and household management. The plantation ledgers of their husbands, calculating the dollar discrepancy paid for mulatto vs. full-blooded African children, both bred for comparative advantage on the domestic market."[1]

Public Spectacles: Such as the October 1858 public humiliation of a Black female abolitionist/feminist forced by white ministers to bare her breasts to prove that she was not an imposter at a woman's rights convention and, indeed, that she was even a woman at all.[2]

"Scientific" Practices: Among them, the codification and display of African bodies in zoos, the 1810 spectacles, and the public exhibition of a nude African female to paying European audiences who ogled her "monstrous" buttocks. Her body and character were described by physicians as primitive, apelike, sexually wanton. After this victimized, totally estranged woman's death, more abuse followed, with the medical dissection of her body and genitals, to be fossilized as "deviant."[3]

Violative Work Rules: Enacted against contemporary Black female "cleaning ladies." One such Black woman routinely was forbidden to use her white employer's telephone, often the only frail link with her own abandoned children, until commanded to do so by her white mistress. For the maid who questioned such quixotic double standards, as did this one who verbally resisted her abuse, condemnation was heaped on her by whites for impudence and "talking back." Her strength of character and courageous speech were rewarded with the imposition of a jail sentence.[4]

Sexual Abuse and Moral Condemnation of Slave Women: None perhaps more extreme than the rape, escape, and seven years' hiding in a dark, nine-by-seven-foot attic crawl space, of one Black female slave who left her story for us. In a desperate attempt to prevent her hated white master from forcing her into concubinage, she relinquished her "purity" to another white man, eventually gaining for herself a measure of emancipation and "self-respect."[5]

The imagination of Zora Neale Hurston thematizes these disparate threads for us, creating an indelible metaphor of Black womanhood. In her 1937 novel, *Their Eyes Were Watching God*, Hurston narrates an extraordinarily poignant moment between an old grandmother and her young granddaughter, the novel's protagonist, Janie. The old nanny, a former slave, seeks to bequeath some security to her grand-daughter, whom she has had to raise alone in the white master's back yard. "I wanted you to . . . pick from a higher bush and a sweeter berry," the old woman confides, offering this description of the power configurations which had so constrained her own life:

> Honey, de white man is de ruler of everything as fur as Ah been able tuh find out . . . So de white man throw down the load and tell de nigger man tuh pick it up. He pick it up because he have to, but he don't tote it. He hand it to his womenfolks. De nigger woman is de mule uh de world so fur as Ah can see. Ah been prayin' fuh it tuh be different wid you.[6]

Hurston gives us a literary signifier of the Black female as a *non-person* — a creature whom white society had consigned to be the ulti-mate menial, the tabooed, dishonored, "unwomanly" figure whose dark attributes, bestial, render her loathesome. The figuration of white womanhood existed in an antithetical relationship.[7] These gender con-ventions, so integral to the racist mythologies of the chivalric cults of Old South, revered the "lady"— chaste, delicate, pure, and passive. The elevation of white womanhood to that nonthreatening space of ornamental powerlessness, the "pedestal," completed the structure of southern patriarchal racism and intensified interracial antagonism between women. Hurston here draws us toward that twisted psycho-sexual discourse of American slavery, in which patriarchy served as its own principal defense. Black female slave narratives tell us that slavery was mythologized as "a beautiful patriarchal institution."[8] But the potency of the ideological construction Hurston reveals of the Black female transcends that historical setting and cannot be reified as an accretion of the American past. The wounds it inflicted and the antagonisms it unleashed inform interracial feminist practices today.

Hurston's is a symbolically savage portrait which in this chapter I wish to treat theoretically, as an ideology of gender against which contemporary Black women continue to struggle. The existential de-nial of self represented in the old nanny's words— and the gesture of transformative hope for her progeny — is emblematic in contempo-rary Black feminist discourse. What bell hooks has called "the continued devaluation of Black womanhood"[9] evokes contradictions and tensions for Black women; of these white feminists are largely ignorant. Such tensions contribute to the skepticism many Black women manifest toward feminism. Racist constructions of womanhood have constricted the potential for sisterhood.

In the process of exercising their militant privilege of flaunting the conventional mores of femininity (the possession of that privilege was taken for granted), many contemporary white feminists are insensitive to lingering stigmas which demean Black women's physical integrity in American culture.[10] Their longing for cultural acceptance as attractive, "respectable" beings is not derived from vanity (the same moralist men who imposed on us the codes of beauty then condemn us for worshipping at the mirror) but is a crucial component of a larger collective effort at self-definition and personhood. Black women historically have been powerless to displace the patriarchy's monopolization of the negative imagery which has cast them variously as depraved sexual temptresses, castrating matriarchs, breeders, or sexless, deferential mammies. The contemporary Black feminist project prioritizes the displacement of such an ideological legacy. Hooks has written that such imagery still "informs the basis of most critical inquiry into the nature of black female experience." And she has implicated white feminists in regarding Black women as "non-women."[11]

How is it that the Black female has been culturally defined as the "mule of the world?" What role have white women played historically as both co-victims and collaborators in the dehumanizing gender constructions of Black women? How have Black women interpreted and resisted structures of symbolic debasement to claim their identity as well as their sexuality? Which scenarios and rituals in the relationships of Black and white women have contributed to intensifying Black women's sense of personal degradation? How do contemporary gender conventions and feminist counterimages often replicate jealousies, competition, and "branding" practices between Black and white feminists?

In order to address these questions, we need to evoke the conceptual terrain Toni Morrison identifies as one of the most destructive ideas in the history of human thought, physical beauty.[12] Beginning, then, with an analysis of the paradoxes of gender constructions as they have pitted Black and white women against one another, we shall move to the conventions of femininity, womanhood, and physical beauty as they operate today in reproducing gender stereotypes and hierarchies. The discussion here will center on phenomenological representations from Black women, as they describe the personal affronts which not only have denied them their womanliness in white eyes, but also have diminished their worth as embodiments of "sensible, moderate women" in the eyes of the Black community.[13]

Through an analysis of one crucial social role and economic locus, domestic household labor — reviled by W.E.B. Du Bois as "a hateful badge of slavery and medievalism"[14] — I point to the functional site most likely to thwart Black women's attempts to discard servile imagery and to fulfill gender expectations of "ladyhood." Not only has the domestic's grueling labor served as Black women's principal means of survival since slavery, but also its context remains the paradigm of inequality between white and Black women. White feminists especially need to understand the volatility of these relations, the barriers to solidarity which still obtain from its rituals. As an ironic counterpoint to the critique of white standards of beauty, I conclude with an inquiry into emerging feminist aesthetics within multicultural feminism around the politics of appearance. I foreground the idealized image of the Third World Feminist of Color as a new model of feminist exotica, and point to emerging orthodoxies of "politically correct" symbols, by which we often wrongfully judge one another's dress, fashion, and hair "statements."

These explorations reveal one of the most powerful threads in the long evolution of Black feminist theory — the transformation of Black women's collective shame into a powerful discourse of affirmation and racial pride. The importance of this reversal must not be overlooked. The rhetorics of inferiority with which African-American images have been stigmatized never have been the airtight casing intended by Western racist ideology. The inscriptions of inferiority in white supremacist ideology must be differentiated from what Black women historically have thought about themselves, even when they internalized their oppression. In this understanding, Zora Neale Hurston's text operates oppositionally, as a strategy of *intervention* against the construction of Black womanhood as mule of the world and not as a sign of the grandmother's own self-definition. The metaphor of the Black female as beast of burden is a statement of a social condition against which the grandmother struggles to provide new options for her progeny. In this she asserts Black women's status as beings of worth, even under conditions of subordination.

There is, however, a troubling paradox involved in my ideological investigations in this chapter around the construction of Black womanhood: I employ a discourse of horror to derive a discourse of affirmation. In order to concretize the full scope of the ideological assault on the bodies and psyches of Black women, I must draw, in part, on the racist pornography embedded in patriarchal mythologies.[15] I want to lay out the horror of this crippling discourse, insert it into feminist theory as an indelible record of where we come from and where, through critique, we are empowered to go next. I want the light of publicity to drain hateful images of their power to dehumanize Black women ever again.[16] I want other white feminists to join me in coming face-to-face with the consequences of the sexual/symbolic victimization of Black women, and to see how we have, perhaps unreflectively, contributed to their gender tyranny. I want us to look forward to a new semiotic politics and new critical understandings of the ambiguities of representation, with feminist knowledge of how to invert the encodings which historically have underwritten all violent inscriptions of "woman." I want us to be able to understand and defuse the rage of someone like the Black feminist playwright Marita Bonner when she asks, "Why do they see a colored woman only as a gross collection of desires? You long to explode and hurt everything white."[17]

I thus want to problematize the context of my inquiry here, to emphasize that a discourse of horror is not a critical discourse. But it can be framed as an oppositional pedagogy. If our goal is affirmative, we can turn words of horror around to create a reading of empowerment, one which prefaces a longer political journey we need to take in the world of structures as well as symbols. Such a reading can take us to another plane of analysis and accountability. The project of horror visited on the bodies and psyches of Black females is an interrogation which we must see as a projection of a collective mind, seething with masculine anxieties (mouthed as they often are by white women), *out of which* emerges an alternative principle of personhood. Black women's strategic deconstruction of that symbolic horror and their struggles for dignity—both in the nineteenth-century mass movement of the Black women's club movement, a mobilization geared primarily to countering society's negative stereotypes of Black women; and today—are giving us the form for that new principle. Their recuperation of a space for diverse embodiment and sexual expression, whether as workers, lovers, teachers, activists, or artists, is an important contribution to a feminist hermeneutic of desire. Their counterimagery of womanhood, threaded throughout this chapter, stands as a stirring example of Black feminist theory as it displaces sexist ideology in political struggle, fiction, and everyday life.

To avoid becoming trapped inside the dominant racist vocabulary, reinforcing its vicious authority, I have tried to utilize commentaries and critiques from African-American women themselves. But in the process of enabling scholarship to go forth, their words and texts have transported white racist images to us as well. They, too, are working them over. The hegemonic discourse of horror is painful, numbing. We can barely imagine the depths of humiliation felt by those many generations of American Black women whose very humanity was systematically denied. But we must imagine, analyze, and critique, even if it means taking the risk of occasionally holding words of revulsion in our mouths. Only when revulsion remains unchallenged can it poison.

Slave Memories: Sexuality and Womanhood

One of the most enduring and divisive segregations of Black and white American women comes from ideological constructions of gender— that is, from the hegemonic discourses, verbal and visual practices, imagery, representations, and symbolizations of "womanhood." Adrienne Rich, in her 1978 essay, "Disloyal to Civilization: Feminism, Racism, Gynephobia," remarked on the destructively complementary character of these patriarchal codes: "The images we have of each other. How black woman and white move as myths through each other's fantasies, myths created by the white male psyche including its perverse ideas of beauty." This splitting of the female image into dualistic caricatures evolved from crippling social relations whereby Black women, as Rich notes, became a "receptacle for white women's fantasies of being mothered," while the black woman more often than not served as the enslaved, underpaid worker in the white household, an icon of strength but lacking access to any form of economic power.[18]

This debilitating dyad of gendered "complementarity" has given rise to structures of resentments, misunderstandings, and alienation dividing women. Its discursive and symbolic implications draw into play feminism's own discourses of gender and sexuality, narratives in which Black women historically have been marked as absence.

In bell hooks's first text on feminist theory, *Ain't I A Woman*, written in 1981, she devoted much analytic energy to critiquing feminist practices which both neglected the impact of sexual violence on Black women and minimized the ideological legacy of the devaluation of Black womanhood. "No other group in America," hooks wrote, "has so had their identity socialized out of existence as have black women." And their efforts to adopt the mores of "womanhood" have seemed, to white America, demonstrations of intolerable arrogance. During the post–Civil War years of Reconstruction, when the preachments of white women and men about their "civilizing" mission to "educate" the brutish ex-slaves to the proprieties of white society were at fever pitch, that same society met Black women's strivings with ridicule and lynching terror. Hooks tells us that

> black women struggled to change negative images of black womanhood perpetuated by whites. Trying to dispel the myth that all black women were sexually loose, they emulated the conduct and mannerisms of white women. But as manumitted black women and men struggled to change stereotypical images of black female sexuality, white society resisted. Everywhere black women went, on public streets, in shops, or at their places of work, they were accosted and subjected to obscene comments and even physical abuse at the hands of white men and women. Those black women suffered most whose behavior best exemplified that of a "lady." A black woman dressed tidy and clean, carrying herself in a dignified manner, was usually the object of mud-slinging by white men who ridiculed and mocked her self-improvements. They reminded her that in the eyes of the white public she would never be seen as worthy of consideration or respect.[19]

In another arena and era, that of contemporary academic feminist discourse on sexuality, Hortense Spillers notes a new form of gendered invisibility for Black women. In this discourse, they stand as the "beached whales of the sexual universe, unvoiced, misseen, not doing, awaiting their verb," their sexual experiences encoded often, though rarely by themselves. The dominant feminist discourse on sexuality failed to record Black women's "structure of values, the spectacle of symbols" under which Black women lived their gendered lives. Recognizing that those who define the problematics of the categories in sexual discourse participate in a conversation of power, Spillers locates in that discursive terrain "another way, in its present practices, that the world divides decisively between the haves/have-nots, those who may speak and those who may not." That is, "Black American women in the public-critical discourse of feminist thought have no acknowledged sexuality because they enter the historical stage from quite another angle of entrance from that of Anglo-American women."[20]

Black women's sexuality has been spoken *for* them, as Spillers argues, because of the violent historical prerogatives of white men under slavery. As historian Darlene Clark Hine has argued, the fundamental tension between Black women and the rest of society has always involved a multifaceted struggle to determine "who would control their productive and reproductive capacities and their sexuality."[21] These readings reinforce for us the Black female's truth that sexuality, womanhood, and slavery have remained interconnected long after formal bondage ended: "Sexually as well as in every other way, Negroes were utterly subordinated. White men extended their dominion over their Negroes to the bed." And for female slaves and white masters, the sex act itself served as a "ritualistic reenactment of the daily pattern of social dominance."[22]

How, though, was the South's veneration of womanhood reconciled with the extracted labor of female slaves? How did the economic dictates of slave labor contradict conventions concerning the proper roles for delicate ladies? Such Western gender expectations did not prevent slave women from being used in heavy fieldwork: "For them the ideals of feminine delicacy proved no shelter from the punishing lash or the lustful whims of slave masters. They were never too pregnant or too young or too frail to be subject to the harsh demands of insensitive owners."[23] Gender ideologies, mediated as they were by the white planter's quest for private profit through the forced labor of Black human beings, thus evolved a dual set of polarized sexual codes that remained in constant tension: the white female's repressed sexuality, the Black female's controlled sexual appetite; the glorified white mother, the Black female breeder.[24]

This dichotomy was upheld uniformly by white plantation mistresses, whose laments over their own "burdens" of overseeing recalcitrant slave "families" far exceeded their capacity to see those same slaves as human. These mistresses were not "slaves of slaves"; and, unlike Black women, they rarely questioned the gender standards to which their society held them.[25] The riddle of womanhood under slavery, as Angela Davis tells us, was "solved" for the Black female slave by placing her, ontologically and symbolically, outside the very boundaries of womanhood: "This was one of the supreme ironies of slavery: in order to approach its strategic goal — to extract the greatest possible surplus from the labor of the slaves — the black woman had to be released from the chains of the myth of femininity. . . . In order to function as slave, the black woman had to be annulled as woman."[26]

But still we must ask the question, Did such a universe of sexual domination wholly define the boundaries of the Black female's sexuality, and indeed her desire? Barbara Omolade's hermeneutic of this tabooed dimension of nineteenth-century Black womanhood, "Hearts of Darkness," gives us a more complex portrait, a vision of the female slave at the center of a web of cruelty and pleasure, love and hate. We need to hold two pictures of enslaved females in our imaginations simultaneously: victims of systematic sexual violence, as no other American women have been; but sexual agents as well, women who brought their erotic power to the beds of both white and Black lovers.[27] Omolade narrates for us the psychology of that strange "commingling of desire and hate" which made of Black females the lustful object of white men. Extraordinarily, Omolade brings this woman's voice to the fore by giving her an inner life. She sketches the shape of a schizophrenic world, from deep within the psyche and point of view of the long-invisible, long-silenced slave woman.

> Racial oppression tends to flow from the external to the internal:
> from political institutions, social structures, the economic system and
> military conquest, into the psyche and consciousness and culture of
> the oppressed and the oppressor. In contrast, sexual oppression tends
> to direct itself directly to the internal, the feeling and emotional
> center, the private and intimate self, existing within the external context of power and social control. Black women fused both racial and
> sexual oppression in their beings and movements in both black and
> white worlds.[28]

Omolade's narrative counters scenarios of victimization with evidence of the female slave's acts of resistance and gestures of sexual autonomy.[29] Just as the "woman could not be separated from the color," neither could the savageries of bondage be separated from moments of her sensual pleasure. Interpretively, we gain here a new sexual history, a revision which makes clear a tabooed mediation, the relationship between the public events and the private acts. Omolade ruptures for the voiceless slave woman the facade of the white man's racist power to expose the hidden private world he constructed to satisfy his desire for her: "He built an exterior world that reflected his fragmented insides." The history of Black women in America, therefore, reflects the juncture where the public and private spheres, as well as personal and political oppression, meet. What a revelatory new landscape of meaning emerges from Omolade's telling of the "true" history:

> The master/lover ruled over the world; he divided it up and called everyone out of their name. During the day, he would call her "wench," "negress," "Sable Venus" . . . He described and wrote about her endurance, ate her biscuits, and suckled her breasts. At night he would chant false endearments and would feel engulfed within her darkness. He would accuse her of raping herself, naming his lesser brothers as the fathers of his and her children. He would record every battle, keep every letter, document each law, building monuments to himself, but he would never tell the true story, the complete story of how he used the rape to make the profit, of how he used the bodies of women to satisfy his needs. He would never tell how he built a society with the aid of dark-skinned women, while telling the world he did it alone.
>
> . . . History would become all that men did during the day, but nothing of what they did during the night.
>
> Only a few daring men, mostly black ones, would recognize that only she understood what it had taken for white men to dominate the world and what it would mean, finally to be free. But some black women who voiced what they knew did not survive. . . . History, however, would obliterate the entire story, occasionally giving it only a false footnote. But deep within the daughters' hearts and minds it would be remembered and this memory would become the historical record everything had to be measured by.[30]

And we know, from those daughters' hearts and minds today, the impact of Omolade's powerful rereading. We can listen to those voices of contemporary Black women as they describe their own inscriptions of otherness flowing from this history.

Symbolic Passing: Deconstructing Femininity

How do current thematizations of gender discourse — femininity, conventions of beauty, and sexuality — operate differently for Black and for white women? This question resides in a context of tension and ambiguity for Black women: vindication of their "womanhood" can seem to depend on embracing those crippling norms of male fantasies — the "soft," "feminine," "passive," "dependent female on a pedestal." That the trap of femininity is a mask for the white woman's powerlessness is too often belied by Black women's subservient social and economic relations with white women. Mutual idealizations further mystify the economic vulnerability of the majority of *all* women. The perceived "luxury" of white women's lives — luxury which often comes at the expense of Black women servants — is an understandable projection, given histories of subordination. Thus white women's monopolization of femininity becomes but another deliberate denial of status to Black women, distilled through the exclusivist practices of past and present feminist institutions. This is our drama, played out on the battleground of gender.

The goal of feminist theory, Teresa de Lauretis argued in 1986, is to define women's sexual difference, "to understand how one becomes a woman, and what gives femaleness (rather than femininity) its meaning as the experience of a female subject." But it is the differentiation and questioning of *femininity* which embodies such contradictions for Black feminists. Their interests lie not so much in ascertaining the differences between biological males and females, but in rejecting the hierarchical definitions of womanhood vis-a-vis white women. But surely it is true, as de Lauretis argued, "that the female subject is engendered across multiple representations of class, race, language, and social relations, it is also the case . . . that gender is a common denominator: the female subject is always constructed and defined in gender, starting from gender."[31] But this terrain has more often been a site of contestation rather than of commonality between women, an internal mechanism of segregation. What has it meant in terms

of the politics of skin color, hair, beauty, and sexuality, that Black and
white women were co-constructed in this same "sign" community?
The forms that signs, or symbolic representations, take, as Hazel Carby
has noted, "are conditioned by the social organization of the participants involved and also by the immediate conditions of their interactions . . . we must be historically specific and aware of the differently
oriented social interests within one and the same sign community."[32]

Carby's argument is an important call for white feminist contex-
tualization, for accountability that white women themselves historically have taken advantage of the hateful stereotypes of Black women
to secure and negotiate their own, albeit subordinate, position within
the racist patriarchy. Carby reminds us that we need to look at how
white women's own practices around gender conventions have contributed to degraded images of Black women. As we shall see in the
following chapter, Black women's reputed "immorality" often served
as a rationalization for their exclusion from white feminist organizations to avoid tarnishing white women's more "virtuous" reputations.
Our white feminist foremothers of the nineteenth century feared, in
bell hooks's term, contamination by their Black sisters. For white
feminists, being "historically specific" means that we acknowledge
the legacy of nineteenth-century white women's willful silence about
the violent consequences for all Black citizens of the symbolic constructions of Black otherness. We must turn to the unequivocal language of Black feminists to be reminded of this record and of the life-
and-death consequences of "ideas" about the bodies of Black folk. For
Michele Russell, these consequences are far from abstract. Ideas about
Black bodies were the vehicles for extermination. Symbols built certain kinds of tactile, material, functional structures throughout America's racial history: "the spits and crossties where we were roasted
after the hunt. Our mutilated body parts smoked and sold as trophies."[33]

These are the stories which are the underside of our wishes today
for sisterhood; they make up a subtext that accounts for the intensity,
the fragility of our efforts now to "recover" or "recreate" that bond.
But the bond of sisterhood was always tenuous, strained by the betrayals of white women. My interpretation of the historical narrative
of nineteenth-century feminism to follow in chapter 5 will document
white women's own positions with regard to the racist ideologies which
stigmatized the bodies of Black women. We long to gloss over those

violations of feminist solidarity, to reflect instead on women's mutual
entrapment within male mythologies and male criteria of female
beauty, to foreground those scenarios where we "move as myths through
each other's fantasies," as Adrienne Rich emphasized.

Wendy Chapkis's text, *Beauty Secrets: Women and the Politics of
Appearance*, provides a powerful reading of the codes of women's
mutual gender entrapment. Her deconstruction of the suffocating
norms of conventional beauty provides the space to situate all women
within that sign of the male imagination, femininity. This is the terrain in which woman comes to know her womanliness through the
policing male gaze which classifies, evaluates, judges us. The politics
of appearance, Chapkis argues, is "hatefully serious business," inex-
tricably bound up with the systems of social, political, and economic
inequality. A cultural practice which is codified, gender, in her reading is denaturalized, unmasked as an "elaborate disguise" which ob-
scures the essential political relationship between gendered appearance and gender privilege. Those arbiters of acceptable "masculine"
and "feminine" desire, the multinational megabeauty factories, demand the projection of a female psychology of inferiority and an
economy of insatiable consumption. This is a semiotic and capitalist
image machine we are caught up in, Chapkis teaches us, our consciousness its raw material. "Appearance is the first, constant commentary of female inadequacy."[34] But this statement resonates with vastly
different meanings when read through the prism of the symbolic genealogies of Black women, for whom "appearance" evoked an intensely
unique form of shame and punishing ridicule.

In such a constellation of structured and manufactured symbolic
inferiority, no woman may feel secure, attractive, or worthy. Through
the cultural apparatuses of communications media, we internalize in-
security about our appearance. These "technologies of gender," in
Teresa de Lauretis's term, inscribe in women a damaged sense of self,
fertile ground for female submissiveness. Chapkis drives home the
sense of deceit and personal fraudulence involved in attempting to
conform to idealized gender codes. The female becomes a *poseur* in
her own "flawed" body:

> We are like foreigners attempting to assimilate into a hostile culture,
> our bodies continually threatening to betray our difference. Each of

us who seeks the rights of citizenship through acceptable femininity shares a secret with all who attempt to pass: my undisguised self is unacceptable, I am not what I seem. To successfully pass is to be momentarily wrapped in the protective cover of conformity. To fail is to experience the vulnerability of the outsider.[35]

It is not insignificant that Chapkis uses a metaphor evoking a particular Black experience of self-effacement — that of *passing* — to describe the consciousness white women employ when confronted with their culturally sanctioned "imperfections." Her perceptiveness gives us a potential point of contact here between white and Black gender outlaws, around which political resistance can coalesce. That white women share a painful aspect of the Black female's sense of inferiority, under the sign of this ideological order, evokes a tentative kind of negative equality.

The legendary Black southern civil rights leader, Fannie Lou Hamer, in her plain-speaking militancy, provides another analysis which weds the unequal socioeconomic relations of Black and white women to their mutual gender confinements. She situates her interpretation of patriarchal ideologies of gender — "that angel feeling," she calls it — in the class structures between Black and white women which intercut the culture's work of gender creation. Like Chapkis, Hamer cautions us to reject the dubious "rewards" promised by sexist conceptions of femininity. And she clearly lays out the power dynamic *inside* this process: the white woman's privileged prerogatives of "ladyhood" come at the expense of Black women's menial labor. Here she speaks as a domestic maid to her white southern female employer:

> You've been caught up in this thing because, you know, you worked my grandmother, and after that you worked my mother, and then finally you got hold of me. And you really thought . . . you was *more* because you was a woman, and especially a white woman, you had this kind of angel feeling that you were untouchable. . . . So we was used as black women over and over. . . . You had been put on a pedestal . . . something like an ivory castle. So what happened to you, we have busted the castle open and whacking like hell for the pedestal. And when you hit the ground, you're gone have to fight like hell, like we've been fighting all this time.[36]

Hamer well knew the conditionality of that pedestal and warned that Black women would no longer subscribe to its tenets. She posited a project of struggle with both Black and white women "fighting like hell" together to resist destructive imposed definitions. She understood the power of the male mythologies which pitted Black and white women against one another in a quest for "purity" and womanhood. "You know the white male," she declared, "he didn't just go and brainwash the black man and the black woman, he brainwashed his wife too. . . . He made her think that she was a angel."[37] But, more vividly, Hamer exposes the white female's culpability in manipulating the symbols of femininity to coerce Black women: "We was used as Black women over and over."

Hamer's discourse is a brutal reminder of the limits of an ethics which argues superficially that both Black and white women are exploited by patriarchy's gendered expectations. Difference undercuts facile accounts which stop there. While the white man's ideology, that "angel feeling," debilitated both Black servant and white mistress, this acknowledgement is extraneous to the system itself. The interrogations of the white woman's complicity and the economic patterns which uphold white "ladyhood" recede into undifferentiated "female" oppression. Hamer's declamation that the white woman "was more" because she was a white woman allows us a more radical point: Black women have always been the "have-nots" in this gender discourse of mutual entrapment. History has divided the empire of women against itself, as Spillers astutely noted, and the too-easy assumptions of gender similarity in my analysis up to this point seem, if not unjustified, incomplete. Black and white women have not suffered equally under the spectacle of symbols which construct sexuality and gender.

I want to be clear, in this critique, about the hierarchy Fannie Lou Hamer asks us to remember, that of the Black female "menial," and about the symbolic resonance which connects that role so powerfully to Black women's diminished self-esteem. This role becomes an archetype, a recurring trope in virtually every genre of Black feminist discourse. Toni Morrison meditates upon it in *The Bluest Eye* with devastating simplicity. We see the roots of psychic and social conditioning, Black women "edging into life from the back door. Becoming." Much of what they would "become" would be translated for them in narratives of subjugation; their physical selves never would be good enough. Judgments and authority would emanate from every quarter. "Everybody in the world was in a position to give them orders. White women said, 'Do this.' White children said, 'Give me that.' White men said, 'Come here.' Black men said, 'Lay down.'"[38]

The conceptual interrogation of Black womanhood has a feminist history, rendered powerfully in Morrison's brief testament, which always takes us back to this painful image. A wounding, but elegantly telling, image which can serve as an essential mechanism for allowing us to capture a lived reality and a political moment which we ought not forget. This image schools us, in our attempted deconstructions of feminine tyranny, to keep our priorities clear, insists that we knot theories about symbols tightly to the deep context of those social relations which call up in Black women a diminished self. Such a deep context of inquiry helps feminist theory avoid the bloodless abstractions Spillers warns us against: "The feminist universe of academic discourse threatens to lose its living and palpable connection to training in the feelings and to become, rather, a mode of theatre for the dominating mythologies."[39]

Gender Signs: The Politics of Skin Color and Hair

Let me now draw from the articulated self-understandings of a small survey of Black women to concretize, in Spillers's terms, the living, palpable connection of ideological abstractions to the historical mappings of Black women's lives. What is the collective self-image of debasement Black women identify in their gender conflicts? The following accounts foreground the range of emotions, practices, and taboos which have impacted on the self-esteem of Black women around the politics of gender, womanhood, sexuality, and beauty.

First historian Gerda Lerner provides a historical context. Her interpretation of a rhetoric of racism, "The Myth of the 'Bad' Black Woman," which arose during Reconstruction, examines a mythology which served as an "effective" and deadly discursive mechanism that supported the increasing lynching of Black men and the rape and sexual exploitation of Black women. Lerner's words point to those subtle indicators of extreme degradation, those "symbolic whips and chains," in Orlando Patterson's words, which contributed during slavery and today to Black women's social death and dishonor.[40]

> A myth was created that all black women were eager for sexual ex-
> ploits, voluntarily "loose" in their morals, and therefore, deserved
> none of the consideration and respect granted to white women. Every
> black woman was, by definition, a slut according to this racist myth-
> ology; therefore, to assault her and exploit her sexually was not repre-
> hensible and carried with it none of the normal communal sanctions
> against such behavior. A wide range of practices reinforcd this myth:
> the laws against intermarriage; the denial of the title "Miss" or "Mrs."
> to any black woman; the taboos against respectable social mixing of
> the races; the refusal to let black women customers try on clothing in
> stores before making a purchase; the assigning of single toilet facili-
> ties to both sexes of blacks; the different legal sanctions against rape,
> abuse of minors and other sex crimes when committed against white
> or black women.[41]

It would be hard to conceive of a more savage construct. How could
the Black female hope to share the symbolic gendered world of white
women if her body were thought to defile commodities of clothing?
How would she avoid being called "girl" or "Aunt Jemima" without
the status of the patriarchy's honorifics? How could she think of herself as a deserving social being, with claims to modesty, when even
architectural structures rebuked her?

   In 1933, the Black feminist educator Mary McLeod Bethune delivered the following address, "A Century of Progress of Negro Women,"
to the Chicago Women's Federation. Thousands of women like Bethune
joined together in the club movement of the late nineteenth century,
to mount massive political campaigns to counter white America's
vilification of Black women as immoral beings. Bethune's speeches re-
sounded in anger and determination against the society which had
tried unsuccessfully to take her humanity away. She began her apologia
with the baggage of history:

> One hundred years ago [the black woman] was the most pathetic
> figure on the American continent. She was not a person, in the opin-
> ion of many, but a thing, a thing whose personality had no claim to
> the respect of mankind. She was a house-hold drudge—a means for
> getting distasteful work done; she was an animated agricultural im-
> plement to augment the service of mules and plows in cultivating and
> harvesting the cotton crop. Then she was an automatic incubator, a
> producer of human live stock, beneath whose heart and lungs more
> potential laborers could be bred and nurtured and brought to the
> light of toilsome day.[42]

The harshness of Bethune's tone equals the brutality of the life world she depicts. This is a legacy which evokes instant recognition in the writings of more recent Black women whose conceptualizations of their own liberatory projects "know" their own "pathetic" configurations to be anchored in some generative way to this savage past. Abbey Lincoln began her 1966 manifesto, "Who Will Revere the Black Woman?", with this theory of internal colonization: "When a country enslaves a people, the first necessary job is to make the world feel that the people to be enslaved are subhuman. The next job is to make his fellow countryman believe that man is inferior, then, the unkindest cut of all is to make that man believe himself inferior." This is Lincoln's discourse of resistance to the gendered inferiority felt in her own life:

> We are the women whose hair is compulsively fried, whose skin is
> bleached, whose nose is 'too big,' whose mouth is 'too big and loud,'
> whose behind is 'too big and broad,' whose feet are 'too big and flat,'
> whose face is 'too black and shiny,' and whose suffering and patience
> is too long and enduring to be believed. . . . Who will revere the
> Black woman? Who will keep our neighborhoods safe for Black inno-
> cent womanhood? Black womanhood is outraged and humiliated.
> Black womanhood cries for dignity and restitution and salvation.
> Black womanhood wants and needs protection, and keeping, and
> holding. Who will assuage her indignation? Who will keep her
> precious and pure? Who will glorify and proclaim her beautiful
> image? To whom will she cry rape?[43]

There is much in the linguistic construction of Lincoln's jeremiad that white feminist theorists may fault: the somewhat overheated language of restitution and salvation, the call for patriarchal "protection," and the yearning for a precious and pure womanhood. But when read across the searing historical account provided by Bethune and in the context of figurations which gave rise to the dynamic of inferiority passed on by the dominant white culture, Lincoln's statement might be seen differently. It can be read as a great refusal of the conventions of beauty, a refusal of the stigmatizing "toos," of physical markings too broad, too fat, too dark, which rendered the Black woman not only *other*, but *less*.

Black feminists today write about their difficulty in coming to accept, love, and cherish their physical selves. Both bell hooks and Alice Walker have employed rhetorics to speak about their hair[44] which resound with harsh metaphors against those rituals of mutilation—

evoked in Lincoln's "fried" hair and "bleached" skin — which Black women have been socialized to inflict upon their bodies. Walker, for instance, has written about her obsession with the "unruly willfulness," the "badness," of her hair; and about how that preoccupation became a barrier to her spiritual development. Her aggression towards her hair, she says, blocked her development as an ethical person. "Oppressed hair puts a ceiling on the brain," she discovered. It was not until her fortieth birthday that she came to reject the "missionary work" of dominating, suppressing, and controlling her hair. When she came to accept "my friend hair" for its own true self — "springy, soft, almost sensually responsive to moisture"— the ceiling on her brain lifted.[45]

Bell hooks has written about the complexities and emotional resonance of the Black female world which evolved, ironically, from white standards of beauty. Black women developed cultural practices and communal "female-only" spaces for beauty rituals; they made of these spaces reservoirs of political and cultural enhancement. Hooks has reflected on the intimate bonding she felt as a child on Saturday mornings when the "real women" of her family gathered in the kitchen to have their hair straightened, listen to soul music, and savor the cooking smells. For hooks, these memories embodied rich cultural meaning, a time for Black women to enjoy one another's company and to communicate about the struggles and joys of their daily lives. She points to what might be a universal contradiction, or slippage, in the dictates of gender conventions: women everywhere can and do manipulate the social spaces and behavior allowed them by the hegemonic culture for their own ends of community-building, often subverting the "vanity" dimension in reversals of accepted ideas of femininity.[46] Because of these empowering dimensions, hooks confesses that for many years she could not reflect critically about the racist implications of "hair pressing." The kitchen rituals provided a space of Black sisterhood, safety, and empowerment, free of restrictive white judgments. "It was a world where the images constructed as barriers between one's self and the world were briefly let go, before they were made again. It was a moment of creativity, a moment of change."

As hooks began to develop her own critical consciousness about the connections between white supremacy and Black women's obsession with hair, she noted the pragmatics of economic necessity as a factor in Black women's rejection of natural or Afro hairdos. The need to look white and wear "straight hair" forces an aesthetic assimiliationism upon Black women: to get jobs their "Blackness" has to be played down, the African-inspired braids and dreads being too threatening to the white world. Hooks describes a doubly oppressive scenario involving Black women's own internalized sense of their hair as "ugly, frightening," as well as their rejection by Black men, who often preferred "white" straightened hair. Hooks's subsequent conversations with young Black women about these issues reveal, she says, low self-esteem, low self-actualization, internalized inferiority. "We talk about the extent to which black women perceive our hair as the enemy, as a problem we must solve, a territory we must conquer. Above all it is a part of our black female body that must be controlled."[47]

Black culture provides its own normative discourse on the bodies and hair of Black women. From the earliest African-American literature, readers can find admiring passages praising "fine" European hair, "delicate" features, "chistled noses," and "silky hair." Often "Black" female heroines were portrayed with these colonized images not their own. The cruel "blue-vein" and "paper-bag" skin color tests employed by bourgeois Black social clubs early in this century instituted hierarchies of "whiteness as rightness," conjoining color-consciousness with class privilege. Even the 1960s, Black Power rhetoric of "Black is beautiful"[48] could not excise the pathology of colorism, preference for light-skinned women, in the Black community. Contemporary Black women remain victimized by — and often perpetrators of — the "wannabe" (as in the "I wannabe white" phenomenon dramatized in Spike Lee's film *School Daze*) ideology that contributes to their own and their Black sisters' oppression. Three feminist women of color recently provided this critique of Blacks' internalized white-skin preference at a national feminist conference:

> When black women within this racist and color-conscious society despise and degrade darker women, identification with the racist oppressor is complete. And when black women turn against lighter black women, this is the subconscious frustration and envy better directed toward a racist and sexist society, which assigns status and power to one's race and gender. By attaching values to skin colors, black women buy into the notion that beauty and femininity are a black woman's most important virtue, thereby relinquishing the power of self-definition.[49]

Building on Trellie Jeffers's exposure of the "dirty little secret" of
colorism in African-American life, Alice Walker's manifesto to the
"black Black Woman" is a biting rejoinder not only to the racism of
the bourgeois class of African Americans, but also to the hostility many
Black women direct to darker-skinned Black women. In Jeffers's reading, white-identified "beauty" rituals which purport to "improve"
Black women's own embodiment become self-destructive "insanities,"
collusions that only help "whites turn blacks on themselves," causing
Blacks to "claw [themselves] into a form of psychic annihilation."[50]
Walker radicalizes W.E.B. Du Bois's 1903 statement, "The problem
of the twentieth century is the problem of the color-line," as a male
formulation, problematizing instead the relations between the darker
and lighter people of the same races. In Walker's commitment to align
herself with dark-skinned Black women, we see just how vast and
punishing are the ideological spillovers of white supremacy, how destructive to Blacks' own efforts at solidarity. But Walker provides a
powerful context and counter-self-image for Black women, a model
of dark-skinned female militancy located in Black women's own past.
Walker's analysis makes clear how colorism both stigmatizes dark-
skinned Black women and denigrates the lighter-skinned female, pre-
venting solidarity between the two.

> And who is being rejected? . . . Harriet Tubman, for one, Sojourner
> Truth, Mary McLeod Bethune. . . . You who are black-skinned and
> fighting and screaming through the solid rock of America up to your
> hip pockets every day since you arrived. . . . Light and white-skinned
> black women will lose their only link to rebellion against white
> America if they cut themselves off from the black black woman.
> Their children will have no hip pockets in which to keep their
> weapons, no teeth with which to chew up racist laws. And black
> women will lose the full meaning of their history in America (as well
> as the humor, love, and support of good sisters) if they see light and
> white black women only as extensions of white and black male op-
> pression, while allowing themselves to be made ashamed of their own
> strength and fighting spirit: that fighting spirit that is our birth-right,
> and, for some of us, our "rusty black" joy.[51]

Walker is able to turn a white-induced discourse of self-hatred into
a collective call for Black feminist unity and self-actualization. Her
paean is a retrieval of skin, color, and hair — those signifiers of gender

battles which require psychological defenses, practices, and strategies of re-valuation, always working across the grain of white supremacy. She offers a different model of female empowerment from that of Abbey Lincoln. In militant pride, Black women need not be dependent and vulnerable, seeking the approval of male "reverence" and looking outward for sources of female protection. By a feminist *will* and a self-sustaining symbolic entity — the black Black woman — Black women can find richness, integrity, and glory in the bodies and tones before them. By celebrating the beauty and strength of Black women themselves, Walker undercuts the "feminine" need for a protective patriarchal "defender." In this, she reclaims Black women's own bodies, sexuality, and fighting spirit as vehicles for liberation and self-perception.

But for many Black women, their defense against the plethora of negativities surrounding their bodies and sexuality is confronted as vulnerable individuals. The world of racist gender signs — cultural messages and images "always already" there defining the Black woman's physical worth — can penetrate even the strongest psychological barriers. The following comments from one young Black woman remind us of the internal self-censoring mechanisms which come into play to thwart Black women's desire, to pervert their pleasures and suppress their sexuality.

> As a Black woman . . . all eyes seem to be focused on you. That means I am constantly aware of the need not to confirm stereotypes in any way . . . I also notice that I choose my clothing with some care not to appear sexually provocative. As a Black woman you are seen as something of a whore to begin with and I just refuse to play to that stereotype. . . . Since I was eleven, I've been aware of how white men look at Black women — the exotic sex object . . . always available.[52]

Doesn't this help us understand the pressures on Black women to conform, to assimiliate their physicality to white acceptability, to curb their erotic selves? The world of feminine codifications often does not yield so easily to gender resisters; defiance often exacts a high cost. Listen to another young Black woman whose nascent sense of sexual exploration was brought up short by the wall of racist ideology:

> A lot of women do their utmost to be good rather than following their own fantasies. And especially for Black women that is a never ending race, because you are never good enough. You can look really

beautiful, you can even be seen as sexually attractive, but the very next moment, *someone may just spit in your face.*[53]

No woman should have to live her daily life is the shadow of such a fear. Can we feel its weight? That word, *denigration?* In Alice Walker's meditation occasioned by Zora Neale Hurston's "mule of the world" epithet, we find some sort of solace, interpretive grounding, a bridge past oppressive internalizations. Walker's words suggest the diminution of self experienced by Black women whose skin and bodies, on our streets, invite the white assaults described above. We might imagine, as Walker does, the collective pain felt by Black women: How many moments have they "considered themselves unworthy even of hope"? How many women abandoned their bodies into selfless abstractions? In order to survive, Black women must have, in Walker's words, "forced their minds to desert their bodies." And there are those Black women, "even whose plainer gifts, labors of fidelity and love, have been knocked down our throats."[54]

An anecdote from Pauli Murray's life sums up the testimony. Murray, the accomplished Black female attorney and theologian, stood before fifteen hundred people in 1979 at the First National Scholarly Conference on the History of Black Women and told a revealing story. Thirty years prior, Murray had been the sole female graduate in her class from Howard University Law School; after great difficulty, she finally secured a post with a New York law firm. One of Murray's first cases was serving as counsel for a poor woman from Harlem who was accused of prostitution. The chief witness against the woman was the "john" who had contracted for her sexual services. After having presented in detail every facet of the sexual transaction, the prosecutor asked the witness to identify the woman whom he had hired. Without a moment's hesitation, Murray recounted, the witness turned before the courtroom and broadly pointed *to her as the prostitute.*

Murray's largely female scholarly audience burst into laughter upon hearing this incredible story—as did she. But despite the laughter, Murray's intent in conveying that story, as she said, was to assure that each woman present understood the total humiliation to which she had been subjected.[55] In sharing that part of her past, Murray transferred her private pain into a public act of resistance for herself and other Black women who had been similarly slandered.

Pedestals, Maids, and Rituals of Deference

The record of the enormity of the frauds which have been marshaled to convince Black women that her presence was an assault to the very idea of being is long. Adrienne Rich's words, with which I began, frame the next contradiction and take us to one of the rawest symbolic segregations of Black from white women: "That flesh encloses a foreign country. You cannot know it. It speaks a foreign language. It is alien territory."[56] This story talks about our misreadings of one other, about the screen that ideologies, mythologies, codes of representation place between our feminist selves. The master frauds of patriarchy create their own contradictions, mystifications, in our minds. In our efforts to deconstruct the colonizing male stereotypes which "create" images and icons of our physical appearance, we often come close to analyses which describe how both Black and white women are pawns in the game of male-created iconography. We see a certain symmetry in the polarized images — the white woman's body a shrine, the Black woman's a sexual receptacle — as co-dependents in assuring the other's debasement. But then the male mythologies put "their" words into our mouths, induce "us" to believe in one another's alienness. Thus begin our own mystification discourses, idealizations, projections. Our participation in the patriarchy's stories about the "meaning" of one another's images segregates us, thwarts feminist connections.

In a series of 1977 interviews, members of the National Alliance of Black Feminists (echoing many previous such efforts by Black women in American history) defined as their primary project educating the white public about Black women's dignity. "Black women should reach the white community and let them know that black women are *not dirt*," one member declared. Another identified Black women's sense of debasement and dishonor as a deterrent to feminist organizing: "Many black women have deep enmity for white women because black women don't fit the white standard of beauty and because white women have always been ladies and black women haven't been eligible for 'lady-hood.'" Another member argued that "black women have always held the lower position in society . . . white women were placed on a pedestal that black women were never afforded. . . . Black women were forced to go out and work because they often had the only jobs open to blacks at the time." Not only did the Black female often internalize these gender symbols, but also "the black man adopted the white man's belief. He felt that a real woman would not be out working but would be nice and feminine, smelling sweet when he came home."[57]

We know that these presumptions about pedestals rest on slippery empirical ground, belied by the economic vulnerability of the majority of women. We know that most white women, like most women of color, are exploited and underpaid in the service economy, victims of the feminization of poverty.[58] But we know, too, that for Black women, the brutalities of poverty resonate historically in profound and cyclical ways.[59] As a group, Black women historically have been white women's "menials," with divergent working lives forming the greatest gulf between Black and middle-class white women.[60] While touting the liberating potential of work, white feminists often have been insensitive to the onerous history of Black women's working lives in America. Not only has Black women's collective work experience been far from rewarding, but most have performed the dirtiest, most dangerous, most reviled tasks under the supervision of white women "superiors." This history gives rise to the most painful assumptions which challenge at every turn the Black female's "femininity." One such scenario involved a white female employer of a Black maid who demanded to see a health card, fearing the germs her family might contract from the Black maid's unhygienic "filthy" Harlem lifestyle.[61] Or consider the insistence of a queasy white housewife that her live-in maid never eat in her family's presence. This rhetoric of sanitized control of the domestic physical space segregated the maid, when not laboring, to the one allowable space, the kitchen—"the black town, the nigger room of the white house," in Trudier Harris's sardonic characterization. The kitchen becomes a spatial metaphor, a realm of insult which reinforces both the domestic's place in the kitchen and the "intrafamilal hierarchy of worth."[62]

Whether in the historical plantation household or in modernity's urban apartment, the arena of household labor has been the Black female's domestic ghetto, an arena of "no money, no respect and long hours" one domestic decried, which became for contemporary Black women "a second slavery."[63] Within the invisibility and imposed silence of the white household, the Black "cleaning lady" is isolated from other workers, without benefit of union protection, subject to the potential of rape and sexual assault from male employers, as are all female domestics. On another taxing, though less physically threatening front, the Black domestic is subject to the whims of the condescending and suspicious white women who dictate the day-to-day conditions of their labor. Black domestics have always been forced to devise individual strategies for dealing with white employers. Their work, more than any other sort, has depended on the possession of intricate skills at maneuvering through white attitudes, adopting demeaning "rituals of deference," in Judith Rollins's term. But such indignities were resisted in many subtle daily sabotages which enabled domestics to endure the arduous, boring, and repetitive work. They became skilled performers, adept at ingratiating subservient behaviors that flattered the egos of white housewives. Despite having spent time on their knees, these Black women struggled to maintain their self-esteem and dignity. The Black domestic knew, even if whites deluded themselves to the contrary, that she never was "one of the family."[64]

But in countless ways the domestic's own family life was shattered; laboring in a well-ordered, attractive white home inevitably elicited comparisons with the domestic's own usually substandard, cramped, and often dangerous tenement or shack. Such transitions from luxury to squalor often made "coming home hard" for the domestic, as Toni Morrison has her character Pauline Breedlove admit in *The Bluest Eye*. The alienating vicariousness of the employer's home provided a surrogate "haven" for the domestic, a world denied her, with "beauty, order, cleanliness, and praise."[65]

The potency of this legacy — and the critical interpretation of its dynamics by contemporary Black feminists, whose own families often bear witness to its scars — should not be underestimated. The centrality of the role of domestic presents an image of Black women most common to their history, replicating in so many ways the relationships learned in the bondage of slavery. The novels, poetry, and scholarly analyses of African-American feminists are filled with stories of the burdens their own families have suffered from their mothers', grandmothers', sisters', and even their own service as household laborers. These violations of the domestic's own sense of family structure were commonplace, merely aspects of the job that were to be expected and endured. Usually a single parent, the Black domestic had to train her own children to survive her absence; this imposed neglect of her own children, who were left to cook and clean for themselves and do their homework alone, meant that the Black domestic's nurturing and attention sometimes became a perishable commodity. The loving daily care of the white children in her charge often left little time for her own obligations of motherhood. The responsibility of parenting often became an imposition curtailing the childhood of the daughters.[66] Then there is the indignity of receiving second-hand clothing and other detritus from white benefactors; the shameful sense of dependence on leftover food brought home on buses and subways late at night. Dorothy Bolden remembers vividly the "service pans," bacon drippings, leftover food, old clothes and shoes bequeathed by white employers, "thinking they had paid you off."[67]

Contemporary Black feminists have provided powerful analyses of the socioeconomic and psychological burdens which this most intensely exploitative role has meant in terms of relating to white women. This scholarship can inform white feminists as to why this kind of work has been an insult to Black women as human beings; it should prioritize feminist resources and organizing. But beyond the need for committed activism on behalf of such exploited female workers, white women must be able to comprehend the social construction of racism, in the context of gender, as it is played out between Black and white women in this volatile historical mistress-servant relationship. As in slavery, the "explosive intimacy"[68] between white mistress and Black servant assured that their interactions would be complexly cruel, occasionally tender, competitive, distrustful, and inevitably unsatisfying. Sisterhood was anathema to these relations, despite the sway of patriarchal control over both groups of women. Because the white woman's sense of superiority was bolstered by the "defilement" of the Black female, their conflicting images of womanhood always would be combustible. And, as in the plantation setting, the Black female domestic's humanity rarely would come alive to her white mistress, who more often than not viewed her Black servant only in terms of an ability to render services and to serve as a receptacle for white images. Minrose Gwin's assessment of these tensions, gleaned from analyses of slave narratives and plantation mistresses' diaries, applies with equal validity to contemporary domestic-employer scenarios:

> White women . . . rarely perceive or acknowledge . . . the humanity
> of their black sisters. Most of these white women in life and litera-
> ture, see black women as a color, as servants, as children, as adjuncts,
> as sexual competition, as dark sides of their own sexual selves — as
> black other. They beat black women, nurture them, sentimentalize
> them, despise them — but they seldom see them as individuals with
> selves commensurate to their own.[69]

From this myopic context white America's most pernicious stereotypes about Black women have derived. Through the work of Judith
Rollins, in particular, we can begin to understand the degrading in-
terpersonal patterns which have so dispirited Black female domestics.
The essence of the relationship between domestics and their white
employers, Rollins argues, is inherently psychologically exploitative in
a specifically gendered context; the typical employer "extracts more
than labor." The particular gendered form of racist oppression analyzed
by Rollins is the "maternalism" of white female employers, a kind of
social and structural patterning affecting both white and Black women
under patriarchy. For both groups, having internalized a belief in
their inherent inferiority as women and being beholden to a male external power holding higher social status than either of them

> make their interrelations different from those in which one or both
> parties is male. The employer might herself be a material and
> psychological dependent. She has the luxury of identifying with
> power but she is not the ultimate power. Both she and the domestic
> know this. The domestic must show deference to an agent of a real
> power; she must show deference to a second-class power figure for
> survival.[70]

Rollins's unraveling of this dynamic sheds conceptual light on just
why it is that the realm of domestic labor, and those who engage in
it, are held in such low regard. Because the white female employer
is "inferior" in gender to the male and a "pseudo-authority" under his
dispensation, both women internalize disdain for such labor, concur-
rent with society's devaluation of "woman's work." A descending cycle
of internalized debasement is enacted; but there is never any doubt
about the white woman's class and race advantages. The employer's
low regard for this work combines with her own sexism, racism, and
class prejudice further to degrade the work and those groups of women
most subordinated in American society.

> One can begin to see why the lower-class woman of color, just *because* of this society's sexism, racism, and class prejudice might be psychologically the most desirable "type" for a position of servitude and why being associated with this archetypical "women's work" further degrades her — even, or perhaps especially, in the eyes of her female employer. The employer benefits from the degradation because it underscores the power and advantage (easily interpreted as the rightness) of being white and middle-class.[71]

This is the *mentalité* which must be fathomed in order to see how Black women's very sense of femaleness, womanhood, and dignity is questioned daily through the mechanism of their most demanding work identity. The Black female domestic toils in a physical and mental universe which defines them with a logic based on a kind of guilt and inferiority by association with dirt and uncleanliness. Defilement in labor spills over to defilement in spiritual capacity. Patriarchal conceptions of womanhood long have associated the idea of female softness and delicacy with a corresponding moral character; but the dark female, capable of grinding work and fatigue, is at odds with such imagery. As in slavery, Black servants/slaves "were not represented as the same order of being as their mistresses; they lacked the physical, external evidence of the presence of a pure soul."[72] Even their names have been taken away, capriciously replaced by denominations preferred by their white employers.[73] The insult of renaming constitutes one mechanism of "keeping Black maids in their place." What is achieved in psychic terms by such practices is deference, requiring the adoption of a personality and posture "low down"; as one Black domestic reiterated, "act like you're down there." Being low down there (physically and ethically, the spatial dictates of the metaphor apply) hardly enhances one's sense of attractiveness and physical appeal.

Rollins, who herself worked as a domestic while researching her book *Between Women*, remarked on the aesthetic aspect of the domestic experience, the depression which comes from knowing that one is not "presentable." Rollins discovered that an enforced ugliness became part of the domestic persona; competition with the white employer always was to be avoided, as was any comportment which suggested equality. Such equality could not be tolerated. The domestic was required to be nonthreatening in all ways, especially physical attractiveness. Rollins describes how one's personal pride is diminished by the drab, dull, ugly clothing required of one whose functional goal is hard cleaning work.

> Not only did I feel no encouragement for grooming and working at attractiveness, but unlike any other type of job I've held, I felt the worse I looked . . . the more my employers liked it. . . . I submit that on some level [domestics] were aware as I was, that the female employer prefered the presence of another woman whose appearance, as well as other attributes, was inferior to her own.[74]

Perhaps in the scenarios described above are to be found the most devastating denials of physical worthiness. These small dramas of hostility between Black and white women leave an indelible mark of bitterness and resentment; they chart the vast patterns of symbolic otherness which often texture the intersection of white and Black worlds.[75] Black women's images as domestics, low down there, have been, are, the negative contrast enhancing the white woman's own reflection. While the former holds white families together, her own communities and children are left to the vicissitudes of daily survival struggles; such women worry about housing, children, drugs, endemic poverty, and institutionalized racism, as they nurture the children of others.[76] These women do, however, as Alice Childress shows us so vividly in her stories, survive dehumanizing patterns, resist and carry on, working to bring some sense of security and equity to the personal interstices where their physical and emotional labor is performed. And in this struggle, they "refused to exchange dignity for pay."[77]

Class privilege and hierarchies do shift with skin color. But exploitive relations also obtain when Black domestics labor for more privileged Black women. Those relations, perhaps more susceptible to exchanges of sisterly empathy and equity than are those with the white female employer, nevertheless are framed in the context of the capitalist service economy. Such relationships often exhibit their own forms of intraracial tensions. June Jordan has brought us such a scenario. Jordan, a middle-class feminist academic African-American poet visiting in a multinational hotel in the Bahamas, is confronted with her exploitative relation to the unseen maid, "Olive," who cleans her room while the poet relaxes on the beach during her first vacation in years. The scope of Jordan's power over the Third World maid's very livelihood is brought home when Jordan reflects on the sterile white card placed on her hotel bureau, "Dear Guests:" it says, under the name "Olive." "I am your maid for the day. Please rate me: Excellent. Good. Average. Poor. Thank you." This awkward nonencounter between Jordan and "Olive" becomes an occasion for Jordan's critical resistance to the structures of class, race, and gender which polarize these two women. The economics of international tourism subvert feminist alliance and are designed to square women off as antagonists: "We are not particularly women anymore; we are parties to a transaction designed to set us against one another."[78]

Jordan tries to imagine the night-shift "Olive," as she dutifully manicures the room for her—clean sheets, dustless furniture, fresh towels for tomorrow's swim in the azure ocean. "Olive" may be older than Jordan, she may smoke a cigarette while she changes the sheets on the bed. Jordan would want to tell her how much she needed this vacation, to leave the stress of overwork and underpay in North American universities, why she chose the colonial Sheraton Hotel for her safety as a Black woman alone. These entreaties would be delivered, as Jordan rationalizes, in a feminist discourse of "New World Values," assertively legitimizing Jordan's own "rights," "freedom," and "desires." Jordan asks herself, what would such declarations sound like to this Black woman described in the card atop her hotel bureau as "Olive." "Whose rights? Whose freedom? Whose desire? And why should she give a shit about mine unless I do something, for real, about hers?"[79]

Jordan teaches a vital lesson here by validating the experience and oppression of the other, by assuming "Olive's" perspective and fragile living conditions to be the crucial political anchorage. Rate "Olive"? "How would Olive rate *me*? What would it mean for us to seem 'good' to each other? What would that rating require?"[80] The ultimate political connection between two such women is, of course, the economic structure which requires the creation of evaluation cards in the first place, the geopolitical availability of Third World havens for vacationers who take but who do not give. But the essential analysis for reversing the oppression which Jordan gives us is the potential for solidarity. The rest of us, like Jordan, need to be "burning up" with commitment to build toward that "ultimate connection" between "us" and those women who labor as "Olives." The connection must be the need that we find between us—not "who we are," but what we can do for each other that will determine the connection. We can, in building up solidarity, *take responsibility* for the conditions of "others." As committed feminist activists willing actually to see beyond our own lives, we need to inquire into how those women whose labor underwrites our existence, rate us. Then we act, as Jordan urges, to do something *for real* to change their lives.

These stories give us a context, then, when we read in Black feminist texts angry idealizations of that icon, the Privileged White Feminist. The assumptions about white female's lives of leisure do come from somewhere, don't they? But Jordan's story tells us that Black women, too, can have pedestals and privilege over the Black women who serve them. Lorraine Bethel's trenchant poem, "What 'Chou Mean 'We' White Girl," is emblematic of the ease with which generalizations about "white woman" are naturalized as a part of Blacks' political understanding.

> I bought a sweater at a yard sale from a white-skinned . . . woman. When wearing it I am struck by the smell — it reeks of a soft, privileged life without stress, sweat, or struggle. When wearing it I often think to myself: this sweater smells of a comfort, a way of being in the world I have never known in my life, and never will.[81]

This theme is repeated in an earlier poem by June Jordan entitled "What Would I Do White?" Jordan depicts white women as rich, haughty, lazy, and acquisitive, and muses about what she would do as a white woman: "I would do nothing. That would be enough." The Black feminist literary critic Mary Helen Washington centers us about this pedestal discourse, tells us why these negative stereotypes of white women abound in the contemporary literature of Black female writers:

> [Jordan's poem] implies, of course, the worthlessness of white women's lives. The hostility expressed in this poem is often found in the black woman writer's attitude toward white women. The white woman as she appears in the literature of black women is almost always described in negative terms: a callous and indifferent employer of black domestics, a phony liberal, a southern racist participating with her men in a lynching, the snobbish upper-class woman. And without exception she is always condescending to the black woman.[82]

I was angered when I first read Bethel and Jordan's poems; I resisted the assumptions that all white women are selfish, spoiled, and oppressing. But their words evoke histories and practices white feminists need to know in order to go forward. We white feminists can know the origin of these narratives, the interactions and practices from which they arise, and finally be able to see how they are connected to the man-made myths about one another's beauty, privileges, womanhood. Only then may we develop a theory which can reveal how all women's images are stolen, entrapped in men's judgments, judgments that women often uphold, pursue, and pass on to our daughters. Washington points to that historical ground which spawned the practices of reiterating polarities. When Black feminists attack white feminists for not forfeiting their gender privilege and the invisible "pedestals" (which *some* of us and *some* Black women take for granted), they are acting not so much out of a demonstrated socioeconomic reality as out of a collective memory of being rated, ranked, and classified by a white world. In interpreting fictional texts of Black female writers in which white women are depicted as pampered, spoiled, and essentially weak, Washington articulates this history of indignities:

> The black women . . . are forced to confront their feelings about
> white women. In neither case are the black women reacting to
> an individual white woman. They are reacting to centuries of
> abuse, alienation, and hostility, in short to what White Woman has
> meant to Black Woman. They are reacting to the privileged status of
> white women in this country; they are reacting to all the years that
> black women have done slave work and daywork in the homes of
> white women while neglecting their own; to all those white women
> who called them by their first names no matter how old they were,
> while they continued to address their employer as Mrs. So-and-So; to
> all the times white women were given jobs up front in the store while
> they were stuck back in the stock room or in the kitchen, where they
> would not be seen; to all the years when it was possible for a white
> woman to pretend rape and have a black man executed and no one to
> whom a black woman could cry rape. . . . The relationship between
> them is still tied to the past.[83]

Washington's interpretation of this deep cycle of hierarchies can be read as telling white feminists "not to take it personally." She might be suggesting to us an antidote to the cycle of misperceptions, idealizations, and projections. We can listen, we can know the histories, assuming our part in seeing they won't occur again, and accept tensions. We ought not to resist being accountable for this history; it is our collective responsibility to be grounded in the historical and economic conditions that have made our current misperceptions possible. To accept this antidote of accountability is not to fall back on a reactionary infinite regression — "But I wasn't alive then, I didn't do those things," "I've never had a maid." To acknowledge those practices, such as the inequalities in the relationship of maid to mistress, once and for all, is to free us to see where our alliances today need to be and what our priorities need to be.

Images and Counterimages:
Mystifications of the Feminist Other

Black women's experiences of humiliation cast a long shadow over our attempts to carve out spaces for feminist diversity and differences and a new aesthetics of self. We continue, in many ways, to image one another wrongly, we become propagandists for the male myths — white woman on the pedestal; Black woman, "something less," always on the bottom of something. White feminists' efforts to ameliorate the gender tyranny inflicted on Black women, the culture's own gynophobia (hatred of the female body), often work troubling kinds of voodoo on our consciousness. In the process of trying to right the wrongs, why do we sometimes create omniscient fantasies and mythic misperceptions of Black women? Why do Black or other women of color sometimes become in white minds mysterious, possessors of magic or special truth?[84]

Where does a new feminist archetype I have seen fit into these constellations? In recent years, the high visibility of Black feminists, the power of their critiques and texts, the excitement, beauty, and drama of their dress — African robes, scarves, jewelry, elaborate hair fashions, braids, and dredlocks — has created an entirely new feminist aesthetic. Such women's appearances at feminist conferences carry a brand new kind of visual charisma and female power. No-one misses them. They are a presence, a vision. This excites me greatly.

Recently, in a Berkeley bookstore, I was captivated by a photograph of a beautiful dark-skinned woman on the wall. I later realized it was from a magazine, an expensive French perfume ad. The woman in the photograph is riding a horse on a white-sand beach, with brilliant aqua water behind her; her hair, in long kinky masses, is held in front by an ethnic woven headband, and it flies in the wind. She is wearing a rough-looking fringed shawl, ripped blue jeans, and boots. The image is muscular, energetic, and powerful. Then you focus on the perfume ad's message: "Tender and impetuous Amazone." When I remarked on the image to a feminist woman of color who was with me, she grinned ironically and said, "That's how you all want us to look now, isn't it?" I protested that it was not *I* who was eroticizing the woman of color's image of "Amazone," the classic signifier of the sexualized woman of color, but the corporate marketing hacks who designed the ad copy.

But as we engaged in dialogue about the image, it became clear to both of us that such an image was saturated in conflicting meanings which couldn't easily be separated. Was my admiration of the beauty and "ethnic" power of women of color somehow implicated in the magazine's iconography? My motives were feminist, truly admiring, celebratory of a new kind of feminist representation. Was this a harmful, manipulative projection? My friend and I determined that since the image had not originated from the imagination of feminist women of color themselves, but in the mercenary mills of Madison Avenue, it was a warning about the ambiguities of fantasizing images in general. In the context of racism and the practices of consumer capitalism, was there any other perspective in which my admiration could be framed?

If that was "how 'we' wanted women of color to be imaged nowadays," how, I asked my friend, were white feminists envisioned? What was the coded imagery into which white representations were supposed to "fit"? She jokingly responded, "Oh, WASP, colorless, plain, and definitely 'unfunky.'" My friend's answer, while ironically meant, did put us onto something troubling. Was the negativitity about white images more "true" than our bantering allowed? After more repartee about the ambivalences involved in attempting to fantasize our political, racial, and gender politics, my friend remarked, "There's really no 'good' image for you to have; however you appear, it's probably going to backfire, no matter how you 'mean it.'"

In subsequent conversations with other feminist women of color,

I've found that the issue of projecting a new counterfeminist image (counter, that is, to the white, blue-eyed, blond icon) evokes conflicting expectations. Some women of color have told me of their feelings of inadequacy about their own "plainness," their inability to fit the image of the colorfully dressed "Radical Woman of Color." They say the "exotic" image of Afrocentric feminists excludes and exploits them, creates a style-induced segregation in their own communities. They say they get judged negatively or ignored (by both white and Black progressive women) if they don't "look like Black feminists are supposed to look."[85]

In my own feminist classroom, discussions with students about the political implications of oppositional standards of beauty often become contentious, revealing intense commitments to often contradictory notions of race and gender representations of self. When an outspoken, beautiful Black woman with "white" features and straightened hair asserts that it is her "right" to choose to wear blue contact lenses and "preppy" rather than "ethnic" clothing, she is met with admonitions from radical *white* female students. It is they who expect her to be the badge of "her people"; they urge her not to deny or invalidate her "Blackness," her "special" beauty. The white radical students seem to love the *frisson* that "Blackness" gives, while the Black student resists, as she said, being trapped into any "racial mold." We debate about the potential for appropriation in our Hawaiian community when *haole* (white) women wear Zulu African bracelets or Hawaiian-style dress or jewelry, or dance the *hula*, insisting that such sartorial symbolism can be fraudulent. Casual appropriation of the cultural symbols of people of color can represent a co-optation of those people who are in struggle against racist colonial heritages if it is not conjoined with activism on behalf of such peoples.

We commiserate about the confusions around feminist practices of "confrontational dressing" and around readings of politically-correct symbolism.[86] We don't come up with too much clarity, but we agree the questions are important: Do certain self-designated people stand as radical "vanguards" to judge others' purity? Who, in our oppositional community, *owns* the images, artifacts, and clothing of Third World peoples? What principles legitimize such ownership? By what criteria do we "know" who can justly dispense scorn or praise to regulate "our" use of "their" cultural artifacts? How does one send off visual signals that one is wearing such adornments in a spirit of anti-capitalism, anticonsumerism, political solidarity? When bourgeois Western women of color adopt the style or dress of Third World village women, is this "speaking for the oppressed" or hypocrisy?[87] Wary of corporate marketing trends and the particularly odious exploitation of "native" Third World producers of indigenous materials, from whom do we purchase these items?[88] Who benefits from our fashion pro-clivities? Are our hands clean?[89]

That women of color often become "otherness machines," as Sara Suleri puts it,[90] is manifested in other feminist scenarios. Some feminists of color have identified strategies of co-optation in white feminist organizations, conferences, publications, and countercultural artistic projects. They criticise this new form of tokenism, which draws on their "difference," as manipulative. Has the symbol of our new multicultural feminism really become "women of color," with no white peeking through, rather than a rainbow? Has the ideological assertion of a distinctive, politicized new form of feminism been conflated into style-ism, a romanticization, a new kind of receptacle for white women's fantasies? Bell hooks has noted certain of these tendencies in recent progressive, multiracial art films. Even when such art is meant to challenge the politics of domination, its dangers include the politics of inclusion and appropriation, both territorial acts. Of the British film *Sammy and Rosie Get Laid* (its director and screenwriter Anglo-Pakistani), for instance, hooks writes:

> The experiences of oppressed black people, specifically dark-skinned black people, are appropriated as colorful exciting backdrop. They are included to stimulate interest (just seeing all the different black people on the screen is definitely new), yet often their reality is submerged or obscured so that we focus even more intensely on the characters whose reality really matters.[91]

Trinh T. Minh-ha also has resisted appropriating practices in white feminism. As one of the token women of color to be included in a "special Third World Women's issue" of a feminist journal, Trinh writes of her dismay at being distanced from other women of color not "privileged" to be included. Her own "specialness" sets her apart from them in ways which encourage unwelcome feelings of competitiveness. Her "specialness" to the white feminist coordinators of a conference, she realizes, is merely a soporofic, an artifice. They not only privilege her to speak, but encourage her to express her difference: "My audience expects and demands it; otherwise people would feel as if they have been cheated." We, the white women say, "came to listen to that voice of difference likely to bring us *what we can't have* and to divert us from the monotony of sameness." The woman of color must, above all, be *authentic*, against white standards of who is and who isn't "authentic." Trinh must paint herself "thick with authenticity":

> Eager not to disappoint, I try my best to offer my benefactors and benefactresses what they most anxiously yearn for; the possibility of a difference, yet a difference or an otherness that will not go so far as to question the foundation of their beings and makings. Their situation is not unlike that of the American tourists who, looking for a change of scenery and pace in a foreign land . . . strike out in search for what they believe to be the "real" Japan.[92]

But these mystifications also work to empower (this kind of power is dangerous) feminists of color as well: they are thick with authenticity, righteousness; white feminists are thin with inauthenticity, pretentiousness, un-funk. Might we not broaden our critique to include the rhetoric of authenticity itself? Perhaps my own veneration of the photo of the woman of color evokes this dangerously policing discourse itself. Should one question as well the stereotyping of white women by feminists of color?

Comment heard on a Mainland campus after a conference on gender and colonialism: "Who was that white-bread woman you were talking to?"

"Hey, she's OK, we were talking about how Asian women are exploited by sex tourism and the mail-order bride industry."

Or the dismissal of a progressive white male, a longtime anti-apartheid activist, wearing a Nelson Mandela button, by a group of women of color: "Look at him. You'd think he owned Mandela."

Expressions of cultural private property abound: A part-Hawaiian woman watching a performance of a *hula halau* (dance school of the hula) says to another "local" woman, "What's that *haole* [white] woman doing up there dancing the *hula*?" Are there subtle new forms of social/spatial segregations operating today, cues which convey a "keeping one another in their places" rhetoric, only in racial reversals? Why would a group of mainly female Black scholars ignore and render invisible a white woman who comes to a public lecture on a major campus to hear a Black professor speak about "African Goddess Myths"?

White women, too, in multicultural feminist settings can learn to despise their physical embodiment, realize that their color prevents them from being "thick with authenticity." That cardboard "white woman," too, can be reified, can be read as a hollow shell whose politics and commitments are judged by stylism and by her (lack of) color. She, with her undifferentiated "whiteness," is homogenized, trapped in images which define her in a certain way, align her with politics she doesn't support. The white woman can be dismissed as "cultureless," parasitic on the literature, customs, food, music of Third World people. Listen to this comment by a young Black woman from Harlem: "Like white people have nothing of their own. Can't identify with the American culture. Can't sing old country tunes. So they latch onto ours. Take from everybody else."[93]

But isn't it America's assimiliationist crimes which have deprived us all of the cultural moorings and symbols which could enrich us? Voices like the above don't think so, but whites often experience cultural alienation as our loss, not our crime. Perhaps cultural resources could be thought of as mediating glue, shared meditations on primal human connectedness, rather than as territorial possessions around which boundaries are erected. Exploitative colonial histories make these hopes fragile, we know.

Misreadings of "our" (I mean this as an omnibus designator) images can erect walls. I might want to distance myself as far as I can from the careerist, individualistic, dress-for-success, white professional woman's image. But still I often look like that. (What kinds of admonitions are to be made about the consumer-crazy Buppie women who grace the pages of *Essence*?) Who likes sending off signals which misrepresent our own lives and struggles? Can "signs" really *communicate* these attributes of our political lives, anyway? Our glances and image-seductions do, though, assign fictive lives, conditions, backgrounds, putative "privileges," and politics to one another. Most often they bury what "we" deeply are or would like to think we are. In a constantly refracting mirror of signs and meanings, the ambiguities of gender assure that our bodies, hair, skin color, and even desires inevitably will be fluid, complex, unstable — and open to misinterpretation. (Is there a "true" representation?) Often our intentions of affiliation, our political commitments, and the "looks" we live behind are betrayed by these ambiguities, destroying what is good in those intentions. Perhaps "we" are (I am?) fixated on surface images too much and judge one another accordingly.

We can try to see one another materially, in the flesh, not as "pictures they own"[94] but as sometimes coalition-mates groping our way toward just relationships amid what we all know to be traps of feminine gender tryanny. Often the images we project have taken on lives of their own, embedded as they are in the conflicting meanings of a racist, sexist, homophobic society. Our attempts at counterimagery and signs of feminist solidarity always "speak us," requiring chastened and reflective interpretations of their possible meanings. For balance, we need other, more solidly political criteria for character-assigning. Images that we cultivate, such as the woman of color riding the horse, can either inspire us, challenging us to play with alternative identities for feminist struggle, or trap us in new kinds of repressive stereotypes. When we mean to open up new spaces between the reified order of the body and the wayward lawlessness of desire, we can shut them down. Tolerance for cultural blunders in these fantasy projects ought to be forthcoming; what looks like appropriations in fact can be aesthetic and cultural appreciation. Politics is the test.

In these, as in all aspects of symbolic politics, we ought not substitute style, imagery, or aesthetics for concrete political engagement. Oppositional dress and appearance cannot displace coherent political actions in the material world. Neither should we base our political judgments and ethical assessments of one another on the chimera of what our eyes "see." Walter Benjamin identified this aestheticization of politics as a real danger, a step toward fascism. When political activity or political agents are evaluated in terms of "beauty" rather than substantive political commitments, we come dangerously close to a fascist elevation of style.[95]

Conclusion

We are coming to understand the tenacity of our legacies of gender—the ways in which our perceptions of one another as physically embodied persons are inevitably opaque, hard to read, in those polarized dichotomies of masculine and feminine. White feminists must recognize our past bad faith in cavalierly flaunting the perquisites of "femininity" and understand the material context and daily rituals of humiliation — in which we participated — which told Black women that they lacked "class," in Tina Turner's word, that their bodies and appearance could never mean "lady."[96] Black women can recognize that idealizing, stereotyping, and envying (and the contempt which underlies these emotions) white women's "beauty" displaces their own self-defining energies. As feminists, we can enjoy being "femininity" outlaws, dodging its traps, fighting like hell, as Fannie Lou Hamer taught us, to crack *all* pedestals.

A critical feminist politics of appearance empowers us all to experiment with the rich diversities of styles and adornments from plural cultural sources. And, in this, above all, our experiments must respect and honor the original "first people" creators. We can acknowledge that counterhegemonic, alternative feminist "looks" can be oppressive and arrogant if they are employed as new kinds of elitism or normalizing maps. As Wendy Chapkis reminds us, it is hard to enjoy looking "it," when, by so doing, we distance ourselves from those who cannot afford the style, or whose color or body doesn't "fit." All women need to feel safe about representations of self, certainly within feminist worlds. That space ought to be a site of gender play, an alternative playground of diversity. Only then can we recognize each other, in Chapkis's forceful words, as "different *and therefore exciting*, imperfect *and as such enough*."[97]

Chapter 5

"Now I Am Here": Black Women
and the First Wave of Feminism

*Any attempt at dialogue between black women and white feminists
must begin with a knowledge of the history of black women as they
understand it . . . [Their] separate paths . . . come directly from the
histories of black and white women.*

Barbara Omolade

*The Negro race has suffered more from the antipathy and narrowness
of [white] women both North and South than from any other single
source.*

W.E.B. Du Bois

The popular interpretation of the origins of American feminism—
conceptualized as the "first wave" in the nineteenth century and early
twentieth century—constructs a mythology that reads as follows. Bound
by the crippling patriarchal ideology of the nineteenth-century "cult
of true womanhood," American white women such as the Grimké
sisters and Lucretia Mott broke their domestic bonds to join with
antislavery crusader William Lloyd Garrison to initiate a national
abolitionist movement. Acting on their religious fervor and on Enlightenment theories of natural rights, the white women reformers
were radicalized by their public activism and sympathy for Black
slaves to resist their own oppression. The epochal manifestation of this
newly-found feminist consciousness in women such as Elizabeth Cady
Stanton and Susan B. Anthony was the Seneca Falls convention in

1848 — the first women's rights meeting and the official symbol of its genesis. After the Civil War, white women's energies were liberated from concern with Black freedom and turned toward the broader and more revolutionary struggle for women's rights and the crusade for suffrage.

Standard feminist histories of the first wave contain obligatory references to "great Black women" such as Sojourner Truth and Harriet Tubman. Their feminism is depicted as "exceptional" and as not shared by other Black women, whose deficiencies as producers and consumers of feminist theory have rendered them minor characters in the overall feminist drama. It then follows that Black women's historical role as objects of exploitation meant that they lacked the requisite political agency to be significant in the early feminist struggle. During the long and volatile struggle for the vote, white feminists welcomed, and even attempted to recruit, Black women into the movement. But their efforts were largely ignored, since Black women were disinterested and unresponsive to their white sisters, preferring instead to organize separately or with Black men to consider solely racial issues.[1]

It is against such biased interpretations that Black feminist scholars today are reacting. And from the point of view of the protest literature comprised of these scholars' texts, white women have defined white women's experience as "feminist history," while for Black women all feminist history is prehistory.[2] As Omolade challenges in the epigram with which I began this chapter, such a historical encounter is a prerequisite for current attempts at interracial unity. This historical rereading inevitably displaces the comfortably accepted fiction of benevolent nineteenth-century white feminist pioneers. The political and theoretical silencing of Black women's contributions to first-wave feminism, and the absent space the Black woman represents in white narratives have eclipsed a legacy of democratic feminist politics, social practices, and moral courage. Because this legacy has been silenced, the important contributions contemporary feminism needs to make towards a transformed world are diminished.

It was in the first wave of feminism that the battle for hegemony over feminist discourse itself smoldered. Who would be legitimized as a feminist? What sources of oppression and domination would warrant feminist resistance? What priorities and strategies would be designed to contest the race and gender barriers which arose to prevent democratization in this expectant period of the American Republic? What coalitions advanced the broad emancipation movements of the day? And, importantly, how did language itself inscribe one as a "woman's rights' advocate," "antislavery crusader," "abolitionist," or "suffragist"? Those defining categories became frozen, circumscribed for later generations of feminist thinkers to reify; in the process, such thinkers were allowed to deny the dialectical character of political action in general and of black women's feminism in particular.

This recent body of revisionist history explores just such questions as highly contestable subjects, with the aim of retrieving and reclaiming a *diverse* feminist identity. The new Black feminist histories are built upon the foundation of an enriching Black first-wave feminist theory which stimulated counterinstitutions and counterphilosophies. The creative vision of feminism which is evident in the texts and actions of nineteenth-century Black female intellectuals belies the dismissals of some contemporary white feminist historians that black women "felt far more restricted by class or race than by sex" and thus "put their needs as Blacks before their needs as women."[3] Where white feminists temporize about the uncharacteristic racist slippages of their legendary foremothers and rationalize the latter's repeated abandonment of Black freedom struggles as inevitable, modern Black feminists name names, issue judgments, and construct alternatives. A new story of sisterhood emerges. The assertion of a white feminist historian that Black women were "relatively late" in organizing sex-segregated groups, did not perceive Black men "as antagonistic to them or as being their oppressors," and lacked the "self-conscious feminism of white women during the early decades of the 20th century," elicits profound critiques.[4]

The texts of Barbara Omolade, bell hooks, Hazel Carby, Angela Davis, Rosalyn Terborg-Penn, Sharon Harley, Darlene Clark Hine, and Paula Giddings have created a revisionist historical project of immense critical importance.[5] Not only do their texts serve to elaborate a powerful feminist knowledge which was lost to American political consciousness, but they also show how Black women led the way in articulating the necessity of coalitions for universal human rights. The fresh understanding of feminism's first wave allows white feminists to consider more seriously how early Black feminists conceptualized possibilities for resisting sexual and racial oppression and established criteria for reassessing this primary episode in American feminism. Paula Giddings's account indicates that nineteenth-century Black feminists exhibited a radicalized knowledge of patriarchal power and organized to struggle against it and all the other forces which constricted their lives. Black women never were the passive beneficiaries of white feminist activism, but put themselves on the front lines of progressive struggles:

> Black women have always been at the center of the feminist struggle in this country. On issues such as the right to vote, to earn a fair wage, to have control over one's body, no group has held stronger convictions or acted upon them more intently.
>
> In slavery, black women, cast to perpetuate the system through their wombs, used contraceptives . . . and physical violence as acts of subversion. As free women, they were often in the feminist activist vanguard. In 1831, 17 years before the Seneca Falls convention, the black abolitionist Maria Stewart — probably the first recorded American-born woman to speak in public — urged women to seek economic independence . . . Later with the formation of the National Assn. of Colored Women in 1896, black women activists — among them Frances Ellen Watkins Harper and Mary Church Terrell — engaged in the organized suffrage campaign with as much determination, and less race and class prejudice than white counterparts such as Susan B. Anthony.[6]

The overall assessment by Black feminists of the founding period of white first-wave feminism is intensely negative. Bell hooks's interpretation of this period illustrates the bitterness felt by many contemporary black feminists when they reflect on the limitations of white sisterhood. Hooks emphasizes that the antislavery sentiments of white female abolitionists did not extend to antiracist attitudes:

> The racial apartheid social structure that characterized 19th and early 20th century American life was mirrored in the women's rights movement. The first white women's rights advocates were never seeking social equality for all women; they were seeking social equality for white women. Because many 19th century white women's rights advocates were also active in the abolitionist movement, it is often assumed they were anti-racist. Historiographers and especially recent feminist writing have created a version of American history in which

white women's rights advocates are presented as champions of oppressed black people. . . . In actuality, most white abolitionists, male
and female, though vehement in their anti-slavery protest, were
totally opposed to granting social equality to black people.[7]

Angela Davis offers a similar indictment of white suffragists whose
priorities placed courting the racist South in order to further suffrage
above the pursuit of broad interracial alliances.

Black women had been more than willing to contribute those
"clear powers of observation and judgement" toward the creation of a
multi-racial movement for women's political rights. But at every
turn, they were betrayed, spurned and rejected by the leaders of the
lily-white woman suffrage movement. For suffragists and clubwomen
alike, Black women were simply expendable entities when it came
time to woo Southern support with a white complexion.[8]

And Rosalyn Terborg-Penn's research in nineteenth-century African-
American sources has documented the epic role of Black female activists in both racial and women's rights struggles. She criticizes the
"historical fallacy" of white-centered feminist history for its "distor-
tion of reality."

The black feminist movement in the United states during the
mid-1970s is a continuation of a trend that began over 150 years ago.
Institutionalized discrimination against black women by white
women has traditionally led to the development of racially separate
groups that address themselves to race-determined problems as well
as to the common plight of women in America. At the same time,
Afro-American women, motivated by a sense of racial solidarity and
a special identity arising out of the uniqueness of the black experience, have tended to identify in their own way with the larger
social movements in American society.[9]

These are the themes — exclusion, betrayal, and racism — which will
animate the analyses in this chapter. Narrating the diverse activism
of first-wave Black women is an essential aspect of recent scholarship.
Coupled with the theoretical insight of contemporary Afrocentric
feminists, such a project has operated to suggest a multiple-oppressions
model to understand how Black women strategized against and interpreted the variety of factors they faced in their lives. The body of
knowledge which has been produced reveals a historic feminist praxis

which revolutionizes the assumptions of feminist theory. Black women's multiple commitments to gender, poverty, and racial issues form the crucial thread connecting both first and current Black feminism. The nineteenth-century record will show that only rarely could white feminists grasp the significance of the Black woman's perspective, even as it related to and advanced their own causes. The translation of interracial, trans-class experience, tenuously begun in the framework of abolitionism, was largely an accomplishment of Black insight, not white.

Much white feminist scholarship views this era only from the perspective of white women. The authors of a popular text, *A History of Women in America* (which briefly mentions less than a dozen Black women in 373 pages covering the period 1620 to 1974), can make the statement: "The cause of woman's suffrage, [Stanton and Anthony] insisted, should be led by women who put their sex first."[10] The authors of this text allow their statement to stand with no hint of the fatalistic implications such a fragmenting strategy would have held for Black women. Black females who attempted to align with white reformers routinely were subjected to such "tests," requiring of them intolerable choices of prioritizing sex over race. They did not, however, adopt the practice of focusing solely on achieving sexual equality at the expense of their racial concerns — as if such an option could have been a rational choice for them at all.

The ability to conceive of racial oppression did not dull Black women's awareness of patriarchy, however. The submerged record of Black female resistance to Black patriarchy was motivated by activism for "justice, simple justice," in Frances Ellen Watkins Harper's motto, in any realm which restricted them. Black women such as Harper saw themselves as rooted in a larger community of being; for Black men and women survived slavery only by leaning upon one another. As Harper traveled the South during and after the Civil War, she spoke to men and women of her race in a language symbolizing this anchorage: "I belong to this race, and when it is down I belong to a down race; when it is up, I belong to a risen race."

But she emphasized the necessity for women to voice their own experience and challenged the Black men who sought to speak for them. To this end, she sought out Black women from plantation shacks, lecturing without payment sometimes as often as twice a day and requesting that her public events not be dominated by male community figures. As a northern intellectual, Harper dedicated her talents to empowering those southern Black women. She encouraged them to meet with her and to "talk about their daughters, and about things connected with the welfare of the race." Harper campaigned against wife abuse and exhorted Black women to "plant the roots of progress under the hearthstone" by not acceding to male privilege. The message she imparted to the nominally freed African-Americans in the wake of Emancipation was the same one she proclaimed as an "ambassador" to the white South — one of sensitivity toward, and militance on behalf of, her Black sisters: "The condition of the women is not very enviable in some cases. They have had a terribly hard time in Slavery and their subjugation has not ceased in freedom."[11]

From the previous discussion, it should be emphasized that during and after slavery, Black women understood only too well their dual victimization along an eroticized color-line. The ideology of southern patriarchy visited both symbolic and physical victimization on slave women. This rendered her "more aware of sexist oppression than any other female group in American society has ever been."[12] Without the protection of social or legal redress, Black women accepted their responsibility for survival of self and survival of community. And they imparted spiritual sustenance to Black culture. Black women were told "to have the sole management of the primal lights and shadows," as Anna Julia Cooper wrote in her autobiography, *A Voice from the South by a Black Woman of the South* in 1892.[13] Black female intellectuals like Cooper understood their dual loyalties to sex and race and the inevitability of confrontations with "both a woman question and a race problem." Cooper's sophisticated understanding of the interconnections between slavery, colonialism, imperialism, and patriarchy not only emphasizes the scope of nineteenth-century Black feminism but constitutes another theoretical and political linkage with the postcolonial perspective of contemporary Black feminism. With Cooper, the private and public spheres conjoined to politicize personal and political forms of domination. And although Cooper was often critical of Black males, she identified Afro-American bondage as collective tragedies to be overcome by all Black people. One of her poems illustrates the common struggle of Black women and men: "For woman's cause is man's, they rise or sink together, dwarfed or godlike, bond or free."[14]

The creative redefinition of feminism revealed in the discourse of nineteenth-century Black female intellectuals reflects a broad commitment to a democratic, antiracist civic culture as well as a determination to aid in the "uplifting of the race." The rhetoric of "progress" often evoked in the writings of certain white female reformers of the last century took on a deeper meaning for Black clubwoman Fannie Barrier Williams. She understood that "progress includes a great deal more than what is generally meant by the terms culture, education and contact."[15] Black women in the nineteenth century challenged white women as "would-be leaders of reform," as Hazel Carby has written, "to transform their provincial determination to secure gender and class interests at the expense of the rights of the oppressed."[16]

Contemporary Black feminist scholars have retrieved this remarkable tradition of feminist activism; one becomes witness to a legacy of Black women who demonstrated a profound engagement with the interrelation of sexual and racial oppression. "Throughout history, Black women did not see their relationship to racial or feminist aspirations as a problematic one. For they saw themselves at the center of both, and acted accordingly, helping to liberates blacks and women in the process."[17]

In this chapter I will examine certain aspects of the controversy over historical interpretations of first-wave feminism and of nineteenth-century Black women's place in that history. This examination will include discussions of several historical "flashpoints" or sites of interracial feminist conflict in both abolitionist and suffragist politics. I shall elaborate on arguments made in contemporary Black feminist discourse on the project of redefining the roots of feminist identity and politics. The analysis will conclude with an interpretation of feminism embodied in the work of Black female intellectuals in the Black club movement and the antilynching crusades. These women shaped an alternative feminist contribution to a future America, based on the conviction that "women's" interests would not be advanced at the expense of others' freedoms.

A Contested History and Feminist Identity

The initial critique offered by Black feminist scholars regarding the first wave of feminism is a methodological one. They reject certain assumptions held by white feminist historians in their approach to historical reportage. Black feminist challenges to the construction and representation of the feminist past bear directly on the tradition of African-American solidarity, which Black feminists wish to emphasize. Historian Barbara Omolade provides a context which is essential in understanding the complex manifestations of Black historical resistance in this country: Black struggle in the United States has been deeply grounded in a developing Black culture. As Omolade notes, the forging of a Black contribution to nationhood, with cultural integrity as its "binding force" and "human civil rights" as its goal, long has been neglected in the study of the history of Blacks in America. This neglect has resulted in historiography which reflects the perspectives and status of "exemplary" individuals. Black feminist theoretical approaches to history are critical of white feminist scholarship which has included as token "heroines" Black historical figures such as Sojourner Truth and Harriet Tubman. Omolade views such practices as condescending and racist on the part of white feminist scholars who discuss Truth and Tubman "as if their achievements were miracles for Black people to obtain." Omolade's work emphasizes that Blacks' experience of oppression in America has been built on a collective response to oppression. She argues that a figure like Tubman, great though she was, could not have emerged in isolation. Tubman's revolutionary consciousness was shaped by those collective aspirations which enabled her to "see" herself as an instrument of her people.[18]

As the editors of a recent Black feminist anthology argue, it has been ordinary Black women whose "unexceptional actions" have inspired generations of Black women to forge their own resistance.[19] Omolade's point can be pushed further. In denying Blacks' sense of collective solidarity, historians evade discussion of the ideologies which dehumanized both Black men and women as "other" Americans. One illustration of the top-down, white-centered approach to history which ignores Blacks' contributions to securing their own liberation, is the case of the Female Anti-Slavery Society of Salem, Massachusetts.[20] When the famed white abolitionist William Lloyd Garrison lectured in Salem in 1832, he mentioned the absence of any Black antislavery societies. The Black female activists of the area promptly wrote to the local newspaper correcting Garrison's oversight and indicated that "females of color" had organized themselves the previous year. The Black female activists set the record straight that, in fact, yet another Black female organization—the Salem Colored Female Religious and Moral Society—had been formed fifteen years earlier, quite independent of white assistance.[21]

The methodological critiques of Black feminist scholars regarding first-wave feminism comprise an important part of a larger project to redefine criteria for American interracial historical interpretation in general. Historians Robert Allen and Pamela Allen have approached the study of white American social reformers from a specifically African-American perspective. Such a perspective foregrounds the issue of white racism, along with its origins and evolution, as a crucial analytical and political focus. Their 1983 text, *Reluctant Reformers: Racism and Social Reform Movements in the United States,* poses a series of questions which ought to be especially germane to white feminists.

> What have white reformers done to abate racism, especially before the racial militancy of the 1950's and 1960's made opposition to segregation and discrimination popular "causes"? As part of their battle for social justice, did early white reformers carry the message of racial equality to their more bigoted brothers and sisters? Did they oppose segregationist and exclusionist movements organized by racists? Did they open their own organizations to participation by nonwhites? In short, if white society is in need of basic changes to purge it of racism, can we say that progressive whites, enlightened social reformers, historically have been a source of such anti-racist thinking and development?[22]

By these arresting standards, first-wave white feminists do not fare well. As we shall see, they failed to demonstrate the kind of political insight needed to sustain the multifaceted human rights alliances that nineteenth-century politics demanded. Further, many contemporary white feminist accounts of first-wave interracial feminism have been woefully silent on the immensity of this breakdown. The disintegration of those interracial experiments surely was the crucial impediment to the achievement of a feminist project which truly could have been said to have enacted a philosophy of social justice.[23] This judgment derives not solely from the fact that most white feminist scholarship has erased the contributions of Black women to the development of feminist theory and politics — although that is a serious indictment — but also from the silence about the implications of those racist exclusions. Contemporary feminism has yet to make this history an object lesson for current feminist pedagogy.

As a preface to examining specific historical events, I want to reflect upon the somewhat arbitrary use of the term "feminist" as it is applied to nineteenth-century female activists by some white scholars. Why are white feminist scholars so reluctant to characterize first-wave Black females as "feminist"? Why have the projects for human equality which comprised Black women's activism in the nineteenth century not been interpreted as pertinent to a feminist ideal of liberation? The answer given by contemporary Black feminist historians centers on the conceptual framework passed down by early white suffragists and replicated by recent feminists. The theoretical blockage which hovers above contemporary as well as nineteenth-century feminist understandings has rested on a prioritizing of oppression. White feminist thinkers have been incapable of incorporating the political reality of Black women's concern with both race and gender. Thus those first-wave Black women whose politics incorporated both experiences have been excluded linguistically from the concept "feminist." Given this context, one of the most significant contributions of contemporary Black feminist discourse has been the legitimation of nineteenth-century Black women's diverse reformism as inherently feminist. This revision has gone largely unrecognized.

For instance, white historians Carol Hymowitz and Michaele Weissman identify white female reformers such as Abby Kelly as "feminist abolitionists" and discuss Lucy Stone as an "abolitionist and women's right activist." The same historians label Frances Ellen Watkins Harper "a black writer from Baltimore" and Josephine St. Pierre Ruffin "a black clubwoman from Massachusetts," while both women were highly visible suffragists and feminists as well.[24] Bell hooks points out a damning double standard which relates to these interpretive strategies. No white feminist historian, she argues, would label the activism of women like Stone, Elizabeth Stanton, or Lucretia Mott, which focused only on reforms aimed primarily at white women, as unfeminist or unrelated to women's rights concerns. "Yet historians who label themselves feminist continually minimize the contribution of black women's rights advocates by implying that their focus was solely on racial reform measures."[25]

When Alice Rossi's edited volume, *The Feminist Papers: From Adams to de Beauvoir*, was published in 1973, it became a textual landmark for white feminists—the intellectual manifestos and private lives of Western feminist pioneers came alive to fuel the emerging politics of women's liberation. Absent from this timely work is the voice of Black feminism, textured with its own history, vocabulary, and political imagination.[26] The white story became feminism *tout court*, inscribing the feminist canon with a white face to be passed on to the next generation of American feminists. This partial history would remain academically respectable for another decade. What an expanded radical consciousness those feminists of the 1970s could have been exposed to, had the "papers" of Black women been included. White feminists would have been challenged by a powerful militant voice, of the type manifested by Black women such as Nannie Rice Burroughs, who wrote of a "glorified womanhood that can look any man in the face—white, red, yellow, brown or black."[27] They could have learned much about the dimensions of struggle and resistance from Mary Church Terrell, the feminist, suffragist, antilynching crusader, and educator. She wrote in 1940, near the end of her long life which spanned three generations of Black feminists, that the tale of her life as a "colored woman living in a white world" could not possibly be like a story written by a white woman. A white woman, she said, "has only one handicap to overcome—that of sex. I have two—both sex and race. I belong to the only group in this country which has two such huge obstacles to surmount."[28]

And a figure like Anna Julia Cooper—novelist, suffragist, Sorbonne-trained linguist, and racial activist—agitated in an unmistakably feminist voice during the horror of the turn-of-the-century Jim Crow era. Cooper's insights are remarkable, precursors of the "innovations" found in contemporary feminist theory. While dedicated to uplifting the entire Black community, Cooper encouraged Black women to speak for themselves and to project their own unique voices. She was convinced that no-one else could "more accurately tell the weight and fret of the long dull pain than the open-eyed but hitherto voiceless black woman of America." She projected a woman-centered radicalism which insisted on female autonomy: "Woman is not underdeveloped man but diverse." Cooper lectured Black women not to subscribe to patriarchal prohibitions which discouraged women from seeking an education on the grounds that it would destabilize marriage. Her deconstruction of naturalistic claims that knowledge would "unsex" women matches today's most sophisticated feminist theories. Patriarchal ideology discouraged education for women, she realized, by constructing "woman" as a "lisping, clinging, tenderly helpless, and beautifully dependent creature(s) whom men would so heroically think for and so gallantly fight for."[29]

Much of Cooper's feminist theory was devoted to demystifying nineteenth-century Victorianism, as the above quotation indicates. She attacked Black males' attachment to chivalry as "sixteenth century logic" and exhorted Black women to stop "worshipping masculinity."[30] This same critique of gender stereotypes would be repeated in the 1920s by the fiery Amy Jacques Garvey, who ran her jailed husband's Black nationalist movement with a powerful feminist spirit. "This doll baby type of woman is a thing of the past," she declared, "and the wide-awake woman is forging ahead." She warned fellow Black revolutionaries that her version of the "back-to-Africa" vision was matriarchal: "We are tired of hearing Negro men say, 'There is a better day coming' while they do nothing to usher in the day. We . . . are getting in the front ranks, and serve notice on the world that we will brush aside the halting, cowardly Negro men, and . . . will press on. . . . Mr. Black man, watch your step! Ethiopia's queens will reign again."[31]

One of the most serious omissions from our feminist past is the story of Maria Stewart, a free Black woman who lectured in Boston in the early 1830s. She was a forerunner to Frederick Douglass and Sojourner Truth and the first Black American to lecture in defense of women's rights. If she is mentioned at all in white feminist histories, she is generally described as a religious figure and the first American-born woman to have lectured in public.[32] Stewart's feminism, however, plays a central role in recent Black feminist accounts of this period. For instance, Paula Giddings's 1984 history, *When and Where I Enter: The Impact of Black Women on Race and Sex in America,* rightly describes Stewart as having established the moral tone and premises upon which future Black female activism would be based. Stewart's thinking—"what would later become known as modernist thinking—gave Black women a freer rein to express and act upon ideas that liberated them from the oppression of both sex and race. . . . [Her] perspective also enabled Black women to see a world not of fixed proportions, but of change."[33]

Where white interpretations stretch just so far, Giddings is able to "see" in Stewart the feminist visionary white feminists have overlooked. A figure who "suffused Black women with a tenacious feminism, which was articulated before that of Whites like Sarah Grimké, who is credited with providing the first rationale for American women's political activism." The key to Giddings's insight is her understanding that Stewart's racial consciousness actually stimulated her feminism, rather than curtailed it.[34] Stewart projected a religious and moral ethic which framed nineteenth-century Black women's feminism for generations to come. In 1832, sixteen years before Stanton and Mott convened the Seneca Falls women's rights conference, Stewart legitimated her activism to mixed audiences in Boston: "What if I am a woman. Did not Queen Esther save the lives of the Jews? . . . . What if such women . . . should rise among our sable race? And it is not impossible; for it is not the color of the skin that makes the man or the woman, but the principle formed in the soul."[35] She challenged Black women to fight for their economic independence.

> Do you ask what we can do? Unite and build a store of your
> own. . . . Do you ask where is the money? . . . We have never had an
> opportunity of displaying our talents; therefore the world thinks we
> know nothing. Possess the spirit of men, bold and enterprising,
> fearless and undaunted. Sue for your rights and privileges. Know the
> reason that you cannot attain them. Weary them [men] with your
> importunities.[36]

And as Giddings points out, Stewart understood that the forces oppressing Black women lay primarily outside themselves; she hotly rejected the idea that Black women were to blame for their own degradation. White America and its slave culture were the source: "She [America] is indeed a seller of slaves and the souls of men; she has made the Africans drunk with the wines of her fornication . . . who caused the daughters of Africa to commit whoredoms . . . upon thee be their curse."[37] Like many Black women to follow, Stewart viewed education as an antidote to self-pity and poverty. "Knowledge is power," she preached, urging Black women to "raise a fund ourselves" to build a high school. "It is of no use to sit with our hands folded, hanging our heads like bulrushes, lamenting our wretched condition. . . . Let every female heart become united." Stewart, herself an impoverished household worker, spoke to audiences of other workers and day laborers, understanding well the condition which later revolutionary theory would label "alienated labor": "How long shall the fair daughters of Africa be compelled to bury their minds and talents beneath a load of iron pots and kettles?" Her own grinding work experience told her that "continued hard labor deadens the energies of the soul, and benumbs the faculties of the mind; the ideas become confined, the mind barren." Stewart did not fail to note the discrepancy between Black and white women's conditions; she realized that often her own and her sisters' labor provided the ground for white women's superior life: "Oh, ye fairer sisters, whose hands are never soiled, whose nerves and muscles are never strained, go learn by experience."[38]

To complete the logic of Stewart's radical message, she castigated Black males for their laxity in political action. She did not hesitate to call the Black community's attention to the internalized passivity caused by slavery. She demanded Black activism in every political arena of the day; and, by encouraging Black men aggressively to assume the obligations of citizenship, made them believe it possible.

> Is it blindness of mind or stupidity of soul or want of education that has caused our men never to let their voices be heard nor their hands be raised on behalf of their color? Or has it been for fear of offending the whites? . . . Here is the grand cause which hinders the rise and progress of the people of color. It is the want of laudable ambition and requisite courage. . . . O ye sons of Africa, when will your voices be heard in our legislative halls, in defiance of your enemies, contending for equal rights and liberty?[39]

If a firebrand feminist like Stewart has been an unknown actor in the feminist drama, the same cannot be said of Sojourner Truth. Truth's feminism has been amply documented by white feminist scholars; in fact, she has assumed a stature near mythic in the writings of many white feminists. Truth's status, however, reveals some complex ambiguities about how white women have symbolized strong Black women.[40] How did Sojourner Truth, an illiterate Black woman, a slave for forty years, come to insinuate herself historically as a white feminist heroine? Her uninvited participation in white women's rights conventions of the 1850s is the source of the mystique that surrounds this charismatic figure. Truth was not the only Black woman to align with white contemporaries in abolitionist and suffragist circles, but her powerful presence at these gatherings has become legendary. Her power to galvanize public attention was carefully recorded in the suffrage histories of the period. Truth's performance at the 1851 Akron, Ohio, women's rights convention is a familiar feminist narrative. The only Black woman present at this gathering, she thundered her famous "Ain't I A Woman?" speech, silencing the male hecklers who were attempting to intimidate the white women delegates. With the riveting story of her triumph over the indignities of slavery and her demonstration of a fierce physical strength, Truth deflated the male shibboleth that female weakness was incompatible with suffrage.[41]

Feminist historian Gerda Lerner, whose documentary history of Black women in America stands as a landmark in feminist scholarship on Black women, projects a thesis that Black and white American women have a history of "ambivalent interdependence."[42] And nowhere is that relationship better symbolized than in the figure of Sojourner Truth. Despite Truth's presence at many women's rights gatherings — due largely to her own initiative — nineteenth-century white women's rights activists nevertheless failed to fight collectively against the overall racism directed against her. Frances Gage, the white reformer who recorded suffragist history in her diaries, coyly referred to the "buzz of disapprobation" emanating from racist white women delegates at the 1851 Akron meeting. "Don't let her speak," they admonished Gage, with a rationale which would become emblematic of suffrage history: "Our cause will be mixed up with abolition and niggers."[43]

Angela Davis takes this context into account and reads an important analysis into Truth's story. Her "Ain't I A Woman?" address had deeper implications, according to Davis, for it was also "a comment on the racist attitudes of the same white women who later praised their Black sister. . . . no less than four times, [Truth] exposed the class-bias and racism of the new women's movement. All women were not white and all women did not enjoy the material comfort of the middle classes and the bourgeoisie."[44] Truth continued to draw hostility from white women at such meetings. And in her defiant speeches, she incorporated her critique of white women's racism into her analyses of male power. Defending herself from racist attacks, Truth nevertheless kept on speaking publicly and lecturing her white audiences about her own dignity and that of other Black women:

> I know that it feels a kind of hissing and tickling like to see a colored
> woman get up and tell you about things and Woman's Rights. We
> have all been thrown down so low that nobody thought we'd ever get
> up again; but we have been long enough trodden now; we will come
> up again, and now I am here.[45]

As Davis points out, it was Truth's ability to represent her Black sisters — both slave and "free"— and her courage in imparting a "fighting spirit" to the campaign for women's rights that is Truth's unique historic contribution to the feminist legacy. In addition, Truth's strength and physical endurance were living refutations of the stifling gender ideologies projected by the patriarchy on all women.

A large part of our contentious multicultural feminist projects today center on the contested terrain of history and feminist identity, or, more accurately, on the struggle to expand the definition of what it meant to be a feminist in the first wave. These abbreviated portraits of activist feminist women — Stewart, Terrell, Cooper, Burroughs, Garvey, Harper, Truth — demonstrate a tradition of little-known feminist pioneers. The recognition that these Black female activists were indeed "feminists" who, as we shall see, creatively redefined feminist politics and existing gender ideologies, is long overdue. And the work of contemporary Black feminist scholars has created a space in which Truth's maxim can resonate: "Now I am here." We need to know that these women were imbued with a passionate rejection of female inferiority. And we need to know as well that their efforts to align with white women reformers in the nineteenth century were systematically rejected — a story to which we next turn. A haunting epithet of segregated sisterhood comes to us from these historical expressions.

The confession of two southern white women to a group of Black female activist clubwomen in the early part of this century is both moving and disturbing: "A race [of women] has grown up in our very midst that we do not know."[46]

The Suffrage Movement:
Racism, Betrayals, and Abandonment

The early first-wave women's movement drew its moral tone and political impetus from the abolitionist movement. As the Black abolitionist Frederick Douglass wrote in his autobiography, women both Black and white were an integral part of Black emancipation from the beginning: "When the true history of the antislavery cause shall be written, women will occupy a large space in its pages, for the cause of the slave has been peculiarly the woman's cause."[47] This decisive conjoining of racial and gender issues proved to be the formative progressive moment in engendering American feminism. Historian Bettina Aptheker rightly has identified this epic intersection as a "revolutionary" event, in organization and personnel, in American movement history. Her analysis shows how the interdependence of the antislavery and women's rights agendas let them "create" one another by revealing new connections and pushing mutual boundaries: "The female presence helped to shape the revolutionary character of abolitionism, and practical engagement in the struggle against slavery impelled a consciousness of a distinctly feminist vision."[48]

That white feminists, if only briefly, contributed to this epochal struggle for human freedom gives symbolic meaning to our contemporary experiments. It is thus important to sketch the contours of this critical period in feminist history—again, from the perspective of recent Black feminist scholars. As has often been overlooked, Black Americans initiated their own organizations to end slavery long before whites became moved by their cause. But Black groups always were overshadowed by the greater prominence given to predominantly white associations. Although the case is popularly assumed to have been otherwise, Black women found themselves unwelcome in most white women's antislavery groups.[49] This contradiction can be accounted for by stressing, as has bell hooks, that early-nineteenth-century reformers attacked slavery, not racism: "When white women reformers in the 1830s chose to work to free the slave, they were motivated by religious sentiment. They attacked slavery, not racism. The basis of their attack was moral reform. That they were not demanding social equality for black people is an indication that they remained committed to white racist supremacy despite their anti-slavery work."[50] The historical research of Pamela Allen and Robert Allen on the abolitionist period makes the same important distinction — that whites' support for ending slavery was balanced by their fear of "amalgamation."[51]

Given this important dimension of the abolitionist experience, it is clear why so many contemporary Black feminists have criticized the practice employed by early white feminist abolitionists of drawing parallels between themselves and Black slaves. Ending slavery could be conceived by whites abstractly as a gesture demanded by Christian morality, but the prospect of relating to Black persons as equal and worthy beings was lost in the emotionalism of rhetorics of amalgamation. Identifying their oppression with that of slaves can be seen, from one point of view, as a valuable referent in white female consciousness. Northern white women, whatever their motivations, were drawn to the antislavery crusades and began to identify their own condition as women with that of Black women and men. They quickly began to invoke the metaphor of slavery as they sought to articulate their own oppression. But Angela Davis has written about the violation of solidarity which ought to have been recognized in such comparisons. When women like Elizabeth Cady Stanton polemicized against the institution of marriage as slavery, as Davis argued, it may have provided "shock value." But such practices also trivialized the depth of suffering of enslaved Black men and women "for whom slavery meant whips and chains."[52]

Bell hooks's reading of white women's rights advocate *cum* abolitionist Abby Kelly's much-praised statement is indicative of this kind of interpretation. Kelly said: "We have good cause to be grateful to the slave for the benefit we have received to ourselves, in working for him. In striving to strike his irons off, we found most surely, that we were manacled ourselves." Hooks disagrees with white feminists who have quoted this expression as evidence that white women became conscious of their own rights as they worked to end slavery, arguing instead that the brutal material differences between the lives of slaves and those of white women rendered such comparisons illegitimate. Furthermore, women such as Kelly "were simply appropriating the horror of the slave experience to enhance their own cause."[53]

Recognition of the contradictions and the undercurrent of racism in these early interracial abolitionist encounters is essential to an honest understanding of these fragile beginnings. We can discern a recurring pattern in these incipient Black and white female relationships. The responsibility fell to Blacks, allied with whites in radical causes, to educate their white allies as to the realities and implications of racism.

> Despite the close linkage of the movements for Negro rights and women's emancipation in the early 19th century, which might make it appear as though white women were just "naturally" advocates of and sympathetic to the cause of Blacks, interaction between black and white women was much more ambivalent and problematical. Not infrequently there was confrontation, competition and conflict.[54]

The southern white sisters, Sarah and Angelina Grimké, however, provided an extraordinarily rich example of the transforming power of abolitionism to generate a profound consciousness of social injustice and feminist awakening. Their achievements and their embodiment of interracial feminism are all the more remarkable when seen against the normative backdrop sketched above. The Grimkés are among the few white women who made the principled stand of linking white women's freedom to that of Blacks — never wavering in that commitment. The solidarity which they created is a model for our own multicultural feminist strategies. But some contemporary feminist scholars, in their praise of the Grimkés' achievements, have written as though Black women in antislavery work had not demonstrated equally egalitarian politics and political courage. Historians Hymowitz and Weissman claim that the Grimkés were the first "respectable" American women to speak in public.[55] In unreflectively using the term *respectable*, they imply that Black activists like Maria Stewart, who preceded the Grimkés, somehow were immoral or irrelevant. And the white historian Sarah Evans praises the Grimkés as so exceptional that "there is literally no one to compare them with." She clearly is — but does not say so — speaking of white women, because she employs a quotation pertaining to southern "ladies" — a term no historian would ever mistake as referring to Black women. Further, she makes the claim that "in the 1830s and again in the 1960s the first voices to link racial and sexual oppression were those of southern white women."[56]

Although the Grimkés are deserving of respect, there is a certain arrogance in attempting to appropriate for white female activists the status of solitary excellence in feminist perception. A more accurate reading of the abolitionist experience might situate white feminist reformers as political ingenues whose moral and political acuity was sharply heightened under the leadership and moral inspiration of Blacks who struggled to enhance the freedom of all citizens. Feminist scholars have recognized the importance of the antislavery movement in imparting a sense of personal confidence to white women as well as in educating them in the tactics of public protest. And, indeed, without the skills learned in this crucial political training ground for women's rights activists, it is doubtful that women's rights would have moved as it did to the center of reform activity in the antebellum period. The extraordinary interracial feminist discourse of the Grimkés and their determined activism reflect such a generative process.[57]

Not only were some white women politicized, through antislavery work, to recognize and act on the oppression in their own lives, but also they found a public arena in which to voice these grievances collectively. Along with Black female reformers, they learned vital political skills such as petitioning, speaking, and organizing, which were necessary for their own struggles. In this process women began shattering the gender stereotypes of themselves as secondary partners to men and violating taboos against female participation in public life. By the example of the Grimkés, other Black and white activists perceived the acts of public speaking and writing as new and vital tools to express their indignation in what Angelina Grimké called that "high school of morals in the land." In contrast to bell hooks, Angela Davis reads more altruism into white women's participation in the abolitionist movement, characterizing their experience as a "baptism in fire." White women, she notes,

> learned about the nature of human oppression. . . . If they did not yet know how to present their own grievances collectively, at least they could plead the cause of a people who were also oppressed. . . . [women had] the opportunity to prove their worth according to standards that were not tied to their role as wives and mothers. In this

> sense, the abolitionist campaign was a home where they could be valued for their concrete *works*. . . . They discovered that sexism, which seemed unalterable inside their marriages, could be questioned and fought in the arena of political struggle.[58]

The Grimké sisters' loyalty to their "home" in the antislavery crusade provided them with a profound understanding of the inseparability of race and gender oppressions. Their philosophy was: "I want to be identified with the Negro. Until he gets his rights, we shall never have ours." If this view had been embraced by the next generation of white suffragists, the bitter interracial splits over Black male suffrage might have been circumvented.[59]

During the Civil War, the incipient woman's rights movement had channeled all its energies into the Union cause. By the decade of the 1860s, the Grimkés' reformist activities had subsided as they retreated into private domestic responsibilities, but women like Elizabeth Cady Stanton and Susan B. Anthony, who had become active in the antislavery movement during the 1850s, continued to make connections between antislavery and women's rights. Stanton, speaking to the American Anti-Slavery Society meeting in 1860, spoke of the "subjective" link between white women and slaves, both of whom knew oppression from the inside.[60]

After the Civil War, Black suffrage became the issue which would dominate reform politics. Feminists, abolitionists, and their allies in the Republican Party, known as Radicals (as the three reform categories had begun to be articulated), embraced this cause as their foremost postwar goal. The period of Reconstruction was a time of intense public concern with political issues, and particularly with the vulnerable status of southern "freed" Black men and women. Bettina Aptheker describes the postwar climate as one in which explosive social and political issues were debated: What would replace the old slaveholding regime of the Old South? Who would determine political and economic structures? And, importantly, "What is the position of the newly freed slaves? Are they 'persons'? Are they 'citizens'? Should they exercise all the rights and privileges of citizenship? Should they vote?"[61]

Having benefited from the discussions on the legal urgency of suffrage for Blacks at the war's end, feminists of both races were convinced that suffrage was the key to the legal position of women as well.

They devised an agenda focusing on convincing their allies to advocate woman suffrage along with Black suffrage (the common meaning of which was "Black male suffrage") as the foundation of Reconstruction. The organizational culmination of this strategy resulted in the formation of the American Equal Rights Association (ERA) in 1866, with Stanton, Anthony, Frederick Douglass, and the Black feminist activist Frances Ellen Watkins Harper as officers.

Stanton opened the ERA's founding convention with the following statement: "Has not the time come to bury the black man and the woman in the citizen?"[62] And Anthony made an extraordinary call for unity, insisting it was necessary" to broaden our Woman's Rights platform and make it in name what it has always been in spirit — a Human Rights platform."[63] The united front for universal suffrage was the logical culmination of common struggle, "a fusion cemented in the trauma of a thirty-year war for emancipation."[64] Anthony's challenge at the ERA's first annual meeting the following year rang with optimism: "This is the harvest time for all citizens who pay taxes, obey the laws and are loyal to the government."[65] But it was an alliance unable to survive the crucible of post–Civil War racism. The divisions came over the Fourteenth and Fifteenth Amendments.

The tensions and expectations of white feminists, which led to the crises over these amendments, centered on their prodigious efforts to end slavery during the war years. Stanton and Anthony had formed the Women's Loyalty League in 1863 and pledged to collect a million signatures on a petition asking Congress to pass the Thirteenth Amendment for total abolition of slavery (the 1863 Emancipation Proclamation had freed slaves only in certain Rebel states). Not meeting their ambitious goal, the women nevertheless had gathered nearly 400,000 signatures by the next year. This effort, along with equally forceful work by African-Americans, resulted in ratification of the Thirteenth Amendment by 1865. Thus the expectation was that the women's rights leaders, who had "sacrificed" their own cause for the duration of the Civil War, would be rewarded with suffrage by a grateful nation and the Republican Party.[66]

But when the Fourteenth Amendment, conferring citizenship, equal protection, and due process of law, was proposed to Congress in 1866, not only did it have no mention of woman suffrage, but the word "male" had been inserted into the Constitution for the first time. The

Fifteenth Amendment, proposed soon after, guaranteed Black male suffrage.[67]

The shock of this action stunned both white and Black feminists and their few male allies; for the word "male" in the Fourteenth Amendment, used three times in connection with the term "citizen," raised the issue of whether women were indeed United States citizens at all. But feminists' subsequent reactions in the fierce debates surrounding the ratification process comprise a disappointing chapter in feminist history, one that saw the total breakdown of interracial politics. Anthony and Stanton perceived wholesale "betrayal" by their abolitionist friends. The latter now eschewed women's rights in this time of the "Negro's Hour," meaning Negro males. The "perfidious" Radical Republicans, fearful that association with women's suffrage would "trammel" their efforts to secure voting rights for Black males, also had failed to endorse woman suffrage.[68]

This series of political crises led Stanton and Anthony to adopt a rhetoric of scathingly ugly racism, hardening their position into outright campaigns to defeat the Fourteenth and Fifteenth Amendments. As suffrage historian Eleanor Flexner wrote of Stanton's reaction, "Her indignation and that of Miss Anthony knew no bounds." An enraged Anthony pledged that "I will cut off this right arm of mine before I will ever work for or demand the ballot for the Negro and not the woman."[69]

Stanton's public speeches embodied a tone of vitriolic white supremacy; she scapegoated Black men and women, "Sambo and Dinah," children of mere "bootblacks and gardeners," who were not fit to share citizenship with "the daughters of Jefferson and Washington."[70] And her words were dangerously close to those which were inciting a lynching furor against Black men, in suggesting that the Black male vote would lead to violence against white women. Stanton threatened that the vote would create "an antagonism between black men and all women that will culminate in fearful outrages on womanhood, especially in the Southern states."[71] Further, Stanton's attacks displayed the colonial mindset which sought acculturation of the immigrant class into WASP mores. Included in Stanton's nativistic diatribes now were not just Blacks, but the "foreign menace," which could only be controlled by a series of literacy tests for those "unfit voters" to ensure white native-born control. She argued that it was "degrading" for educated Anglo-Saxon women to be voteless while "two million ignorant men are being ushered into legislative halls. What can we hope for at the hands of the Chinese, Indians and Africans?"[72]

In such a tone, Stanton and Anthony presided over the degeneration of the common struggle of the ERA for universal human rights into a strategy of "opposing feminism to Black suffrage." The pair "attempted to build feminism on the basis of white women's racism."[73] In traveling around the nation actively attempting to defeat Black male suffrage, Stanton paraded statistics to display whites' superior class numbers over the "bestial" underclasses. "We point to official statistics for proof that there are more white women in the United States than colored men and women combined. . . . Therefore we urge that this large proportion of patriotism, temperance, morality, religion and intelligence be allowed to impress itself upon the government through the medium of the ballot box."[74]

Of all the pioneer feminists of the first wave, none presents as troubling a legacy vis-a-vis the thesis of this book as do Stanton and Anthony. The attempt to produce a "sacred" feminist tradition out of these contradictory thinkers causes a continuing dilemma.[75] One wonders how the story of racism organized itself inside the heads of these revolutionary women who had so defiantly created their feminism in and through the spirit of abolitionism. Part of the answer lies in the complexity and chaos of Reconstruction politics. A scenario evolved which worked to play the "rights" of one group against those of the other. Another part of the answer stems from the inability of white feminists to see the question of Black male suffrage as more than an abstract question of legal rights. For Black Americans, it was a question "involving the freedom and indeed survival of an entire race."[76]

The attainment of suffrage was perceived by both white feminists and Black people as a highly significant validation of full civil rights and political equality. The franchise was particularly vital to emancipated Blacks' sense of citizenship and security, since most of the militant abolitionist associations had disbanded at the war's end, leaving the Black population without institutional resources. This was a period, as Robert Allen notes, when organized support for Blacks' rights was weakening, when several defenders of Black equality in Congress had died, and when the coalition of Radical Republicans (who previously could be counted on to enforce Blacks' civil rights) was breaking apart.[77]

Had white feminists understood just how fragile were Blacks' claims on establishment politicians and the public at large, they might have been motivated to regroup and solidify their reliable alliances with Blacks. That the Republicans were manipulating both groups' rights off against the others' does not justify the feminists' treating Blacks' rights as targets upon which to vent their anger. White feminists' resistance to the postwar amendments was based in part on their un-warranted optimism that woman's liberation could be linked com-fortably to Black liberation *at that historical moment.* Slavery and the status of African-Americans had been a "boiling national issue" for over thirty-five years; a bloody and wrenching Civil War had been fought over it. No such popular intensity of feeling yet obtained for women's rights, even among most women.[78] This acknowledgment does not imply, however, that white suffragists should have diminished their efforts; quite the contrary. The "united front" strategy of linking women's rights with the question of Black male suffrage was an im-portant demonstration of political solidarity. What needed to be theo-rized and strategized by the principals involved was a *long-term* frame-work capable of articulating the goal of universal suffrage within a resilient organizational structure that could take advantage of what-ever short-term advancements the political climate availed. This under-standing, as we shall see, and the mutual trust required by such coali-tion prospects, failed to provide a cohesive rallying point around which white suffragists and Black activists could unite.

The Degeneration of Interracial Suffrage Alliances

The crucial event of this period, around which these tensions coalesced, was the 1869 final meeting of the American Equal Rights Association. This event symbolized the abandonment of Black civil rights as a feminist principle and set the racist tone the American suffrage move-ment would enunciate for the next decades. The issue at hand was whether the association should endorse the Fifteenth Amendment, which gave the franchise to Black men but not to women of any race. Two resolutions were before the delegates. The Stanton-Anthony Resolution was opposed to the amendment: "Until the Constitution shall know neither black nor white, neither male nor female, but only the equal rights of all classes, we renew our solemn indictment against that instrument as defective, unworthy, and an oppressive charter for the self-government of a free people." Frederick Douglass offered a contrary proposal which implied an evolutionary, long-term strategy to accommodate both Black males and all females' rights. The ERA, Douglass said, "hails the extension of suffrage to any class heretofore disfranchised as a cheering part of the triumph of our whole idea . . . and gratefully welcomes the pending fifteenth amendment." Douglass went on to make clear that the amendment represented "the culmination of one half of our demands," and he called for redoubling "of our energy to secure the further amendment guaranteeing the same sacred rights without limitation to sex."[79]

Two years prior, Sojourner Truth had taken the position of not supporting the amendment, fearing that putting more power into the hands of men would only serve to keep women down. "There is a great stir about colored men getting their rights," she said, "but not a word about the colored women." Truth's feminism made her alert to the perils of domestic tyranny, and she criticized Black males for increasing the burdens of Black women. Women, Truth argued, "go out washing, which is about as high as a colored woman gets, and their men go about idle, strutting up and down." As Paula Giddings points out, inflated attacks on Black male privilege were often articulated by white feminists on the lecture circuits. Susan B. Anthony earlier that year had declared that Black men trained so well by their Saxon rulers in the ways of "tyranny and despotism" would adopt patriarchal ways. Stanton followed up on the same theme with a statement that must have been viewed by Black women as reflecting a perverse logic. She warned that if Black women weren't given the ballot, they would be fated to a "triple bondage that man never knows. It would be better to be the slave of an educated white man than of an ignorant black one."[80]

As the debate roared on in the 1869 ERA meeting, Frederick Douglass made an impassioned plea for the greater urgency of Black male suffrage:

> When women, because they are women, are hunted down through the cities of New York and New Orleans, when they are dragged from their houses and hung upon lamp posts; when their children are torn from their arms, and their brains dashed upon the pavement; when

they are objects of insult and outrage at every turn; when they are in
danger of having their homes burnt down over their heads; when
their children are not allowed to enter schools; then they will have an
urgency to obtain the ballot equal to our own.[81]

But was this horror not also true for the Black woman, someone asked
Douglass. "Yes, yes, yes," he replied. "It is true for the Black woman
but not because she is a woman but because she is Black!" Douglass
was unable to persuade his lifelong allies in the feminist movement,
Stanton and Anthony, of the critical life-and-death struggle of Blacks.
Douglass's credentials as a militant feminist were impeccable. He,
after all, had persuaded a cautious Stanton to include suffrage as one
of the demands of the Seneca Falls women's rights meeting twenty-
one years earlier. And the pages of his newspaper, *The North Star*,
had been an important forum for promoting feminist ideas.

Conspicuously absent from the white feminists' arguments for
woman suffrage was any discussion of racial oppression, as Robert
Allen has argued. Douglass and others labored to impress upon the
white women the objective differences between their lives and the condition of all Blacks. Anthony's legalistic conception of citizenship
blinded her to the distinction which Douglass was attempting to convey.[82] Anthony could not comprehend the regime of brutality which
confronted Blacks during every waking hour, resulting in a vulnerability which reflected a qualitative difference from middle-class white
women's condition. She answered Douglass's speech by personalizing
the problem, a move which again deflected attention from the physical
jeopardy and apprehensions of the Black population: "When he tells
us that the cause of black men is so perilous, I tell him that even out-
raged as they are by the hateful prejudice against color, he himself
would not today exchange his sex and color with Elizabeth Cady
Stanton."[83]

Paula Giddings's account of the ERA debates on the amendments
reveals that the feminist and abolitionist camps were not neatly divided
on the issue; many whites supported Douglass's resolution, while other
Blacks endorsed enfranchising women in tandem with, or even before,
Black men. Black feminist Frances Ellen Watkins Harper supported
Douglass in a manner which emphasized her "bottom-line" assessment of the issue. "If the nation could handle only one question," she
lamented, she would not have the Black woman "put a single straw

in the way." According to Giddings, Harper realized that white feminists were incapable of the empathy required of dependable allies; she was skeptical of their ability to transcend their own gender interests. "The white women all go for sex, letting race occupy a minor position," Harper said. But for her, "Being Black means that every white, including every white working-class woman, can discriminate against you."[84] The white feminist abolitionist Lucy Stone, however, endorsed Douglass's and Harper's strategy of "not putting a straw" in the way of Black men's achieving the vote. Stone's understanding of interracial solidarity around the suffrage issue contrasted sharply with Stanton and Anthony's. This is how she expressed her decision to adopt any policy which would ameliorate the status of Blacks: "There are two great oceans; in the one is the black man, and in the other is woman. But I thank God for the XV Amendment, and hope that it will be adopted in every state. I will be thankful in my soul if anybody can get out of this terrible pit."[85]

Posed in the language of priorities, the dilemma over the Fifteenth Amendment was insoluble. That the debates were framed in this manner assured the brokering of race over sex. And the white suffragists' response to the "false historical necessity" terminated an important human rights coalition.[86] The split in the ERA was by no means inevitable, however. White women could have seen that the long-term strategy proposed by Frederick Douglass would have enhanced, not limited, their own freedom. It may have been, as Harper remarked, that the nation, at that historical juncture, could "handle only one question." But white feminists such as Stanton and Anthony refused this tactical plan. Their resentments of Black men (resentments which lay just beneath the surface of their human rights commitments) led them to embrace a reactionary politics which American feminism is still struggling to live down.

Given their penchant for constructing a hierarchy of rights, with those of white women on top, Stanton and Anthony interpreted the situation in their own short-term self-interest. They could not comprehend, or would not trust, Douglass's commitment to agitate for womens' rights *from the platform of a strengthened Black male electorate*. The issue became for the white suffragist leaders a question of conflicting interests. Barbara Andolsen reiterates their conflict: "Did concern for black people entail that white women must set aside their own claims in order to help black men take advantage of the political opportunity open to them? Or could white women legitimately pursue their own self-interest regardless of the effects of their actions on the political fortunes of black men?"[87] That they chose to exercise the latter position not only squandered white women's moral capital in nineteenth-century interracial politics, but failed in pragmatic terms as well. Aligning themselves with the nation's most reactionary forces did not advance, but rather isolated, their cause.

Other white suffragists, however, challenged Stanton's intransigence on the suffrage question. Abby Kelly described, as Anthony and Stanton could not, the vivid details of the ex-slaves' dilemma and just what they were up against. Kelly questioned Stanton's priorities, exhorting that whites were committing atrocities against Black people in former slave states, and arguing that it was imperative that Black men be offered full civil rights immediately for self-protection. Kelly asked, "Are we not dead to the sentiment of humanity if we shall wish to postpone his security against present woes and future enslavement till woman shall obtain political rights?"[88] Stanton and Anthony refused to recognize the physical danger in which many Blacks still lived, blinded as they were by abstract misreadings of Blacks' civil status. They were erroneously convinced that emancipation had "equalized" the legal rights of Black people and white women.

While the Fourteenth and Fifteenth Amendments were detrimental to woman suffrage, they provided important benefits to Black men, and, potentially, to Black women. The Fourteenth Amendment protected the civil rights of both groups in general, if not the specific right to vote. The amendment offered Blacks *some access* to the electoral system and potential legal protection against racist crimes. As Aptheker has argued, precisely because the Fourteenth Amendment was intended to advance the cause of African-American freedom, it inevitably would have "rebounded to the benefit of [all] women, but only a class-conscious element could have seen that point in 1869."[89]

Other coalition scenarios attempting to resolve the ambiguities over the civil rights amendments were conceivable, had so many whites not succumbed to the ugly class and race biases which surfaced when their former abolitionist sentiments were put to the test. Aptheker posits an alternative historical possibility, given the political configurations surrounding the suffrage question, one which would have placed white feminists in the center of a resistance movement from which they could have strengthened the women's cause. The issue of Black suffrage, she argues, was not the "Negro's Hour" in an abstract moral sense, but a moment of failure in progressive civil and women's rights alliances. Had not the unity of the ERA dissolved over a contest of priorities, "the betrayal of Reconstruction would have at least been tempered by an organized opposition."[90]

Black women clearly understood and accepted the viability of such a coalition scenario. Paula Giddings's analysis illustrates that Black women had no intention of curtailing their own demands for equal citizenship, nor did they view the victory of Black male suffrage as detrimental to their own autonomy:

> The support of the Fifteenth Amendment by Black women did not mean that they had less interest in their suffrage, economic independence, education, or any other issue that pertained to them. And their support certainly didn't mean a collective willingness to be oppressed by men, Black or White. But Harper and others understood that the rights of Black men had to be secured before Black women could assert theirs. If the race had no rights, the women's struggle was meaningless. But after the Fifteenth Amendment was assured, Black women continued their own struggle throughout the 1870's with renewed vigor.[91]

They did so in a segregated movement culture. From this moment on, the alienation of the organized women's movement from the cause of Black liberation was assured. When the 1869 ERA convention passed Douglass's resolution supporting the Fifteenth Amendment, the organization split, resulting in two competing white women's suffrage organizations—the American Women's Suffrage Association (AWSA), led by Lucy Stone; and the National Woman Suffrage Association (NWSA), led by Stanton and Anthony.

In assessing how Black and white feminists have interpreted the significance of these interracial breakdowns, one can see the inadequacy of certain interpretations. Some white feminist historians tend to minimize the extent of Stanton and Anthony's racism, rationalizing it as symptomatic of the times, or to deflect criticism to Republican Party leaders as the truly culpable actors. One can weigh the *realpolitik* of antebellum Republican politicians just so far; but in no way can this analysis justify the torrent of anti-Black rancor unleashed by Stanton and Anthony.

For instance, Ellen Carol DuBois, biographer and editor of Stanton and Anthony's correspondence, stresses the sense of "immense betrayal" experienced by the two women over the Fourteenth and Fifteenth Amendments, the enormous sacrifice of their own cause which had been made during the Civil War. DuBois cites "political forces beyond their control" which made it impossible to unite the demands of women and the freedmen; she is silent on the question of betrayal of Black freedom.[92] And she blames antifeminist Republican men for "driving a wedge" between Blacks' and women's rights, further downplaying the factor of white racism.[93] But the texts of Black feminists make clear just who actually betrayed whom. Commenting on the example of white feminists in the postwar period, Frances White states, "When Black feminists look at the first wave, the problems inherent in alliances with white women are highlighted."[94]

More damaging still is the tendency to evaluate this traumatic split between Black and white reformers as a revolutionary, progressive step which facilitated and advanced, independent feminist movement. DuBois writes approvingly of Stanton and Anthony's radical feminist newspaper, *The Revolution* (which was funded by the racist Democrat George Train), as flourishing only when Stanton and Anthony became "entirely independent of abolitionist influence." She praises Stanton and Anthony for producing "a bold and comprehensive portrait of the exploitation of women." How could a comprehensive portrait of "women" derive from a discourse based on "the subtle habit of seeing women's grievances from the viewpoint of white women," as DuBois herself admits? DuBois's ability to view the subsequent segregated and racist suffrage movement as a "radical and multifaceted feminism" itself serves to jeopardize the potential for feminist unity today.[95]

Narratives of Expediency

As the two competing national women's suffrage groups became mass movements in the last two decades of the nineteenth century, they were increasingly influenced by the leading scientific dogma of Negro racial inferiority. Feminists like Stanton and Anthony acquiesced to what historians have labeled "strategies of expediency."[96] Drifting toward a nativistic rationale for woman's suffrage as a policy to ensure white supremacy, the women's movement increasingly narrowed its interests from earlier radical concerns promoted by Stanton's theories on divorce, the patriarchal roots of organized religion, battery, female education, housework, and reproductive rights, to an obsessive drive for the vote. A pattern of pandering to southern racist prejudices became accepted practice, as white suffragists condoned and even fostered the institutionalization of American apartheid. Anthony, who came to lead the suffrage movement, adopted a *status quo* policy. "I do not want controversy," she told Frances E.W. Harper in 1888; and the NWSA's policy of working with anyone, whatever their views on other matters such as race, became an accepted criterion for coalition.[97]

The failure to actualize the potential for an integrated women's movement is dramatically illustrated by several incidents taken from suffrage history. "As the Black leaders discovered, it wasn't just racist politicians who put up obstacles to their enfranchisement. White women, including suffragists who should have been their natural allies, often became their most formidable adversaries."[98] In 1890, the two suffragist factions which had split in 1869 over the Fifteenth Amendment reunited as the National American Women's Suffrage Association (NAWSA). As suffrage historian Aileen Kraditor has noted, suffragists no longer were motivated by the same liberal ideals of natural rights and equality of all persons, or by the Christian morality which animated earlier abolitionist crusades. White suffragists embodied a posture of racist instrumentalism.[99] The "expediency" strategy of organized suffrage activism is illustrated by this 1893 NAWSA resolution:

> Resolved, that without expressing any opinion on the proper qualifications for voting, we call attention to the significant facts that in every State there are more women who can read and write than all negro voters; more American women who can read and write than all foreign voters; so that the enfranchisement of such women would settle the vexed question of rule by illiteracy whether of home-grown or foreign-born production.[100]

Historians cite the NAWSA conventions of 1899 and 1903 as the final separation of the suffrage movement from the Black cause. The records of these meetings provide a discourse of exclusion and segregation of

Black women, cooperation with southern racist practices, and a degeneration of former reformist goals. The white suffragist movement became an elitist, bigoted instrument for the advancement of white class privilege. As head of this influential mass organization, Susan B. Anthony contributed to such a legacy by endorsing a "neutral" stance on racial issues. At the 1899 convention, the black suffragist Lottie Wilson Jackson took advantage of the meeting's location in Michigan — home of one of the few NAWSA chapters to admit Black women — to encourage her white sisters to join Blacks in protesting Jim Crow policies.

Jackson communicated to the assembly the indignities Black women had endured on the segregated trains en route to the meeting. She explained that Black women were compelled to ride in unsanitary smoking cars despite the fact that they had paid for better accommodations. She expressed her dismay that many uncouth, often drunk male passengers created an atmosphere which was repugnant to decent women. Jackson proposed a resolution "that colored women ought not to be compelled to ride in smoking cars and that suitable accommodations should be provided for them."[101] Influenced by the denials of southern white delegates that such conditions existed, and tacitly refusing to interfere in "local customs," Anthony delivered the following rationale: "We women are a helpless disfranchised class. Our hands are tied. While we are in this condition, it is not for us to go passing resolutions against railroad corporations or anybody else."[102]

Stanton's position and the fact that the majority of the white delegates voted to table Jackson's resolution demonstrated two important features of segregated "sisterhood" in the 1890s. First was the callous disregard of the physical and psychological assaults on Black women traveling on southern railroads. Second was Anthony's assumption that, without the vote, white women were politically powerless to effect social change. This statement is indicative of the emphasis white suffragists placed on the vote as a panacea for women's oppression.

For middle-class Black women, the separate car system was one of the harshest indignities they had to suffer in Jim Crow. As historian Barbara Hilkert Andolsen has pointed out, segregated public institutions *were* a woman's issue, since Black women in those cars often were at risk for sexual harassment, assault, and other forms of violence. Susan Anthony's lack of sympathy for Black women's slighted sense of womanhood was a cruel demonstration that white suffragists "were not willing to take even mild symbolic action to support the special priorities of black delegates. . . . The assaults on the spirits of black women traveling on the railroad system were as damaging as the threats to their bodies."[103]

The theme of Jim Crow humiliations experienced by Black women is a common one in first-wave Black feminist narratives; it so frustrated their efforts to maintain "respectability" in a hostile cultural environment. These struggles of Black women, in the most violent period since the Civil War, failed to evoke sisterly concern from white suffragist leaders, as the Anthony example indicates. The era of the 1890s was replete with lynchings and rigid "black codes" of segregation; ideologies of "pure womanhood" existed simultaneously with eugenic theories of Black "bestiality." These forces created a climate of terror and psychological tension for all Blacks. As Lerone Bennett has written, by 1890 the "southern view had become the American view."[104] In 1893, the Supreme Court reversed the Civil Rights Act of 1875; three years later, it announced the "separate but equal" doctrine of *Plessy v. Ferguson*, which consolidated the South's legal system of segregation. KKK lynch mobs began to terrorize the entire Black population, and northern white society watched the South reenslave Black citizens through literacy laws, intimidation, and poll taxes. "The last decade of the nineteenth century was a critical moment in the development of modern racism — its major institutional supports as well as its attendant ideological justifications."[105]

During this volatile period, the lack of interracial affiliation by white suffragists was felt most acutely. It is important, then, to look at the critiques which Black clubwoman Anna Julia Cooper made of the white suffragist movement during this period. Her analysis of the position of women was a radically insightful one. It was exemplary of the project of nineteenth-century Black female intellectuals to develop a feminist theory capable of liberating all persons and exposing nativist racism, particularly the politics of expediency of the suffragist movement. Cooper combined her keen literary and political skills in a brilliant essay entitled "Woman versus the Indian." In the vein of the most critical contemporary feminist postcolonial views, Cooper deflated patriotic myths about American expansionism, railing against colonial exploitation and white supremacy; she allied African Americans with

Native American Indians as both victimized and stereotyped by the dominant white society. But, as political satire, the essay most brilliantly exposed the practices of white suffragists in forsaking alliances with Blacks, the poor, and other disenfranchised classes of Americans to gain the support of racist southern states for suffrage. She framed her analysis in a metaphorical form, writing of the courting of a petulant "southern belle" who demanded to keep her "pet" institution, slavery, under another name. Cooper similarly identified the suffragist movement as "courting the southern lady" (white) and southern "woman" (Black), two groups with radically different interests. In Hazel Carby's reading of Cooper's text, Cooper was pointedly criticizing the courting of the lady at the expense of the woman as the cause of the constrained and parochial politics embodied by the white women's movement. Cooper's essay highlighted the limits of the "all or nothing" strategy which had destroyed the ERA coalition, forcing Black feminist Frances E.W. Harper and Frederick Douglass to oppose Anthony's prioritization of suffrage exclusively for white women.[106]

Cooper attacked the suffrage movement for becoming what she characterized as the plaintiff "Eye" in a suit "Eye vs. Foot." Cooper's critique focused on white women's denigration of both African Americans and Native American Indians as "ignorant and gross and depraved" so long as "lofty-souled white women" were denied the franchise. Cooper challenged the racist white women to abandon their exclusionary policies and the pursuit of their own gender and class interests for a concern with all oppressed persons:

> Is not this hitching our wagon to something much lower than a star? Is not woman's cause broader, and deeper, and grander, than a blue stocking debate or an aristocratic pink tea? Why should woman become plaintiff in a suit versus the Indian, or the Negro or any other race or class who have been crushed under the iron heel of Anglo-Saxon power and selfishness? If the Indian has been wronged or cheated by the puissance of this American government, it is woman's mission to plead with her country to cease to do evil and to pay its honest debts. . . . [Let] her rest her plea, not on Indian inferiority, nor or Negro depravity, but on the obligation of legislators.[107]

In contrast to the exclusionary ethnocentrism of the white suffragist's ideology, Cooper's essay is a remarkably important document of nineteenth-century feminist theory. She exposed the racist collaborations of white feminism and redefined woman's cause as not that of "the white woman, nor the black woman nor the red woman, but the cause of every man or woman who has writhed silently under a mighty wrong." She refused the alliance-shattering tactic (encouraged by white suffragists) which attempted to pit one oppressed group against the other, elaborating instead a clear commitment to mutual support and advocacy. The egalitarian political framework Cooper established provided a ground for the widest possible coalition paradigm. Had the suffragist movement not been immobilized by white racism, Reconstruction politics might have been redirected by the radically democratic discourse of Black feminists such as Cooper. She proferred a feminist strategy which "intended to expand the rubric of the concerns of women to include 'all undefended woe, all helpless suffering' and to encompass an ideal and set of practices that could become a movement for the liberation of all oppressed peoples, not remain a movement for the defense of parochial and sectional interests in the name of 'woman.'"[108]

As Cooper's critique reveals, white suffrage politics contributed to the racist climate and apartheid flourishing in the 1890s. Her insight into this problem can be brought to bear again in the context of the NAWSA's 1903 convention in New Orleans. Susan Anthony presided over this conference, which sat silently as white Mississippi suffragist Belle Kerney exhorted northern feminists to "look to our Anglo-Saxon women as the medium through which to retain its supremacy of the white race over the African."[109] Such blatantly divisive sentiments, however, were not new in NAWSA debates. Two years earlier, in one of her many gestures to placate southerners, Anthony declared that it was time for women to become "saviors of the Race."[110] The politics of expediency which accommodated white feminists' single-minded drive for woman suffrage meant that their desire for southern support superseded any claims Blacks might make on behalf of their own civil rights. When the convention opened in New Orleans, the local newspaper (ironically) assailed the northern feminists for encouraging "social equality" between the races — to which the NAWSA board responded by stating the association had *no official view on the question of equality for Black Americans.*[111]

Black feminists were familiar with the coded social messages in both the tactics of neutrality and the discourse of social mixing. Designed to whip up southern fears, the suggestion of interracial mixing had, of course, sexual overtones, but not those which would have protested the rape of Black females or the lynching of Black men. In order to defuse such inflammatory rhetoric, Black feminists consistently had stressed that their concerns were for *justice* — not forced intimacy between the races. In her 1892 collection of essays, Anna Julia Cooper distinguished clearly between the right of access to, and civil treatment in, public facilities, on the one hand, and coerced intermixing on the other. She insisted that "the social equality which means forced or unbidden association would be as much deprecated and as strenuously opposed by . . . [black women] as by the most hide-bound Southerner."[112] Cooper aggressively exposed the forced association implications of the "social equality" debates as a divisive tactic; for her it was Black citizenship and the right of Blacks to self-determination that were at issue, not social mingling. "She understood that behind the smoke screen of the controversy over social equality was a barrage of questions of heritage and inheritance which gained consensus in both North and South."[113]

That Susan B. Anthony contributed her reputation and leadership to a suffragist movement which had deviated so drastically from the spirit of the ERA is a forceful indicator of the racist complexities of nineteenth-century reform politics. The conflict between Susan B. Anthony's egalitarian personal values and her public manifestations of racism should serve as a warning about the limitations of personal commitments to decency; those private goals yield easily to other perceived interests. In 1894, Anthony betrayed her old ally Frederick Douglass by asking him not to attend the forthcoming NAWSA meeting in Atlanta so as not to embarrass either himself or the southern suffragists. According to Terborg-Penn's account in her important essay, "Discrimination Against Afro-American Women in the Woman's Movement, 1830–1920," Anthony explained to her Black friend Ida B. Wells, the antilynching feminist activist, that Douglass's presence on the stage with the honored guests would have "offended the southern hosts."[114]

The friendship between Anthony and Wells and their 1894 conversation about this event offer revealing insights into first-wave interracial sisterhood. In her autobiography, *Crusade for Justice*, Wells relates an episode which took place on one of her long stays at Anthony's home. Realizing that Wells needed help with some important correspondence, Anthony instructed her white stenographer to take dictation. When the stenographer failed to appear, Wells sensed that the reason was racial prejudice and informed Anthony of this upon her return. Anthony was so angry at the stenographers's refusal "to take dictation from a colored woman," she dismissed her immediately.[115] Wells wrote that she greatly admired Anthony during those "precious days in which I sat at the feet of this pioneer and veteran." Yet Wells, one of the boldest, most intelligent, and most daring social activists of the nineteenth century, felt that it was necessary openly to criticize Anthony for failing to make her personal fight against racism a public issue of the suffrage movement. On the issues of Anthony's spurning Douglass's participation in suffragist conventions and Anthony's refusal to assist black women in forming their own suffragist organizations, Wells made clear her disgust at her mentor's hypocrisy: "'And you think I [Anthony] was wrong in so doing,' she asked. I answered uncompromisingly yes, for I [Wells] felt that although she may have made gains for suffrage, she had also confirmed white women in their attitude of segregation."[116]

Yet this tacit endorsement of racism characterized Anthony's public stance on the issue until she resigned from the NAWSA in 1900. Her white successors would continue to exclude Black women from suffrage activities and to manifest racist attitudes well into the twentieth century, through the final push for the Nineteenth Amendment in 1920.[117] By the last decade of the century, the political and moral bankruptcy of the white woman's rights movement was apparent. White suffragists had abandoned their earlier egalitarian moral principles of universal human freedom. They used the resources of their movement and their privilege to strengthen racist Anglo-Saxon pretensions to human superiority, subordinating Black claims to personhood and citizenship. And they became apologists for the systematic exclusion of Black women from a shared public world of feminist reform politics. The strategies of expediency employed by white suffragists after Reconstruction were rooted in class bias as well as racial and ethnic prejudice.

After the women's movement severed its link with African-American freedom, it lacked the moral accountability and empathy which had awakened white women to their own sense of injustice. The women's rights movement had become a conservative element in American politics by the last decade of the century, eventually turning on even its own radical feminist mentors. The revolutionary premises of feminist thought, spawned in part by the Grimkés and Stanton and Anthony, had begun to shatter the hegemony of American patriarchy. Such radical challenges to sexist institutions, however, had become liabilities to the suffrage-dominated reform groups, dedicated to the single issue of the vote. The volatile issues which Stanton earlier had raised—women's domestic duties, divorce restrictions, marriage, and free love—were silenced by all but a few women. At its 1896 convention, the NAWSA officially dissociated itself from Elizabeth Cady Stanton's scathing feminist critique of the Bible as promoting female subservience.[118] That "feminists" could so publicly rebuke one of its most radical theorists—not for her racial prejudices but for her truly revolutionary deconstruction of patriarchy—is evidence of the movement's increasingly reactionary turn.

But Stanton and Anthony themselves betrayed their Black sisters who so desperately sought their leadership and political alliance. How might we evaluate these two contradictory feminists? Bettina Aptheker's principled and wise historical perspective on these issues provides a context of understanding which accomplishes two important political achievements: she allows us the constructive path of learning from the limits of white feminist pioneers, while dissuading us from a misguided expectation of their innocence. One aspect of this legacy is clear: the human rights of Black Americans rarely were legitimated by white feminist leaders, whose instrumental approach to reform politics rendered Blacks, at best, occasional pawns to be manipulated for their own ends. We might easily "blame" Stanton and Anthony for derailing a potentially transformative coalition for justice; the evidence exists to do so. But a more productive approach demands that we not stop there; we ought to focus then, and now, on combating the vast display of indifference which collectively underwrote this feminist shame. Aptheker's assessment has merit:

> The point is not to defend or excoriate Stanton or Anthony. They were no more, and probably less, racist than many of their contemporaries in the abolitionist movement, although they have been more prominently rebuked. The point is to learn what we can from their experience and process. Neither one ever really felt the urgency, the

pain, the dailiness of Afro-American oppression and struggle. Neither one ever grasped the extent to which the liberation of woman was bound up with the emancipation of the Afro-American woman and her people. . . . Anthony had several significant relationships with Afro-American women, including Sojourner Truth, Ida B. Wells, and Mary Church Terrell. Evidence suggests that Sojourner Truth especially influenced her ideas. Overall, however, Anthony's role was one of soliciting Black support for woman suffrage without granting reciprocal support for Afro-American rights.[119]

Intellectuals, Activists, Agitators: First-Wave Black Feminists

The suffrage record makes clear why Black women's ample social reform activity at the turn of the century took the form of separate organizations. As new Black feminist histories celebrate, Black female intellectuals in this period sacrificed their middle-class lives to go South, to teach and cajole funds to build schools and clinics for the impoverished former slaves[120]; to write novels as political acts; to tour the country as public speakers and reformers[121]; to agitate for suffrage and women's rights[122]; to publicize, report on, and resist mob violence by organizing international antilynching crusades[123]; and to institutionalize mass club networks to honor and redeem their womanhood.[124] They were reconstructing womanhood, as Hazel Carby's research shows us, and developing feminist theories committed to a radical transformation of social relations. In the words of the brilliant feminist polemicist Frances Harper, women's rights must extend to "the grand and holy purpose of uplifting the human race." Vanguards on the "threshold of woman's era," Black women were ready "to add their quota of good citizenship to the best welfare of the nation."[125] Unlike Susan Anthony, Harper did not believe that women were paralyzed without the vote; by her example and exhortation, she encouraged Black women to engage every important issue and activity of the day.

The racist exclusions of white suffragists did not prevent Black women from working for the vote. It is important to establish the extent to which Black women both contributed to its success and linked electoral freedoms to their economic and material survival. As the work of Terborg-Penn and others have shown, Black women's extensive suffrage history is rarely written about by white scholars. But their commitment to achieving the vote, as an integral part of full female citizenship, was a central part of first-wave Black feminist theory and conceptions of female liberation. As Mary Church Terrell, a lifelong member of NAWSA, said in 1898, on the fiftieth anniversary of the Seneca Falls women's rights convention, "Thus to me this semi-centennial of the National American Woman Suffrage Association is a double jubilee, rejoicing as I do, not only in the prospective enfranchisement of my sex but in the emancipation of my race."[126]

Giddings's history of Black women's activism makes clear also that, despite the segregated practices of NAWSA, Black female activists organized their own suffrage clubs and marshalled their considerable energies to get the vote. "In fact," she notes, "the racist attitudes provided additional impetus for their own struggle." The fiery Fannie Barrier Williams declared that *any* tactic, the vote included, would be embraced against the racism of white women: "We should never forget that the exclusion of colored women and girls from nearly all places of respectable employment is due mostly to the meanness of American women, and every way that we can check this unkindness by the force of the franchise should be religiously done."[127]

Black women were incensed that certain of their men violated the integrity of the franchise for personal gain. They routinely castigated Black male freedmen for "selling" their votes during Reconstruction. Frances Harper's satirical poem, *Dialogue on Woman's Rights*, attacks Black patriarchy for thinking "that women's voting's wrong. . . . How can you push your wife aside and try to hold her back?" Harper's protagonists in the dialogue, Jacob and John, are redeemed, however, by becoming advocates of woman suffrage: "Well, wrong is wrong and right is right, for woman as for man, I almost think that I will go and vote with Betsy Ann."[128] African Americans demonstrated more consistency and democracy about suffrage than did whites. They maintained a broad political philosophy of universal suffrage, while whites systematically erected more and more exemptions (foreigners, uneducated, poor, Blacks, Asians, Indians) to curtail citizen participation.

Black feminist analyses viewed suffrage as a political vehicle to facilitate broader freedoms, an important theoretical insight which furthered their diverse resistance efforts on many social fronts. They exhibited a keen understanding of the connections among racism, economic exploitation, slavery, sexist practices, and other structures which violated Blacks' freedom. Harper's 1893 address to the World's Congress of Representative Women in Chicago placed in relief white women's timidity in asserting themselves politically, simply because they lacked the formality of suffrage. Harper's feminism was bound neither by those who told her what she could not do, nor by those who adhered to norms of womanhood which confined women's influence to "their place" in domestic affairs. For Harper, suffrage was indelibly linked to race. "It was voters, stated Harper, who tortured, burned and lynched black people. Women's political perspective, she insisted, would have to be wider than a focus on obtaining the franchise."[129]

One would be hard-pressed to identify a nineteenth-century figure with keener understanding of that premise than the redoubtable Ida B. Wells. Her brilliant theoretical and analytical capacities, coupled with a single-minded determination to raise public consciousness about the conditions of Black Americans, rendered her indeed "a brand new thing under the sun," as the New York editor Thomas Fortune put it, praising Wells in 1889.[130] A talented journalist whose passionate and frank pamphlets[131] exposing the southern lynching terror catapulted her into the leadership of an international campaign against the violence visited on Black Americans, Wells also was at the forefront of suffrage agitation and Black women's club activism.

As Hazel Carby's work on Wells tells us, no other historical figure was as dedicated to uncovering the economic and political significance of lynching and exposing the sexual ideologies which fueled it than Ida B. Wells. As a journalist, newspaper editor, and public speaker, Wells traveled throughout the North and Britain to build resistance to the wave of lynchings running rampant in the South.[132] In her lectures, articles, and speeches, Wells exorted Blacks to mobilize political resistance by mounting boycotts of white businesses, and to abandon their passive stance as victims. Wells placed the phenomenon of lynching in the context of American slavery, insisting that the labor, sweat, and toil of slave men and women had for 250 years built the nation, made it "blossom as a rose, created vast wealth for the masters and made the United States one of the mighty nations of the earth."[133] The failed Reconstruction, however, meant that Black freedom had been abandoned, their centuries of labor still went unrewarded, and new forms of control were being exercised. This perspective enabled Wells to interpret lynching as a new economic weapon used by whites to subordinate Blacks. Lynchings, Wells argued, were "an excuse to get rid of Negroes who were acquiring wealth and property . . . to keep the race terrorized and to 'keep the nigger down.'"[134]

Wells's analyses were able to link white society's attack on Black economic power with Black males' newly won suffrage privileges. Not only did lynching serve to thwart Blacks' economic stability, but also it worked to defraud Black males of their votes and the benefits of citizenship. In *Red Record*, Wells both discredited the specious statistics of white newspapers, demystifying the "rape" rationalization for mass lynchings, and illustrated how powerfully suffrage functioned for Black men as a symbol of their manhood and citizenship.[135] Wells understood, as did other Black women and men, that suffrage was an empty political gesture without legal protection against lynching and rape, access to fair trials, and a forum for challenging the ideological war being waged against Blacks' intelligence and moral character in the press.[136]

But Wells's insight as a feminist theorist is most apparent in her interrogation of the manipulation of the racist patriarchal ideologies surrounding Black female and male sexuality. The dialectics of the lynch mentality meant the dehumanization of Black men, the debasement of Black women, and a construction of white women as property. In a scathing 1892 editorial in her Memphis paper, Wells suggested that it was not the "lust" of Black men to "rape" white women which defined the sexual dynamic of antebellum society, but the desire of white women to seduce Black men.[137] Wells understood how, in an effort to tighten their control over the sexuality of both white and Black women, white men had constructed both a culture of lynching and a culture of chivalry as manifestations of patriarchal power. By linking the murder of Blacks with the sexual fears of white males, Wells was able to deconstruct these forces and to reveal the inadequacy of those tenuous Black civil rights purportedly championed by northern Republicans at the war's end.

In her pamphlet *Southern Horrors*, Wells discredited the association of lynching and rape, arguing that few of the cases of murdered Blacks had even involved rape charges. The "rape" of white women, she said, was a recent invention, virtually nonexistent during the Civil War when the white male population was on the front. Wells's feminist analyses of lynching, as Carby tells us, were wide-ranging, complex. Her voice forced white society to acknowledge the sexual victimization of Black women, a fact ignored in the pervasive white propaganda of the day, which advocated the "protection of womanhood."

> She situated the murder of Black men historically within the whole spectrum of black and white social, political and economic relations. But at its core, what was and has remained unique about Wells' theorizing is its dissection of sexual ideologies and mores. Early in her work, Wells indicted the miscegenation laws which, in practice, meant that black women were the victims of rape by white men who had the power to terrorize black men under the pretense of the protection of white womanhood.[138]

Carby describes Wells as an "uppity" Black woman, a woman who refused to adopt the "ladylike" attitudes of compromise and silence. These irreverent qualities, as well as her genius as a theorist and activist, claim for her a place of honor in our feminist past. She helps us see today the pervasive constellations of race, gender, economics, and violence in the lives of all women. We ought to see, as well, that the literature against lynching, to which she so powerfully contributed, was not a construct of victimization. In actuality, it functioned as a discourse of empowerment for Black men, Black women, and white women. In defending the integrity of Black manhood, Wells simultaneously "affirmed the virtue of Black womanhood and the independence of white womanhood" by revealing their entanglement in the murderous cycle of lynching. She and the other Black women of the antilynching campaign made an invaluable contribution to feminist theory by demystifying the patriarchal manipulation of rape. For the first time in United States history, women had forged a movement that made rape a political issue.[139]

As Wells's example makes clear, one of the hallmarks of first-wave Black feminists was their defiant practice of talking back — not only to the males who attempted to subordinate them, but also to the white female reformers whose "sisterly" symbols and rhetoric were, more often than not, honored in the breach.[140] Black female intellectuals and activists, in their writings and speeches, articulated the connection between patriarchal power and white female reformers who practiced racist exclusionism in their organizations and actions. As they participated in club forums, legislative debates, and religious convocations, Black women consistently called white women to account for their segregationist policies and their failure to come to the aid of Black women. Fannie Barrier Williams's 1900 essay, "Club Movement Among Colored Women of America," is a strong demonstration of these themes:

> Afro-American women of the United States have never had the benefit of a discriminating judgment concerning their worth as women made up of the good and bad of human nature. . . . These women have been left to grope their way unassisted toward a realization of those . . . standards of family and social life that are the badges of race respectability. They have had no special teachers to instruct them. No conventions of distinguished women of the more favored race have met to consider their peculiar needs.[141]

Not only did women "of the more favored race" fail to mobilize in solidarity with Black clubwomen, as Williams claimed, but they often proved themselves to be most energetic popularizers of apartheid. Such white indifference could mean death in the Black community. The struggle to dislodge white women's "pride of caste," in Frances Harper's term, and to secure their aid in anti-lynching activism — as well as their help in organizing against the rape of Black women — was a difficult endeavor. But Black clubwomen continually brought these issues to the attention of white women, prodding them to take responsibility for stopping both lynching and sexual violence against Black women. Black club activists wrote and spoke of the chilling atrocities committed against Black women as well as Black men. Mary Church Terrell, a Black feminist activist in every progressive political struggle of the day, recounts the reaction of two white women upon hearing of the lynching of a pregnant Black woman whose baby was torn from her body. "What did she do to deserve it?," the white women queried.[142] Terrell's 1904 essay, "Lynching from a Negro's Point of View," pleaded with white women to recognize their historical responsibility for, and culpability in, lynching:

> The white men who shoot negroes to death and flay them alive, and the white women who apply flaming torches to their oil-soaked bodies today, are the sons and daughters of women who had but

little, if any, compassion on the race when it was enslaved. The men who lynch negroes to-day are, as a rule, the children of women who sat by their firesides happy and proud in the possession and affection of their own children, while they looked with unpitying eye and adamantine heart upon the anguish of slave mothers whose children had been sold away. . . . It is too much to expect, perhaps, that the children of women who for generations looked upon the hardships and the degradation of their sisters of a darker hue with few if any protests. . . . But what a mighty foe to mob violence Southern white women might be, if they would arise . . . to implore their fathers, husbands and sons no longer to stain their hands with the black man's blood![143]

Terrell's vivid recounting of white lynching culture framed the atrocities of her era in a generational context which emphasized the collaboration of mothers of slaveholding families in the turn-of-the-century racist crimes perpetuated by their descendants. The smug and protected ignorance afforded to white women by their domestic isolation, as well as their direct acts as accomplices in the savage mutilation of Black men, both indicted white women and challenged their idealized status as the South's "moral conscience."

Black feminist clubwomen, in the context of lynching, skilfully exposed the hypocrisy of white women, whose possession of "higher" ethical and spiritual values were mythologized as sanctifying southern "civilization." If the "true womanhood" of white women validated them as arbiters of a just social order, as Black clubwomen theorized, then white women justifiably could be held accountable for failing to end not only lynching but also racism in white society. Just as Terrell argued that white women should and could be a powerful social force, the outspoken Black feminist educator Charlotte Hawkins Brown militantly challenged white women to rise to their exalted reputations. Before an interracial meeting in Memphis in 1920, Brown insisted that her white audience "put yourself in my place" and ask themselves, "What would Jesus do if he were in my place?" And she established a potential Christian sisterhood by indicating that Black and white women eventually would have to reach out for the same hand: "But I know that the dear Lord will not receive it, if you are crushing me beneath your feet." Brown made it clear that Black women were tired of struggling alone:

> We have become a little bit discouraged. We have begun to feel that
> you are not, after all, interested in us and I am going still further.
> The Negro women of the South lay everything that happens to the
> members of her race at the door of the Southern white woman . . .
> we all feel that you can control your men. We feel that so far as lynch-
> ing is concerned that, if the white women would take hold of the
> situation, that lynching would be stopped.[144]

As these critiques indicate, white women's inaction constantly
brought their "womanhood" up short. What must have been demoral-
izing defeats did not, however, diminish the vision of Black feminists.
Their legacy is an egalitarian and inclusive political theory which
demonstrates a public voice of advocacy for all women and all oppressed persons. They consistently called for a transformed women's
movement, as *one* project which could align with other human rights,
religious, labor, and racial coalitions for social justice. They demanded
radical structural change and resisted the imperialistic practices of a
state that exploited all the poor and the people of color. The struggle
for women's equality and the formal rights of citizenship was always
balanced by an urgent concern with the economic viability of the entire Black community. These women would not build a new feminist
movement on the discriminatory practices they had experienced at the
hands of whites. Resonating with democratic hope, Anna Julia Cooper
told her Black sisters in 1892:

> Let woman's claim be as broad in the concrete as in the abstract.
> We take our stand on the solidarity of humanity, the oneness of life,
> and the unnaturalness and injustice of all special favoritism, whether
> of sex, race, country, or condition. We want . . . to go . . . demand-
> ing an entrance not through a gateway for ourselves, our race, our
> sex, or our sect, but a grand highway for humanity. . . . Not till then
> is woman's cause won.[145]

And the noted Black clubwoman Josephine St. Pierre Ruffin, despite
the many insulting affronts to her reputation that she endured from white
women's organizations, could project a conception of feminist solidarity
based not on bitterness and expediency, but on the promise of a new form
of political life. Ruffin's feminism did not define itself by race, class, or
color, but appropriated, in the strongest terms, *citizenship* and a vigorous
intellectual passion to leave a unifying mark on the world:

> Our woman's movement is a woman's movement that is led and directed by women for the good of women and men, for the benefit of all humanity . . . we are not drawing the color line; we are women, American women, as intensely interested in all that pertains to us as such as all other American women; we are not alienating or withdrawing, we are only coming to the front, willing to join any others in the same work and cordially inviting and welcoming any others to join us.[146]

Given the leadership and integrity of such women, Black feminists organized themselves into democratic national movements, open to all women who were committed, as *American women*, to the hard political challenges of upholding their dignity through full civic engagement. We ought to remember that their sense of obligation to the multitudes of impoverished, illiterate, and vulnerable Black women was profound. As educated elites, intellectual women like Ruffin, Wells, and Cooper were not "isolated figures of intellectual genius," as Carby tells us. They were organically linked to the daily realities of their Black sisters and brothers, and they framed their public efforts and priorities in response to the needs of the grass roots. Privileged though they were, they nonetheless "tried to develop a cultural and historical perspective that was organic to the wider condition of black womanhood."[147]

Conclusion

The narrative of white feminist history in the first wave is a tragic one. It is a tragedy of which I and, I am sure, most of my white feminist community were ignorant for many years. The first formidable barrier which confronts us, then, relates to the need for historical recovery and accountability. We white feminists can expect little solace from or response to our rhetorics of interracial bonding and sisterhood until this racist memory is absorbed into our collective symbols. Those few instances where interracial commitments flourished, mark them as important turning points in the growth of a self-conscious movement for women's liberation. But those moments alone are thin legacies upon which to build. Those moments cannot erase the larger story of betrayal, manipulation, and even hatred, voiced by white feminist pioneers, those icons which most white feminist scholarship has held in such high esteem. When we look closely, as Black feminists have educated us to do, at the story those nineteenth-century white feminists have told about their struggle for female autonomy and about their psychological strivings in a world of white over Black, we do not see the feminist anticipation of a just society.

A defensive politics of memory might advocate the wholesale purge of this part of our feminist past. But only a nihilistic posture could advocate such a denial. We need to think through a politics of memory which begins with the paradox of assimilating a new identity, one which holds within its bounds both emancipation and shame. And somehow we must convince Black women that we engage this paradox in order to earn both their trust and their forgiveness. This process must not be maudlin; it must be honest and visible. I think there will be much pain and misunderstanding in our ragged attempts to communicate to Black women our knowledge of the hateful collusions of so many nineteenth-century white women. But I think, too, this project can carry us to spaces of important transformative potential. In this way, we can discern in the white story the "usable past" which C. Vann Woodward views as intrinsic to the inheritors of a tragic history.[148]

What intellectual nourishment can advance this urgent recovery of feminist meaning? Which historical fragments from this first-wave legacy might we use to construct a new feminist public memory? What kind of interpretive language might we employ in our attempt to redefine our identities and politics?

We may look to the vision of solidarity and the body of theory which first-wave Black female intellectuals created. The legacy which comes to us in the rich feminism these women created affords a recovery of meaning vital to contemporary feminist thought and politics. The principles of Black abolitionists, suffragists, clubwomen, antilynching activists, and intellectuals redefined the standards of sisterhood and laid the organizational ground for true female solidarity. Theorizing a politics which upheld women's collective efforts toward social change and justice, they created a vision of sisterhood that was based on collective advancement, mutual respect, and individual empowerment.

As the original authors of Black feminist theory, these nineteenth-century women understood — as do contemporary Black feminists —

the methodological insights of multiple oppressions, the exploitation of all persons of color which derive from racist colonialism, and the ideological sweeps of racist patriarchy. In these formulations, current Black feminists can be viewed as the inheritors of this rich tradition. And they have had to fight mightily for this *dénouement*. As the hearts and minds of white feminist scholars and our students begin to fill with the spirit and images of these courageous Black precursors, no longer a silence at our center, we can learn from and pass on a remarkable civic gift. Frances E.W. Harper's claim against the nation for "justice, simple justice" ought to be our shared memory.

Part 3

Conclusion

Chapter 6

Crossover Dreams: Toward a Multicultural Feminist Politics of Solidarity

To assess the damage is a dangerous act.

Cherríe Moraga

In thinking about what political configurations, concepts, and principles multicultural feminism might embody and endorse, I want to revive some of the divergent voices and issues I have discussed in the introduction to this book. I want to bring myself back into dialogue with those dimensions of Black feminist theory — its Afrocentric, postcolonial, and postmodernist moments — which seemed to cohere usefully in the paradigm "feminist theory in the flesh." That concept thematized feminist theory as a materialist map of what I have called deep context, a reading of the particularities of diverse women's lives, historically and culturally situated in vulnerable "identities" and oppressions of protean making. Feminist theory in the flesh is *not*, to be sure, feminism unmodified; it is feminisms in flux, always already in relations of power. And although it draws on some of the aspects of identity politics — the empowerment and affirmation of long-silenced hybrid populations — it differs politically in important ways which I shall spell out.

The kind of politics which I want to suggest in this chapter for multicultural feminism, the symbolic rendering of our emancipatory goals, requires movement. That principle guides my design in employing the crossover metaphor. Crossover politics implies that all parties shift a bit — not forever, but strategically for survival and health. Crossover feminists try (but never truly succeed) to see and hear from "other" vantage points, perhaps sharing some of their experience and knowledge with someone else, some of whose own experience and knowledge might rub off. Hopes for such empathic transfers are restrained, however — viewed as welcome long shots. Because it understands the fragility and limits of reciprocity and mutuality ("put yourself in my shoes"), a feminist crossover community does not draw on the affective models of "organic" collectivities. The histories of segregated "sisterhood" have made us all too wary of these metaphors. Although appealing, such visions of bonding often mask impulses toward conformity, toward silencing differences, dissent, and even "deviance." A crossover model of community is socially more modest, encouraging unassimilated others[1] in somewhat distant but ultimately more egalitarian structures. "Crossovering" requires not a shedding of one's own particular roots, but a willingness to acknowledge the cultural life worlds contained in someone else's roots. It is neither a hierarchical nor an assimilative metaphor — taboos to keep us constantly alert — nor does it aim for a dialectical, "higher" social whole or an unwrinkled unity. The music which gets created in crossover tones is usually hyphenated in genre, far from pure, like "our" lives. But crossover styles are open to and encourage mixing, playing around, experimenting. Process-driven, crossover "we"s know that we will never get it "just right"; we reject the priests and saviors who preach correctness. I shall return to these formulations of feminist *polis* life at the conclusion of this discussion.

The crossover ideal is a vehicle for critique as well. In the context of multicultural feminism, and in my location as a white feminist, I want to think out loud about an enigmatic comment made by Michelle Cliff: "We do not see only issues of color, but we do see coloredly."[2] Now, what could she have meant by that tantalizing statement? Cliff's "we" refers to "writers of color"; there is a clear implication of shared ideological and political consciousness — effects of Afrocentric feminism. The statement illustrates self-consciously the kind of unity ("writers" or "women of color") one ought to expect from the affinities shared by those for whom theory in the flesh resonates in a white supremacist culture. What can theory in the flesh mean, though, if "you" are white? We know what "seeing whitely" has meant, and we want to turn that around. It ought to be apparent that a parallel maxim for white feminists (seeing whitely) is treacherous, given what we know about American apartheid. Elizabeth Spelman has cautioned white feminists in her exemplary work, *Inessential Woman: Problems of Exclusion in Feminist Thought*, about the racist dangers of assuming commonalities in feminist theory. The abstract phrase "as a woman," she argues, is the "Trojan horse of feminist ethnocentrism."[3]

The discourse of Black feminist theory has lucidly shown us how this works in the hegemonic milieu of a principally white movement. Worrying about white essentialism, I want to illustrate the troubling kinds of results when women of color create equally non-negotiable constructions of self. The prospects for democratic politics are short-circuited when "utopias of historical reversal," in Luce Irigaray's term,[4] come to define feminist praxis. How easily deforming seductions take over when even counterhegemonic "mythical norms"[5] which define and suffocate are enacted. The oppositional other is not immune to thinking in totalistic categories; the old dream of symmetry sets in by insistently projecting certain realities onto "others." "We resist your definitions that *we* are this or that," the dialogue goes—while in the next breath declaring, "However, all of *you* are this and that."

I want to return to Spelman's working out of her thesis about homogenizing practices (the "as a woman" problematic) later. What I am interested in exploring now is a question about "the Other's" creation of new closed narratives and identities. I offer the proposition that ethnocentrism is not a spectator sport in feminisms: we all contribute to it through the will to generalize and erase specificity. But one of the ways we contribute to feminist thought at all is by generalizing; so, yes, *all* feminists are essentialists in this basic sense. It's that obstreperous cousin, ethnocentrism, that gets us into trouble by assuming that "seeing coloredly" or "seeing whitely" relates to an unambiguous shared picture of the world. In defining what they are, feminist women of color ought not succumb to the bait of ethnocentrism — as have so many of us white feminists.

Does Spelman's Trojan horse insight about these practices impose some ambivalence or ambiguity on all constructions or claims about "women," including categories such as "women of color"? There are certainly important — indeed, vital — things to be said and actions to be taken on behalf of those who share racist oppression. In previous chapters, I have tried to spell out my view of the significance of Black feminism. But we have some evidence that such a category ("women of color") is far from unambiguous, nor is its membership clearly defined. Chela Sandoval's important work on the oppositional consciousness embodied in the construction "women of color" is different from the naturalized identities of "woman" in some white-centered feminisms. "Women of color" aligns on the basis of conscious coalition, but its membership criteria are somewhat open-ended intentionally.[6] Sandoval's use of quotation marks around "women of color" is an important signifier that suggests even oppositional identities are susceptible to incoherences and contradictions, that those who powerfully "speak coloredly" might not always speak with one voice. That awareness of fallibility ought to be seen as an efficacious, not negative, sign. Evidence of ambiguity speaks to the intricate and nuanced deliberations which go into "our" articulation of locations, identities, and experience.

In the first part of this discussion, I thus want to consider an interpretation of the limits of identity politics which allows us to see how easily reifications of self and other are developed and ontologies embraced. The generic "woman of color" is no advance over the generic "white woman." I want to insert some tension into debates over the content of oppositional identities, to try and discern those tendencies which replicate the essentialist moves feminists of color rightly criticize in white feminism. If we can be alert to the imperialist moment of identity creation *per se*, we might be able to think new grounds for multicultural feminist conversations.

In 1984, Elly Bulkin, also writing about this tendency in identity politics, expressed concern over the silence around "oppression privilege," the code that established who was justified in criticizing whom. Bulkin, a Jewish feminist, wished to speak about the anti-Semitism of some women of color; she resisted the assumption that "certain criticisms can be made only by those who share a given identity; that it is unacceptable, for instance, for a non-Jewish woman to criticize a Jewish woman, for a white woman to take issue with a woman of color." Bulkin admitted that few white women had challenged women of color about the possibility that an adherence to "identity" and one's own oppression concealed the "less comfortable contours of a more complete picture in which we might exist as oppressor, as well as oppressed."[7] But it is precisely that more complex picture which holds the greatest liberatory potential.

Bulkin worried about her authority to make such critiques. I think she is correct that nothing a non-woman-of-color says can protect against the charge of racism. We certainly can hope, and exert great care to insure, that "our" approach to such issues be free of offensive innuendo. Emma Goldman found herself in a similarly vexing situation in the period following the Bolshevik Revolution. She was insistent in her determination not to "shut up" about her views of a derailed Soviet socialism, even while she contemplated the possibility that her criticisms might work hand-in-hand with those of reactionaries. "I know," she insisted, "that our position is of a different nature."[8] But there is never any firm assurance such distinctions will be accepted. We do know, on good orders, that silence won't protect us and that assessing the damage is inherently dangerous. One way out of this end-game is to recognize silence as a condescending and ultimately racist response to conflict and debate. Perhaps we can be schooled in a healthier, more open attitude toward contestation — realizing full well "our" mutual capacity to function as both "scoundrels as well as excellent militants."[9]

In order to ask some relevant questions about identity politics and to probe some of the discursive edifices (such as our frames for understanding identities/consciousness/experience) which underwrite identity discourses (often played out in the spatial dualisms of margins/centers), I want to set these issues up as a problematic[10] which not only is theoretical but also relates directly to our ability to perform crossover coalition maneuvers.

Our Politics Our Selves:
A Story of Alchemical Identities

I want to begin with an alchemical image — one which offers a dual reading of the contradictions of identity politics.[11] What appears to be a sharply defined configuration of "identity"— including indices of cultural location, politics, and affinity — can break down, meld into new circles of connection, relationships, and intentionalities. The image is a photograph of Sweet Honey in the Rock. Posed in a striking tableau are the six members of the group, led by Bernice Johnson Reagon, Ph.D. in U.S. history, and Smithsonian Institution curator. Wearing elaborate beads, headdresses, and African-inspired tie-dyed costumes, several of the women are holding African percussion gourds with which they accompany themselves. This image powerfully encapsulates the cultural associations embodied in Afrocentric feminism, which I discussed in Chapter 2. To a quite powerful, colorful, and passionate degree, Sweet Honey in the Rock, in its self-presentation, visually proclaims a clear affinity with the African roots and cultural modes of resistance of Diasporic people: they signify these meanings visually. And knowing the celebratory origins of their lyrics — paeans to the African-American civil rights struggle and those courageous Black leaders who continue to inspire these singers — we read a politics deeply infused with feminist postcolonial sentiments "behind the back" of this image. The aesthetic condensation involved in reading this image locates Sweet Honey in the Rock concretely in a particular historical, symbolic, and political domain. The group's allegiances are clear to any observer.

If the image were used, say, in a documentary film about Afrocentric feminism, I can envision scrolled across this image the words of the Combahee River Collective, Black feminists engaged in antiracist, antisexist, antihomophobic struggles and intent on maintaining Black ties with working class and poor as well. In its manifesto, the collective paid tribute to militant Black female pioneers by adopting as its name the famous guerrila action conceived and led by Harriet Tubman in 1863, which freed more than 750 slaves. These are the words which the collective presented in the late 1970s as a statement of identity politics, of which I'm thinking.

> Even our Black women's style of talking, testifying in Black language about what we have experienced, has a resonance that is both cultural and political. We have spent a great deal of energy delving into the cultural and experiential nature of our oppression out of necessity because none of these matters have ever been looked at before. No one before has ever examined the multilayered texture of Black women's lives.[12]

Despite the richness of analysis and politics these associations reflect, what kind of reductionism have I imposed with this "picture thought" construction? By inscribing so tightly my reading of the affinities of Afrocentric feminists, have I inadvertently limited their connections to others? Picture thoughts of this kind operate as "imprecise images that involve an affective response while defying particular differentiations."[13] Have I not "soaked with a vengeance" Afrocentric feminism, soaked it with one unitary identity so marked and prescribed that it makes alliances with other tendencies as difficult as they are inescapable? Am I not employing naturalizing identities which serve to contain unduly the crossover potential of any of our categories of feminisms? If so, perhaps my error can serve some pedagogical function. Critiquing the excessive identification that attends feminist theory's moves to deconstruct and specify "woman," Denise Riley remarks that we

> needn't be tormented by a choice between a political realism which will brook no nonsense about the uncertainties of "women," or deconstructionist moves which have no political allegiances. No one needs to believe in the solidity of "women." . . . Instead of veering between deconstruction and transcendence, we could try another train of speculation: that "women" is indeed an unstable category, that this instability has a historical foundation, and that feminism is the site of the systematic fighting-out of that instability.[14]

Perhaps my moves to *fix* Afrocentric feminism violate the commitments of multicultural feminist theory itself to multiple identities and multiple consciousness, as we learned from Deborah King in chapter 2. As an antidote to the tendency to pinpoint subjectivity as an unproblematic *telos*, perhaps this is an instance when we could benefit from a small dose of Julia Kristeva's discourse of displacement: "It follows that feminist practice can only be negative, at odds with what already exists so that we can say, 'that's not it' and 'that's still not it.'"[15] But then Kristeva's extremism is likely to leave us with a critique and no politics. That is to say, the actual engagements of African-American feminists with specific histories and social realities may surely stretch beyond the parameters of the category "Afrocentrism."

Another warning about our attempts to construct identities and define subjectivities, on the one hand, and to resist assertions of sameness, on the other, concerns the potential allure of kitsch. According to Kathy Ferguson's reading of this concept, as it appears in Milan Kundera's novel *The Unbearable Lightness of Being*, kitsch

> is the aesthetic ideal of the categorial agreement with being. It is a basic faith that all is well in the world, or that all will be well once a different world is made. Kitsch can be generated out of whatever

ground one gives to one's categorical agreement with being: kitsch comes in communist, democratic, feminist, European, and third world varieties. "The identity of kitsch," Kundera tells us, "comes not from a political strategy but from images, metaphors, and vocabulary." Kitsch allows one to belong too well to one's place; it ties up all the loose ends through its too-complete affirmations . . . an alertness to kitsch can warn feminists of the forms of sentimentality and self-delusion that our own formulations make possible.[16]

But if my alchemical treatment of the "identity" of Afrocentric feminism is burdened by the kitsch-inducing sentimentalities I have used, hasn't Sweet Honey in the Rock's Bernice Johnson Reagon helped me in this image-making? More information about the production of the image might seem to bear out my claim. The photograph is self-consciously a publicity photograph; the singers are posed against a studio backdrop. It appears in the national circulation celebrity magazine *People*. But anyone familiar with Reagon's probing feminist writings on coalition politics knows that she is uniquely skilled at disrupting stable identities and secure "homes." Reagon's commentary in *People* which accompanies the photo subversively undercuts the magazine's celebrity *raison d'etre*. She asserts that the group has refused to commercialize itself by turning down offers from four major record companies. "This group is owned by the women in it," she insists. "We are not letting somebody else decide if we're good enough to be onstage." Another of her politicized responses to debunk the escapism of the *People* world: Reagon says to the not specifically African-American but general readership, "I think everything is political. We are about being accountable."[17] In a brilliant crossover move, Reagon delivers a vitally important radical message to American mass readers.

So, the alchemical transformations begin to take place upon a second, more ironic reading of Sweet Honey in the Rock's image. And if we fast-forward to Reagon's celebrated essay, "Coalition Politics: Turning the Century," we are face-to-face with a classic of crossover multicultural feminism: "The only way you can take yourself seriously is if you can throw yourself into the next period beyond your little meager human-body-mouth-talking all the time."[18] Reagon's admonitions to feminists about the rigors and difficulties of coalitions are sober warnings not to confuse our need for nurturing "homes" with the often hardball conflict scenarios which are a part of coalition work. And she is equally aggressive in insisting that the exclusionary practice of separating into little "barred rooms" signals the destruction of feminist political achievement. Reagon herself is totally up front about her "identity" and her political priorities: "I don't start nothing except with Black people," she has said, nudging a deracinated feminist movement into acknowledging its roots and its accountability to African-American struggles. "Black folks started it, Black folks did it, so everything you've done politically rests on the efforts on my people — that's my arrogance."[19]

But Reagon's "identity," as she tells us, has a down side; her politics of location does not shield her from self-criticism. One of her most valuable contributions to deflating our penchant for constructing "pure" identities and self-positions is her critical ability to reflect on and modify her own misreadings of the "identities" she assigns to "others." Veterans of past political struggles, such as her own 1960s activism, she tells us, didn't always get it right. Commenting on a protest song she composed during the Vietnam War, Reagon is able to draw on new multicultural insight and racial sensitivity which mark her past interpretations of Vietnamese and Indians as reductionist, one-dimensional: "Now the songs and the pictures and poems ain't all right, cause you ain't dealing with people who are free from bigotry. . . . If in the future somebody is gonna use that song I sang, they're gonna have to strip it or at least shift it. I'm glad the principle is there for others to build on."[20]

Reagon's work allows room for cultural blunders, rereadings, reinterpretations, rethinking, and relearning without the fear of excommunication from the feminist universe if we ourselves happen someday to "get it wrong" (and who doesn't?). Generosity, Reagon knows, has to accompany prickly coalition struggles *on the important condition* that those of us engaging in the misreadings correct ourselves in the spirit of the first principle of multicultural feminism: accountability. And in a culture of white privilege, this condition imposes a greater burden on white feminists to take the first step toward making things right.

Fight the Power: Can There
Be Margins Without Identities and Centers?

Among the most radical formulations of theory elaborated by Black feminists and other women of color has been the privileging of the perspectives of marginalized groups. Yet the conceptualization of standpoint arguments and the margin/center ideas which accompany it present us with new complications. A crude rendering of this theory denotes the idea that a script[21] is naturally affixed to the identities of the oppressed, making the interpretation of their subjugated knowledges a transparent action. One simply reads from the oppressed's script: by virtue of the experience of exploitation, this vantage point is a more inclusive and radical standpoint for political action and knowledge. The script is often laden with the romanticized assumptions of kitsch, a vehicle for hagiography: the oppressed are pure, innocent, blameless in relation to their suffering, bearers of a "founding myth of original wholeness,"[22] while the oppressors become an undifferentiated, ahistorical bloc of power. I want to return later to some of the political implications of these kinds of essentialisms and the ontologies they construct.

There is some kernel of truth in this example of the dualisms which derive from standpoint strategies. And its materialist arguments are powerful. One of the most forceful examples comes from bell hooks's 1984 text, *Feminist Theory: From Margin to Center.* Hooks prefaced her text with a powerful account of her racial, cultural, and economic history as a young Black girl growing up poor in a segregated southern town: "Living as we did — on the edge — we developed a particular way of seeing reality. We looked both from the outside in and from the inside out. We focused our attention on the center as well as on the margin. We understood both."[23] But hooks's argument then takes a troubling turn:

> As a group, black women are in an unusual position in this society, for not only are we collectively at the bottom of the occupational ladder, but our overall social status lower than that of any other group. Occupying such a position, we bear the brunt of sexist, racist, and classist oppression. At the same time we are the group that has not been socialized to assume the role of exploiter/oppressor in that we are allowed no institutionalized "other" that we can exploit or oppress.[24]

Hooks's argument exerts tremendous force and has the validity of Black women's historical record of subjugation on its side. But her claim risks a series of commitments and assumptions that both her own more recent writings and those of other feminist women of color reject. Jane Flax has pointed out some of the assumptions hidden in standpoint/margin/center claims: beliefs that people act rationally in their own interest, that the oppressed are not in fundamental ways damaged by their marginality, and that they themselves are somehow removed from a will to power.[25] This critique and the shadow of vanguardism in hooks's argument ought to raise some questions. The implication that some sort of unmediated clarity exempts Black women from the exercise of power — despite their undisputedly vulnerable position in economic structures — takes the place of historical analyses and more complex understandings of the kinds of privilege-within-oppression which Elly Bulkin has pointed out. I wish hooks had spelled out the content of the relationship between Black females and others. What would be their mode of political interaction? What practices would obtain? With respect to marginal consciousness, what authority would determine who's got one? The center/margin analytic seems to substitute one hierarchy for another, without specifying the political grounds for collective action between the newly centered and the newly marginalized.

I think this structural critique can be made without taking away from the validity of the claim — which Afrocentric feminism persuasively argues — that racially oppressed women of color indeed have important truths. And middle-class white feminists have much to learn about the dynamics of oppression and the expanded viewpoint of one who has survived hegemonic power. The Marxist literary critic Terry Eagleton has written that oppressed peoples are "natural hermeneuticists, skilled by hard schooling in the necessity of interpreting their oppressors' language. They are spontaneous semioticians, forced for sheer survival to decipher the sign systems of the enemy and adept at deploying their own opaque idioms against them."[26] This understanding speaks to those truths and is vital to a progressive politics. But it is not in itself theoretically adequate to prevent the erection of equally repressive "other" hierarchies.

If we return to the model of overlapping oppressions, given to us by Afrocentric Black feminism, we are drawn back to a crossover position. This position insists that the workings of power, the fragile construction of subjectivities, and the often inharmonious conflicts attendant to multiple identities are much too complex for the frame of margins and centers. We ought to consider hooks's contribution to multicultural feminist theory provisionally, as an important "merely partial" but nevertheless "less false" feminist account of and knowledge about the world. Without clearly articulated democratic political principles — which I hope to suggest in the conclusion of this chapter — to ground the politics of otherness that hooks describes, we are unlikely to create the kinds of self-critical organizations and theories we need.

Audre Lorde's writings serve this purpose as a compelling examination of contradictions in the fragile and tenuous "unities" among Sister Outsiders. Radical social theory is not always accessible, she tells us, to those folks on the margins. Lorde opens up the identity politics debate with self-conscious narratives that work against the grain of those stories which assume and naturalize the links among women of color. And she echoes James Baldwin's admonition to Black writers to avoid the "European error" of assuming racial superiority. Lorde's work problematizes otherness in important ways. There is no exemption from critique for Black females on the margin, no assumption of innocence or distance from power. She knows that the true focus of revolutionary change is never merely the oppressive conditions of patriarchy, "but [is] that piece of the oppressor which is planted deep within each of us, and which knows only the oppressors' tactics, the oppressor's relationships." She forces us all to recognize the oppressor's power, anger, intolerance, and fear "as other faces of myself." And she provides an important caveat to the feminist theorist of otherness who wishes to stand, outside power, on the margin.

> What woman here is so enamored of her own oppression that she cannot see her heel print upon another woman's face? What woman's terms of oppression have become precious and necessary to her as a ticket into the fold of the righteous, away from the cold winds of self-scrutiny?[27]

Lorde's analysis also disrupts the fiction of automatic connection between oppositionally oriented feminist women of color, emphasizing the necessity for historically grounded political struggle. Speaking to Black women, Lorde writes, "We are strong and enduring. We are also deeply scarred. . . . But connections between Black women are not automatic by virtue of our similarities, and the possibilities of genuine communication between us are not easily achieved."[28] We leave Lorde's essays refreshingly enlightened about the provisional, contingent, and fragile character of human allegiances, allowing us to acknowledge the slippages among and between "different" women. This is an important turn in multicultural feminism.

Bell hooks's more recent writings have demonstrated an energetic willingness to reexamine the assumptions of standpoint strategies; she advocates and engages herself in vigorous affirmative critique and debate with other Black feminists. She has not been afraid to speak openly about the hostility, lack of trust, and ideological differences often evident in the currents of Black feminism. Hooks's implicit understanding of her own politics — her consistent advocacy of Black sisterhood and African-American political solidarity is a matter of record — follows Reagon's in insisting on the essentially contested nature of political affinities and identities. Hooks, for instance, might respond to Michelle Cliff's statement about "seeing coloredly" with an invitation to talk about what "coloredly" means, even pointing out possible dissenting hues in her own vision. Hooks has courageously taken elements of the Black community to task for projecting homophobic attitudes toward gays and lesbians, as allies working toward inclusive civil rights. She has criticized as well the apolitical and antifeminist use some Black women have made of Alice Walker's concept of "womanism," arguing that womanist is "not sufficiently linked to a tradition of radical political commitment to struggle and change." What would a womanist politics look like?, she asks: "If it [womanist] is a term for black feminist, then why do those who embrace it reject the other?"[29]

Many of hooks's essays deal with her dismay over the hostility, competitiveness, and lack of solidarity sometimes evident in interactions between Black women, in the academic conferences "in which social interactions mirror sexist norms, including ways black women regard one another." Hooks long has been the target of anger in some Black female circles for her insistent promotion of feminism as a means of empowering Black women and providing them strategies for autonomous self-definition. Feminist commitment, she says, sometimes gets rejected because of the rage many Black women feel toward white women. "In some settings it has become a way of one-upping white women for black women to trivialize feminism."[30]

Writings by other women of color provide additional evidence that women of color don't always easily interact or find grounds for commonality. Exclusionary tendencies and cultural insensitivities can operate "in the margin," as well as in white mainstream feminisms. Mirtha Quintanales, who identifies herself as a "Third World Caribbean" feminist, has written about these issues. Attempting to organize a panel discussion on racial and ethnic minority lesbians in the U.S., she tells us that she is alarmed over the many points of separatism among "Third World feminists." She attempted to bring a high-spirited, aggressive Greek woman into contact with Black feminists on the panel, a strategy they rejected. This Greek woman, Quintanales states, clearly "does not fit" either in the white feminist world or in the "woman of color" affinity as defined by Black women. Asking how and under what conditions diverse feminists of color may act together, Quintanales describes the disintegration of the terms and categories that are supposed to certify one's status as "oppressed":

> Not all Third World women are "women of color"— if by this concept we mean exclusively "non-white," I am only one example. And not all women of color are really Third World — if this term is only used in reference to underedeveloped or developing societies. . . . Clearly then it would be difficult to justify referring to Japanese women, who are women of color, as Third World women. Yet, if we extend the concept of Third World to include internally "colonized" racial and ethnic minority groups in this country, so many different kinds of groups could be conceivably included, that the crucial issue of social and institutional racism and its historic tie to slavery in the U.S. could get diluted, lost in the shuffle. The same thing would likely happen if we extended the meaning of "women of color" to include all those women in this country who are victims of prejudice and discrimination . . . but who nevertheless hold racial privileges and may even be racists.[31]

Quintanales, obviously frustrated by these densities, admits, "I don't know what to think anymore." Things get even more complicated for her when she considers that many Third World women enjoy class and educational privileges denied white working-class women. She is concerned when Latinas put down and generalize about the "white woman," or when Black women dismiss all non-Black women or all women "who are not *strict* women of color." She attempts to blur the certainty of those categories (a crossover gesture) of Blackness: "yellow," "mulatto," "light-skinned Latina," "Afro-Hispanic-American," so that some common space for feminist politics may be found. "We are still seeing racial differences when they don't exist and not seeing them when they are critical. And most disastrously, we are failing to recognize much of what we share. . . . Will we ever really be accepted by our black American sisters?"[32]

Enabling critical conversations among members of historically exploited persons is an extremely difficult endeavor, given the potential for jeopardizing what slight unities have been wrested from the dominant culture. But many feminist women of color have insisted on the need for bold stock-taking and self-reflective principles in their counter-hegemonic projects. Michele Russell's truly radiant short essay on the legacy of female African-American blues singers, "Slave Codes and Liner Notes," does just this. She remarks about the Black population's susceptibility to "all the forms of personal decadence this society markets to prolong our slavery." Russell squarely faces "all the ways we have voluntarily made slaves of ourselves."[33] And the Combahee River Collective's manifesto displays an example of solidarity among "others" gone sour. They wrote of conflict and internal disagreements among themselves "first conceptualized as a Lesbian-straight split but which were also the result of class and political differences."[34] In Bernice Reagon's terms, they didn't "get it right" either. Even in their nurturing "home," the Combahee Collective might not have discerned exactly, specifically, precisely the cause of their conflicts the first go-around.

The point of these examples is not to gloat over divisive splits among women of color, or to take the pressure off oppressive practices of hegemonic white feminisms, but to illustrate the inevitably contradictory, conflict-ridden, and context-specific terrain of all political engagement. We need to keep in mind how our categories and identities blur and leak, as Trinh Minh-ha has remarked, how they resist our desperate need to contain and define them in the discursive/physical barred rooms we create for our "selves." Is this perversity cause for alarm? On the contrary, the recognition of partiality and open-endedness even in the spaces of marginality frees us from potential orthodoxies. Honest recognition of cracks in our oppositional categories and certainties signifies more possibilities for erotic dimensions of radical politics, in the Marcusean sense — a recognition of mystery, spontaneity, innovation. It means that none of us knows everything; that multicultural feminist practice "lacks the assurance that allows one to settle everything." Thus, one "who does not know everything cannot kill everything."[35] Of course, erotic uncertainty and the undercutting of "identities" will remain frustrating enigmas in the process of doing politics, until we convince ourselves that "it" won't go away or straighten out, that the counterhegemonic histories of our "truths" are but the stories "of successive lapses, sometimes corrected, and committed once again."[36]

The recognition of difference within difference and margins within margins is a constant reminder as well that the only posture we can take to fight the power which infuses all human interaction is a vigilant, searching political eye. I think Maxine Hong Kingston understood this riddle of political marginality keenly when she made Wittman Ah Sing, her protagonist in *Tripmaster Monkey*, so paranoid about his own Chinese-American marginality. Skeptical of the singular "Black and white" racial emphasis of the Civil Rights Movement, Ah Sing declares, "I can't wear that civil-rights button with the Black hand and the white hand shaking each other. I have a nightmare — after duking it out, someday Blacks and whites will shake hands over my head. I'm the little yellow man beneath the bridge of their hands and overlooked."[37] The extension of solidarity to marginal "others" is far from axiomatic; it requires a deliberate political struggle, debates about inclusionary commitments.

Joan Cocks points out another dimension to these issues. Her analysis reinforces that we ought not to view dissension in the ranks on the margins, or imperfections in oppositional identities, in a negative light. Portraits of "essential" goodness, correctness, rightness in the consciousness of any oppositional category — radical lesbian feminists, white female proletarians, women of color, indigenous people — serve to flatten out our messiness, gloss over the truly interesting and paradoxical ways we don't get things right in our thoughts, motives, and action. The supposition of purity and correctness in feminist(s') subjectivity, Cocks declares, is actually infantalizing and embalming: "It implies that women are not complex enough in desire, sophisticated enough in imagination, and dynamic enough in will to act in vicious as well as virtuous ways." Cocks urges us to say good riddance to the idea that any subordinate is incapable of thinking and doing "ugly things of its own accord." "Unmitigated goodness," she writes, "is a quality signifying something so spiritless and static that the vital and vigorous are all too happy to impute it to populations they especially despise."[38] In crossover feminism I want readers to meet new populations of spirited, unstatic renegade women.

Cocks's analysis of this essentialist tendency connects it to a certain limited conception of power, to an instrumentalist analysis of power. In this reading, the patriarchy/state/white/heterosexual entity has "it" (power), which is bad, and the oppressed "others" don't have "it" (power), which makes them good. Cocks is aware of the vital political effects for subordinate groups of this understanding of power; it makes radical forms of critique possible. It allows those groups to say, "They have done this to us, *we* are innocent, *they* are guilty; *they* are evil, *we* must be good!" Not discounting the validity of such claims, Cocks nevertheless wants to be skeptical about such oppositions. "Life is not always what it appears to be," Cocks tells us:

> it is a long leap from the claim that a dominant group exerts a tyrannical agency in society to the claim that it exerts sole agency. It is an even longer leap from the claim that one group wields mastery over another in a system of social power, to the claim that that group is master of that system: that it has concocted the idea for it, designed it, executed it, and that it craftily has inculcated the group it oppresses and exploits with appropriately submissive beliefs, tastes, and preoccupations.[39]

Multicultural feminist practice needs to remember modern power's penchant for traveling, discussed here and there in previous chapters, and the microlocations such power is wont to visit. To fight the power and those techniques "aimed at the retooling of deviants as docile and useful bodies to be reinserted in the social machine"[40] can certainly refer to feminisms' own social machines. For crossover feminists, I would think that fighting the power would become something of a routinized, domesticated daily practice that keeps us alert but not necessarily antagonistic.

As a final consideration in the problem of margin/center, I want to point out the assumptions which some analyses by women of color reflect when critiquing the homogenizing tendencies of white feminist theory. In other words, the insistence by women of color that theory be historically grounded, nuanced, often is honored in the breach in treatments of white women. To employ Chandra Mohanty's analytic approach as a model, she rightly has criticized the construction of a profile of the "average Third World woman" in some of the Western feminist development literature. These texts set up oppositions, placing a reductive and monolithic "Third World difference" against an authorial Western feminist possessed of complex agency. Mohanty inserts a crucial methodological and political standard when she exposes the ahistorical assumptions of such work: "the assumption of women as an already constituted and coherent group with identical interests and desires, regardless of class, ethnic or racial location." The normative and ethnocentric bias of such one-dimensional portraits of Third-World women whose real lives are extraordinarily diverse and complex, she argues, results in a discourse that depicts such women as pitiable and leading restricted lives: "This average third-world woman leads an essentially truncated life based on her feminine gender (read: sexually constrained) and being 'third world' (read: ignorant, poor, uneducated, tradition-bound, religious, domesticated, family-oriented, victimized, etc.)."[41]

I want to insist on the need for such contextualized standards in the writings of women of color about the "average First World woman," too, and underscore Mohanty's point that such universal, undifferentiated codifications subvert the political possibilities of coalitions between feminists who inhabit vastly different locations. It simply won't do for any of us to assume that any other of us is an "always already constituted" subject outside of social relations. Such colonialist thinking denies historical specificity all around and easily degenerates into purity-reversal games.

Listen to these demonologies of "white women" and "white culture" constructed by writers who seem to position themselves as innocent opposites:

> Whites . . . have cut themselves off from their spiritual roots, and they take our spiritual art objects in an unconscious attempt to get them back. . . . Anglos [could] lose the white sterility they have in their kitchens, bathrooms, hospitals, mortuaries, and missile bases. . . . Though in the conscious mind, black and dark may be associated with death, evil, and destruction, in the subconscious mind and in our dreams, white is associated with disease, death, and hopelessness.[42]

> [White women] were like clear, dead water . . . they were frivolous, helpless creatures, lazy and without ingenuity. Occasionally one would rise to the level of bitchery."[43]

> We who have been oppressed and silenced . . . because we belong to insular "minorities" . . . will never be tempted by the illusions of leadership, will never be deluded into thinking we can represent anyone but ourselves.[44]

> I couldn't stand the idea of a white person touching me. Eventually I realized that it wasn't the white skin that I hated, but it was their culture of deceit, greed, racism, and violence. . . . Their manner of living appeared devoid of life and bordered on hostility even for one another. . . . The white people always seemed so loud, obnoxious, and vulgar. . . . After spending a day around white people, I was always happy to go back to the reservation where people followed a relaxed yet respectful code of relating with each other. . . . a welcome relief after a day with the plastic faces.[45]

Perhaps I have played fast and loose here in my choices; one excerpt is from a work of fiction, two others from highly personalized polemical essays, the fourth from a scholarly study. And surely dramatic license warrants the skillful use of rhetorical overstatements in discourse, the will to scandalize being one of the dissident's most persuasive weapons. I am not saying that such characterizations of desacralized Western modernity are inaccurate; rather I am asking whether all whites are all that bad all the time. If not, we need to schematize contracts for white allies who are accountable (as they should be) for the totality, and create politics and knowledge which can transform those whites who still participate in oppressive modes of life. Such wholly negative accounts of "whiteness," which are often encountered in writings of women of color, can paralyze rather than mobilize. Massive clouds of *guilt* seem to hover above such statements as outlined above, inducing fatalism rather than political initiative. Totalistic representations encourage me to think: "The only way for me to *absolve* myself from the horrors perpetuated by those of my race is the final solution of total *self-erasure*. When my evilness is gone, perhaps they will be saved." Only pathology here.

The demonizing language of women of color replicates a "Manichean allegory" by asserting the irrevocable barbarism of the white other. Abdul JanMohamed writes of these tendencies in Western colonial literature, discourses which constructed the defiled native other. There is nothing in principle which prevents a reversal of his formulations. "The European [read Third World] writer commodifies the native [read white other] by negating his individuality, his subjectivity, so that he is now perceived as a generic being that can be exchanged for any other native [read white] (they all look alike, act alike, and so on)." Aren't we still engaged in the game of positing worthless alterities, affirming our already-fixed ethnocentrism of whatever variety? The narcissistic text — no longer the colonialist text, but the postcolonialist one — proceeds to fetishize the other:

> This process operates by substituting natural or generic categories for those that are socially or ideologically determined. All the evil characteristics and habits with which the colonialist [read postcolonialist] endows the native [read white] are thereby not presented as the products of social and cultural difference but as characteristics inherent in the race — in the "blood"— of the native [read white]. In its extreme form, this kind of fetishization transmutes all specificity and difference into a magical essence.[46]

The most tragic outcome of the creation of such Manichean oppositions lies in the terms most important to us, the political terms. Instead of seeing "others" as a "bridge toward syncretic possibility," in JanMohamed's potent phrase, we constrain our political imaginations by creating cardboard figures ("average Third World woman," "average white woman") with whom we cannot, will not, try to connect. Bringing deep context back into play in our representational projects can be an important praxis. Instead of the fixation on seamless "identities," we might enumerate all the things "we" are, and all the overlapping conjunctions of our social linkages. We all occupy highly idiosyncratic spaces. We might be friends of taro growers; middle-aged babysitters of our friends' children; servants of uppity, part-Persian female cats; newly enlisted members of AIDS support groups, as well as multicultural feminist activists eager to establish grounds for affinity and mutual support as (always-being-redefined) women enmeshed in gender *as well as* racial constructions. Our specificities, our differences, needn't require that we discontinue exploring the effects of gender.[47] Aren't there points at which protean multiple subjects and fractured identities intersect as "women"? Feminist theory ought to keep working out those points as well as reminding us of our nongender loci.

What do we do, then, about the margin? I am reluctant to abandon the framework because of the politicizing import of margins. Attention to the edges of social and economic life keeps us critically attuned to exploitation, allows us to learn when some new other has been excluded or silenced.[48] It's the imperial center which gives me trouble. Bettina Aptheker's capacity to theorize grounds for feminist solidarity in diversity plays some interesting tricks on centers. Why not, she asks, *pivot the center* "to include the experiences of Afro-American, Asian-American, Native American, Latina, Chicana and Euro-American women, and the diversity within and between them"? Recognizing all the rich pluralities among "us," Aptheker also seeks connection, "as long as the connection remained respectful of the differences and became a point of illumination rather than a mush of obfuscation in a white, ethnocentric, heterocentric landscape."[49] Historian Elsa Barkley Brown has extended Aptheker's strategy of pivoting the center by including overlapping diverse "gumbo ya ya" conversations where everyone talks at once while simultaneously understanding other talking selves. Brown's agenda is appropriate to a communicative model which, to be successful, believes that we are capable of demonstrating considerable capacity for intersubjectivity. Center in another's experience, she urges:

> I do not mean that white or male students can learn to feel what it is
> like to be a Black woman. Rather, I believe that all people can learn
> to center in another experience, validate it, and judge it by its own
> standards without need of comparison or need to adopt that
> framework as their own. Thus, one has no need to "decenter" anyone
> in order to center someone else, one has only to constantly, ap-
> propriately, "pivot the center."[50]

I too am hopeful that multicultural feminist theory can creatively
educate us to such utopian practices. In the meantime, however, I
would like to leaven expectations about pivoting centers with a dose of
Bernice Johnson Reagon's power discourse. We ought to be prepared, as
Reagon candidly tells us, to encounter in our crossover space those folks
who are singularly uninterested in pivoting: "Watch these mono-issue
people. . . . people who prioritize the cutting line of the struggle . . .
saying that whatever's bothering you will be put down if you bring
it up." We ought to know, too, that at times—and we do hope that
our judgment about timing is judicious and clear—we must exercise
our own power "and make people contend with your baggage, whatever it is."[51]

I would like to keep a politics of margins without centers, thinking
instead in other spatial terms: about crossover tracks back and forth
to coalitions and affinity spaces. I would like to retain a conceptualization of identity and experience which is alert to conceits of "possessive
exclusivism." Edward Said renders this tendency in counterhegemonic
discourse as "the sense of being an exclusive insider by virtue of experience."[52] We could think about experience and consciousness not
as given prepolitical essences but via the tropes Donna Haraway has
suggested—a "bush of women's experience." This schema, designed to
foreground the intersections of feminist theory and critical approaches
to colonial discourse, involves two crucial couplings: local/global and
personal/political. Each of these pairs, beginning with "experience,"
splits and bifurcates infinitely. Haraway's diagram of these categories
posits an "experience" which allows political connection, but in an open-
ended framework:

> One can work one's way through the analytical/descriptive bush, mak-
> ing decisions to *exclude* certain regions of the map. . . . But the rest of
> the bush is implicitly present, providing a resonant echo chamber for
> any particular tracing through the bush of "women's experience."[53]

Does Haraway's "bush" promise to lead us to an unmediated construction of identity/experience which we can present as an icon to unlike others? What it does, as she remarks, is to "guarantee an open, branching discourse with a high likelihood of reflexivity about its own interpretive and productive technology."[54] Reflexivity is the keyword here, inscribing our feminist theories with the constant imperative to keep looking back over our shoulders to see what and whom we have left out of the identities we present to the world.

Toward More Solid Solidarity

Drawing on the crossover terms in which I have framed a possible multicultural feminist politics, I think it is important to concretize further the dimensions of community and solidarity. Anyone who has read recent accounts of interracial feminist animus — both personal and institutional — unavoidably must acknowledge the souring of the social contract of sisterhood to hold "us" together.[55] We must begin to think together, from the discourse of politics, about which symbols and principles can best facilitate egalitarian feminism. Obviously, the theoretical tools with which we conceive our identities and experiences need to be free of totalizing ideas, as the previous discussion has emphasized. Whatever status our subject positions accord us along the varied axes of oppression, we need to be open to a modifying dialectic of self/other. These understandings make of us in some sense deconstructionists — theorists wary of unified, innocent "selves." But what about our activist selves? What can nourish our reconstructive goals in our daily interactions and movement practices?

The ideas of radical democracy and radical pluralism propose an important reformulation of the solidarity project among the diverse new social movements of (post)modernity. Political theorist Chantal Mouffe encourages us to define modernity at the political, rather than the exclusively epistemological, level, for it is there that social relations are shaped and symbolically ordered. Mouffe's reading of the shifting coordinates of contemporary political struggle, the space which records the "dissolution of the landmarks of certainty," contributes to a new democratic theory for diverse political agents. In order to capture the crossover referents of diverse multicultural feminists, we can draw from Mouffe's validation of radicalized conceptions of rights. In her model of democracy, rights become dynamic tools unfrozen from previously privatized realms, where the "rights of certain subjects do not entail the subordination of the rights of others." This is her interpretation of solidarity as the key to such a democratic practice:

> The progressive character of a struggle does not depend on its place of origin — we have said that all workers' struggles are not progressive — but rather on its link to other struggles. The longer the chain of equivalences set up between the defense of the rights of one group and those of other groups, the deeper will be the democratization process and the more difficult it will be to neutralize certain struggles or make them serve the ends of the Right. The concept of solidarity can be used to form such a chain of democratic equivalences.[56]

This reengagement with rights and citizenship in the context of radical democratic theory is an interesting turn. Those concepts, having traditionally been claimed by the liberal discourse of possessive individualism and utilized by the hegemonic powers for decidedly unradical ends, become reinvigorated. Mouffe's emphasis on the necessity of "democratic rights" is framed in a broader, coalition-friendly context, a context which sees rights as entities "which, while belonging to the individual, can only be exercised collectively and presuppose the existence of equal rights for others." Theorizing the terms for a critical reinterpretation of the concept of rights is a project endorsed by many contemporary scholars and activists of color — a constellation in which white feminist theorists can participate.[57] Liberty, as well, gets a radical reinterpretation by Mouffe as "an idea . . . that transcends the false dilemma between the liberty of the ancients and the moderns and allows us to think individual liberty and political liberty together."[58]

Crossover feminist politics is marked by an implicit need for ideas such as those provided by Mouffe. Coalitions depend on the ability to think in terms of a *chain of democratic equivalences*, of both individual and political autonomy, and of a concept of collective as well as individual rights. Such resources can help to articulate the grounds for political action between feminist collectivities by stressing our need to translate the material outlines of one feminist life world without absorbing or displacing the material outlines of another feminist life world. Debates about relative power and privilege would ensue once the specifics are laid out. This type of politics sets up a logic of reciprocity grounded not in the visceral, affective terms of sisterhood, with its intensified expectations and membership assumptions,[59] but the more remote — and more reliable — political discourse of democratic practice. The idea of equivalences retains specificity and autonomy for "identities" in the flesh, in self-selected coalition "homes," within the framework of seeking justice for others differently located in related-but-separate "homes." Individuality is maintained, and indeed can only be fulfilled substantively, within a collectivity. Thus, writes Mouffe, "the importance of the postmodern critique for developing a political philosophy aimed at making possible a new form of individuality that would be truly plural and democratic"[60] becomes a reliable hope for future theory.

The standards of radical democracy and radical pluralism afford a possible reconfiguration of our shared public space as multicultural feminist citizens. I wonder whether we might speak of democratic equivalences in both the commission and the overcoming of exploitative acts around our differences. How do white feminists and women of color learn to cross the chasm of difference to engage our similarities? I am not convinced that some of Elizabeth Spelman's formulations further this equivalence aim. It is not Spelman's incisive demonstration of hegemonic white feminism's racist erasure of women of color (the ethnocentric "as a woman" assumptions) to which I object, but certain corrective postures she suggests for white women.

Many of Spelman's critiques and analyses are devoid of any consideration of possible reversals, and few of her admonitions against stereotyping and homogenizing tendencies are reflexively formulated. I wonder about the one-directional focus of her critiques, her lack of power-sensitivity toward possible coercive tendencies in the practices of women of color. One has only to reprise the honest accounts of Quintanales and hooks to be reminded of this reality. Couldn't we all benefit by enacting the democratic stance implicit in Mouffe's analyses? How *could* this urgent political remapping be facilitated asymmetrically, as if change, transformation, and growth were the liberating burden of only some of "us"?

In our *jouissance* over difference, are we liable to forget our potential for those contested commonalities which remind us that feminist political transformation is impossible without some degree of "complementary reciprocity"?[61] Of course, we must insist that as a group white feminists are most in need of "correcting," learning, listening, being educated by the leadership of women of color, working to root out the racist criminality on the streets of the U.S.A. In no way are my remarks intended to deflect such accountability and struggle. Am I demanding a shortcut, a reprieve, a premature absolution for white feminists who don't like a taste of their own medicine? I don't think so. My fear is that if we do not insert the robust and healing structures of democratic political practices into our feminist polity, those resentments, dichotomies, and distrusts will consume whatever is left of "us."

Spelman asks white feminists to "call upon the resources of their imagination and their capacity for tolerance," to hear from "different" women. This requires a kind of apprenticeship, she argues, based on the important inquiry, "What do I and can I know about women from whom I differ in terms of race, culture, class, ethnicity?"[62] But important qualifiers do not follow; it is not clear when and under what conditions the apprenticeship might evolve into a dialogue or debate between equals. Certainly Spelman's critically important pedagogical scenario of cultural learning is one that also can be extended to women of color. The troublingly over-broad term "women of color" wrongly implies that diverse cultural and ethnic particularities do not have their own specific voices within the larger voice of their representation — just as the term "white women" does. Indeed, the voice of the oppressed is more alert to the silences of hegemonic life; but a dose of multicultural sharing about difference would be a welcome pedagogy in any configuration of voices.

Spelman, presumably addressing white feminists, urges us to go to conferences planned by people from whom we wish to learn "and manage not to be intrusive, and so on" (179). Well, yes, there are crucial times when loquacious white mouths need to stay shut, ears opened; but this chillingly elliptical "and so on" makes me nervous. Again, I would want to know what politically evaluative criteria we might envision to bring white feminists out of the shadowy recesses of the conference hall? At what point might we hope for participatory, inclusive settings? And what safeguards ought we to initiate in order to quell dominating voices? Perhaps one could envision rotating apprentices, but even that construction, although it points to the fact that we all may need to learn from one another, signifies a hierarchy. Perhaps a simple racial reversal of talkers and listeners may be strategically inevitable. But I would like a debate about our guidelines for contestation.

It seems to me that Spelman's laudable dictates to white women about the limits of tolerance (182–83) — a gesture of futility if nothing in the lives of white women is changed by encounters with women of color — and the possibilities of imagining, are tremendously empowering possibilities *for all of us.* The ability to find a comfort level within some spaces of the other's life would be a hope of crossover feminism. Reworking Sartre's distinctions between merely imagining images and truly perceiving real objects and persons, Spelman writes:

> When I am perceiving someone, I must be prepared to receive new information all the time, to adapt my actions accordingly. . . . when simply imagining her, I can escape from the demands her reality puts on me . . . make her into someone or something who never talks back, who poses no difficulties for me.(181)

I would want to underscore the mutual obligation of confronting "the demands her reality puts on me," while worrying that perhaps, in the role of apprentice, Spelman has constructed a cardboard white feminist who never talks back. Or at least she has set up a course of study without theorizing the grounds for graduation. I am not urging a rejection or invalidation of Spelman's formulations, only asking for some fine-tuning in the reciprocity field. This implies a recognition that the exclusionary tendencies she outlines operate problematically all around. Part of the problem in Spelman's line of analysis on this point has to do with her choice of conceptual terms. Trying to derive political guidelines from such prepolitical concepts as imagining or perceiving leads toward abstraction. For instance, Spelman proceeds with the imaginary analytic, admitting that doing so is dangerous because it allows the oppressor simply to objectify, without really "knowing" the oppressed as an object of imagination. The imagining oppressor may not truly "perceive" the material reality of the oppressed, whose presence, speech, and anger "may be there" nonetheless. Spelman here cites the following quotation from Maria Lugones: "White/anglo women do one or more of the following to women of color: they ignore us, ostracize us, render us invisible, stereotype us, leave us completely alone, interpret us as crazy. All of this *while we are in their midst"* (n.14, p. 212).

Lugones's anger and pain are palpable; they need to be heard. I would like to suggest, though, that Lugones's experience could be reversed with the white feminist being ostracized, rendered invisible, stereotyped, and interpreted as crazy. Indeed, such reversals are now being demonstrated in feminist interactions. We need to focus on this larger, more complex rectifying strategy. Why can't we admit to the dehumanizing practices of both white feminists and feminists of color?

I think that framing this dynamic in psychological terms, as Spelman does, is insufficient and confusing. I am unable to derive a politicized understanding from her discussion of the limited faculties of imagining and perceiving. What do we *do with* the psychic sketching provided? What of it can we take to our coalition settings and alliance projects? While certainly erudite and fascinating, I wish Spelman's analysis had gone on to the next step. Making moves beyond our segregated and barred rooms requires more concretely political insights — such as a vigorous commitment to debating the conditions for democratic equivalences.

I am not so trusting of my perceptual capacities. I am skeptical that I can avoid confusing "imagining" women with "knowing" them — something Spelman cautions against. Nor am I sure that others might not equally misperceive me. Spelman's suggestion that we "call on the resources of our imagination" asks both too much and too little. I have questions: Would our lingering impoverished misperceptions of one another foreclose our strategic alliances? Ought we to stake our political potential on this ephemeral terrain? Spelman is aware, of course, that simply analyzing the textual tropes we use cannot take us to emancipatory coalition spaces. And she certainly highlights the unintended but pernicious legacies of white privilege in projects of trying-to-know-one-another. I am glad she included her disclaimer that those "we" wish to know may themselves not wish to be known in the ways in which "we" wish to know them. "That is not apprenticeship," she declares, "but imperialism" (185).

I think that Spelman relies too much, as perhaps have I, on notions of reciprocity and mutuality. These ideals are residues of sisterhood-fixation: bonding, caring, intersubjective empathy, and even Seyla Benhabib's term which I invoked above, "complementary reciprocity." As the acerbic Nietzsche was wont to remark: Bad air. Bad air. My skepticism about empathy reflects not primarily a postmodern "cool," but rather the evidence of conflict in so many feminist interactions today. It is the case that many feminists definitely do not want to be known by "others" at this moment. Building trust in multicultural settings involves a long process, a process we cannot weight with too many affective desires. This does not mean we should stop telling our stories to one another, nor hoping that "others" listen.

The notion that interracial cooperation, as Audre Lorde has argued, is possible "between feminists who don't love each other," requires new conceptions of community.[63] I laid the groundwork at the beginning of this chapter for the kind of crossover community which I felt could enhance possibilities for appreciating democratic equivalences and diversity, and the practices of multicultural feminist citizenship. In Bernice Reagon's terms, such a community would be not a "home" for like-minded sisters, but a rather more artificially[64] constructed arena for unassimilated others to politically engage themselves and the larger society. It might be described as a sort of mediated community of feminist strangers rather than sisters. "Stranger" is the term Iris Young employs to theorize an alternative form of public space. She wishes to discard the term community itself — viewing it as too closely linked to those very expectant ideas of homogeneity and comformity and to the ideal of persons "relating to one another through reciprocal recognition of subjectivities as a particular standpoint of moral autonomy."[65] Young fears that such expectations operate out of a totalizing desire to reconcile the differences of subjects. Such desires, she argues, express damaging impulses to overcome the "otherness" of others through reciprocal recognition. "Sisterhood," we know, has been marked by such tendencies in ways which have disadvantaged women of color.

Young is hard-nosed here, a social pragmatist in ways in which Spelman and I, perhaps, are not. If we take to heart Young's skepticism concerning the discourse of organicism, we cannot put much faith in our ability to fathom the maze of imagining and perceiving. In this reading, we might insist that such pursuits might be more adaptable to therapy groups, the sensitivity seminars of particular feminist "homes," but not too useful for broader coalitional fields. Insistence on the ideal of shared subjectivity, for Young, leads to undesirable political implications. Our ability truly to understand the other as we understand ourselves (do we?) is too capricious a test to replace more formal political standards. Thus, Young urges:

> Political theorists and activists should distrust this desire for reciprocal recognition and identification with others, I suggest, because it denies difference in the concrete sense of making it difficult for people to respect those with whom they do not identify. . . . [this ideal] is similar to the desire for identification that underlies racial and ethnic chauvinism.[66]

Our continuing desires for the kinds of identification that are embodied in the term *sisterhood*, I am extending Young's argument, only thwart our principled calls for heterogeneity in feminism. In a multicultural vein, Young wants to deny that difference is alienating to community, arguing instead for a validation of difference and an acceptance of "historical givens." The historical givens of our contemporary feminist world, I argue, are so volatile and so fragile that they preclude our glossing over them and those contradictions of race, sexuality, and class. Appeals to a concept of community based on seamless friendship or sisterly bonding are not viable. The vision of politics as a sphere of love, as Hannah Arendt warned us, contains the seeds of totalitarianism. Affective models, when made public, can destroy politics and the concept of public space.[67] Utopian goals of sisterhood (which potentially could reside in those smaller, more intimate "homes" Bernice Reagon spoke of) did underwrite — in enough cases to alarm us — the collapse of needed boundaries which honored women's differences. Those utopian expectations also broke our hearts when "others" didn't love us in sisterly reciprocity.

Young's "historical given" in her analysis of modern life is the urban landscape, which she wants to portray as potentially other than alienated, massified, and bureaucratic. Without entering into her urbanity debate, I do think her rendering of the contours of public interaction is helpful for feminists to think about in terms of our own coalition relationships. The unoppressive city, Young declares, is defined as "openness to unassimilated otherness." How, she asks, can the relationships of group identities embody "justice, respect, and the absence of oppression"? Only a robust politics of difference can accomplish this goal, aided by this view of social relations: a space "without domination in which persons live together in relations of mediation among strangers with whom they are not in community."[68]

This construction contains some elements useful for my framework. I would, however, substitute the resonant category of "feminists" for Young's "stranger" and change the term *community*, with this result: A crossover politics entails "multicultural coalitions without domination in which persons live together in relations of mediation among feminists with whom they are not in sisterhood but solidarity." I am not ready to abandon the concept of community, as has Young, but I wish to suggest that multicultural feminist coalitions might qualify as a reconstituted kind of community. Changing the concept of sisterhood to "feminists in solidarity" ought to be viewed not as callous but as a sign of our political maturity.

Conclusion

To enact the democratic crossover potential, white feminists need to keep alive a politics of memory. This narrative would relate the stories of segregated sisterhood, reinforcing our accountability for those silences which denied the feminist spirit of countless poor, working-class, lesbian, Black, and other women of color. For feminist theorists, intriguing philosophical challenges abound — contestations and reflections on subjectivity, power, and experience promise important oppositional insights. Shane Phelan's analyses of identity politics within lesbian discourse and practice highlight one of the most important. "Non-negotiable identities," she writes, "will enslave us whether they are imposed from within or without."[69] But when we are performing as theorists, we ought not to overestimate the significance of the symbolic. Bernice Reagon's insistent voice brings us back to our materialist imperative as activists to continue "to deliver the goods of survival in a society that does not know how big we are and how much room we need to stand to our full height."[70] And what of our obligations to enhance feminist movement building? The white civil rights/feminist activist Mary King asks, "If SNCC could thrust up Fannie Lou Hamner, the twentieth child in a family of uneducated sharecroppers and the granddaughter of a slave, as its standard-bearer, why can't the women's movement deliver a union leader from a canning plant, a farmer, or a textile worker among its spokeswomen?"[71]

In order to transform our struggles for social justice and diversity, we require not only the structural commitment to those democratic practices which I have attempted to spell out, but more generous personal elaborations toward one another as well. First, I think we must take the leap of faith that encourages us to believe that we *can change*. With respect to the intransigence of racism within feminism, I think that many of us are now prioritizing anti-racism and teaching it in our classrooms. Many achievements are forthcoming; more and more white feminists are attempting to trace their own "social geography of race" in politicized, self-critical modes.[72] We need to encourage these explorations in open environments which are critically affirmative rather than intimidating. This means allowing for the possibility that those who are attempting, however inadequately, to enter those difficult dialogues are planting the seeds of transformation. The work of Sara Schulman, for example, engages the feminist potential for changing consciousness in powerful ways.

One of the most exuberant moments of Schulman's novel of AIDS, *People in Trouble*, comes when her lesbian protagonist Molly recognizes how HIV-infected male patients are able to transform their masculinist habits of a lifetime.

> This dying had been going on for a long time already. So long, in fact, that there were people alive who didn't remember life before AIDS. And for Molly it had made all her relations with men more deliberate and detailed. First, the men changed. They were more vulnerable and open and needed to talk. So she changed. Passing acquaintances became friends. And when her friends actually did get sick there was a lot of shopping to do, picking up laundry and looking into each other's eyes. She had never held so many crying men before in her life.[73]

That one might see "the other" in more human terms is a hope of multiculturalism as well.

When crossover voices begin to dialogue, a new politics is brought into play. It brings conflict with it. On this daunting edifice multicultural transformation either stands or falls. I want therefore to encourage our animated embrace of this most Socratic virtue of public life. Acceptance of the positive aspects of conflict, however, ought not to serve as a brief for savagery in our dealings with one another. Not scars but mutual respect can condition our conversations. I learned this valuable consideration from Bettina Aptheker. "I presumed the integrity of her purpose," is the way she approaches women with whom she disagrees, as she tells us in her text *Tapestries of Life*.[74] The kind of political and personal engagement I want to endorse gives shelter, as well, to less earnest human expressions. A *mentalité* of paradox and contradiction may one day help to save us from ourselves.[75] Above all, a crossover dream demonstrates our inherent commitment to and appreciation for many social densities beyond those to which our specific skin, culture and history consign us. This is the emancipatory gift of multicultural feminist politics. And we may look to a future whose daily enactment involves that most erotic attribute of politics, what Alice Walker has called the "machete of freedom."[76] Talk. Endless talk.

Notes

Introduction

1. Donna Haraway, "Review: Spirits of Resistance and Capitalist Discipline: Factory Women in Malaysia," *Signs* 14, no. 4 (Summer 1989):946.

2. This is the elegant phrase Cherríe Moraga and Gloria Anzaldúa employ to conceptualize multicultural feminism in their pathbreaking feminist anthology by women of color, *This Bridge Called My Back: Writings by Radical Women of Color* (Watertown, Mass.: Persephone Press, 1981), 23.

3. Renato Rosaldo plays archly with language and politics by employing the construction "others of invention." See her review, "Others of Invention: Ethnicity and Its Discontents," *Village Voice Literary Supplement*, Feb. 1990, p. 27.

4. Michelle Cliff, "A Journey into Speech," in *The Greywolf Annual Five: Multicultural Literary*, ed. Rick Simonson and Scott Walker (St. Paul, Minn.: Graywolf Press, 1988), 60.

5. Audre Lorde, *Sister Outsider* (Trumansburg, N.Y.: Crossing Press, 1984), 60.

6. Donna Haraway, "A Manifesto for Cyborgs: Science, Technology, and Socialist Feminism in the 1980s," *Socialist Review* 15, no. 2 (Mar./Apr. 1985): 65–107.

7. Anders Stephanson, "Interview with Cornel West," in *Universal Abandon?: The Politics of Postmodernism*, ed. Andrew Ross (Minneapolis: Univ. of Minnesota Press, 1988), 277.

8. Moraga and Anzaldúa, *This Bridge*, 23.

9. I have found Cornel West's explication of African-American genealogical materialism fruitful in describing the methodological and political con-

tours of Black feminist theory. West's interpretation of genealogical materialism, in analyzing African-American racist oppression, does not derive solely from linguistic deconstructions of discourses or operations of power within those discourses. West combines those strategies with a deep historical consciousness and attention to specific material forms of domination which confront more candidly, as he notes, "the complex confluence of human bodies, traditions and institutions." West is crucially aware of gender as a feature of prevailing modes of oppression, although he does not provide a fully developed account of its operations. See West, "Race and Social Theory: Towards a Genealogical Materialist Analysis," *The Year Left 2* (London: Verso, 1987), 75–90, esp. 85–86.

10. Moraga and Anzaldúa, *This Bridge*, 23.

11. Haraway, "Cyborgs," 75.

12. Patricia Williams, "Alchemical Notes: Reconstructing Ideals from Deconstructed Rights," *Harvard Civil Rights–Civil Liberties Law Review* 401 (1987):401–33.

13. Toni Morrison's rendering of African-American spirituality in her epic novel of slavery, *Beloved* (New York: Knopf, 1987), 88, is exhilarating and powerful. The scene which depicts the "unchurched preacher" Baby Suggs and her community of slaves in the forest clearing "dancing in the sunlight" is "religious" in a very resonant sense:

> She did not tell them to clean up their lives or go and sin no more. She did not tell them they were the blessed of the earth, its inheriting meek or its glorybound pure. She told them that the only grace they could have was the grace they could imagine. That if they could not see it, they would not have it.
>
> "Here," she said, "in this here place, we flesh; flesh that weeps, laughs, flesh that dances on bare feet in grass. Love it. Love it hard. Yonder they do not love your flesh. They despise it. They don't love your eyes. . . . And O my people they do not love your hands. Those they only use, tie, bind, chop off and leave empty. Love your hands! . . . *You* got to love it, *you!*"

14. This is the title of Cornel West's text on the discourse of radical Black Christianity, *Prophesy Deliverance!: An Afro-American Revolutionary Christianity* (Philadelphia: Westminster Press, 1982).

15. Patricia Williams, "Alchemical Notes," 433.

16. Derrick Bell, *And We Are Not Saved: The Elusive Quest for Racial Justice* (New York: Basic, 1987), 211.

17. Andreas Huyssen, "Mapping the Postmodern," in *Feminism/Postmodernism*, ed. Linda J. Nicholson (New York: Routledge, 1990), 13.

18. Appiah is quoted in Henry Louis Gates, Jr.'s essay, "Writing 'Race' and

the Difference It Makes," in *"Race," Writing and Difference*, ed. Henry Louis Gates, Jr. (Chicago: Univ. of Chicago Press, 1985), 14.

19. Haraway, "Review: Spirits of Resistance," 946.

20. S.P. Mohanty, "Us and Them: On the Philosophical Bases of Political Criticism," *Yale Journal of Criticism* 2, no. 2 (1989):2.

21. Lorde, *Sister Outsider*, 132.

22. I thank Iris Young for this term. It, along with some of her provocative rethinkings of egalitarian communities, appears in chapter 6 of this book. Iris Marion Young, "The Ideal of Community and the Politics of Difference," in *Feminism/Postmodernism*, ed. Linda J. Nicholson (New York: Routledge, 1990), 301.

23. This is Abdul R. JanMohamed's elegant phrase. See his essay, "The Economy of Manichean Allegory: The Function of Racial Difference in Colonialist Literature," in *"Race," Writing and Difference*, ed. Henry Louis Gates, Jr. (Chicago: Univ. of Chicago Press, 1985), 84.

24. bell hooks, "Stylish Nihilism at the Movies," *Z Magazine*, May 1988, p. 26.

25. Eloise Buker beautifully renders this practice in her foreword to *A Time for Sharing: Women's Stories from the Waianae Coast* (Honolulu, Hawaii: Women's Support Group of the Waianae Coast, 1982), vii–xi.

26. Trinh T. Minh-ha, *Woman Native Other* (Bloomington: Indiana Univ. Press, 1989), 2.

27. Trinh, *Woman Native Other*, 94.

28. Breyten Breytenbach, "The South African Wasteland," *New Republic*, 4 Nov. 1985, p. 37.

29. Michael Omi and Howard Winant, *Racial Formation in the United States* (New York: Routlege, 1986), 86.

30. Minnie Bruce Pratt, "Identity: Skin Blood Heart," in *Yours in Struggle*, Minnie Bruce Pratt, Barbara Smith, and Elly Bulkin (Brooklyn: N.Y.: Long Haul Press, 1984), 11–63.

31. Olivia Castellano uses this phrase to describe her own sense of intellectual inadequacy, in her essay, "Canto, Locura y Poesia," *Women's Review of Books* 7, no. 5 (Feb. 1990):18–20.

32. See Kathy Ferguson's review essay, "Knowledge, Politics, and Persons in Feminist Theory," *Political Theory* 17, no. 2 (May 1989):302–313.

33. Rosario Morales, "We're All in the Same Boat," in *This Bridge Called My Back*, ed. Cherríe Moraga and Gloria Anzaldúa (Watertown, Mass.: Persephone Press, 1981), 92–93.

34. Maxine Hong Kingston, *Tripmaster Monkey* (New York: Knopf, 1989), 307–308.

35. Ibid., 318–19. Kathy Ferguson's watchful eye picked up on Ah Sing's male anatomical tropes, reminding me that Ah Sing's gendering of the language works to his male benefit. No "I," then, ever can be unambiguously worthy of our acclaim.

36. Ibid., 306.

37. This is the self-erasing strategy advocated by the white literary critic Minrose Gwin in her "A Theory of Black Women's Texts and White Women's Readings or . . . the Necessity of Being Other," *NWSA Journal* 1, no. 1 (Autumn 1988):21–31.

38. This role, which I critique in chapter 6, is advocated by Elizabeth Spelman, *Inessential Woman: Problems of Exclusion in Feminist Thought* (Boston: Beacon, 1988), 178–79.

39. Cornel West, using Sam Greenlee's notion, criticizes as the "spook who sits by the door" the assimilationist Black academic who "eavesdrops on the conversations among the prominent and reproduces their jargon . . . to imitate the dominant paradigms held in awe by fashionable elites." Were I, as a white feminist, to assume the toadying behavior of West's spook, I would merely join in the nay- or yea-saying of Black feminists either uncritically or opportunistically and, either way, cynically. See West's essay, "The Crisis of Black Leadership," *Z Magazine*, Feb. 1988, p. 24.

40. Françoise Vergès pointed out these tendencies to me in the context of Third-World feminist debates about *mettisage* (creolization) or purity. Vergès to the author, 1 June 1990. For a fascinating feminist critical study of *mettisage* as both a literary and a political metaphor of solidarity and diversity, see Françoise Lionnett, *Autobiographical Voices: Race, Gender, Self-Portraiture* (Ithaca, N.Y.: Cornell Univ. Press, 1989), 1–19.

41. Johnella Butler, "Women's Studies in the '90s: Achieving Transformation," *NWSAction* 2, no. 4 (Winter 1989):1–4. Butler's phrase, "Come discharge cargo!", is a rhetorical tribute to an African-American history teacher from a school in Rappahannock, Virginia, whom Butler's parents lionized. In the 1930s, on April 3, Emancipation Day or Jubilee Day, the teacher would give a rousing speech to celebrate the freeing of the slaves. The teacher exhorted students to "Come see! Come fight! Come discharge cargo!" in fighting the Jim Crow practices and the lynchings of their own day.

Chapter 1

1. Mary E. John, "Postcolonial Feminists in the Western Intellectual Field: Anthropologists and Native Informants?", *Inscriptions* 5 (1989):49–74.

2. Audre Lorde, *A Burst of Light* (Ithaca, N.Y.: Firebrand Books, 1988), 70.

3. See Haraway, "Cyborgs"; and Donna Haraway, "Situated Knowledges: The Science Question in Feminism and the Privilege of Partial Perspective," *Feminist Studies* 14, no. 3 (Fall 1988):575–99.

4. S.P. Mohanty, "Us and Them," 13.

5. bell hooks, *Talking Back* (Boston: South End Press, 1989), 15–16.

6. In this commitment to articulating an African heritage (or "internationalism" in Alice Walker's term), contemporary Black women echo their 19th-century female predecessors. The discussions in chapters 2 and 5 illustrate Black women's historical and cultural consciousness, as well as their organizational strategies to assist in the emancipation of all formerly African peoples.

7. Edward Said, "Representing the Colonized: Anthropology's Interlocutors," *Critical Inquiry* 15 (Winter 1989):205–225, esp. 219.

8. Cornel West, "Minority discourse and the Pitfalls of Canon Formation," *Yale Journal of Criticism* (1987):193–201. For an overview of the debates on alternative canon formation, see: Lillian Robinson, "What Culture Should Mean," *The Nation*, 25 Sept. 1989, pp. 319–21; "Culture Wars," a special issue of *Village Voice Literary Supplement*, Jan./Feb. 1989; Richard Rorty, "The Old-Time Philosophy," *New Republic*, 4 Apr. 1988, pp. 28–33; "The Canons Under Fire," *Time*, 11 Apr. 1988, pp. 66–67; Richard Bernstein, "In Dispute on Bias, Stanford Is Likely to Alter Western Culture Program," *New York Times*, 19 Jan. 1988; Tzvetan Todorov, "The Philosopher and the Everyday," *New Republic*, 14 and 21 Sept. 1987, pp. 34–37; Tzvetan Todorov, "Stalled Thinkers," *New Republic*, 13 Apr. 1987, pp. 26–27; Rick Simonson and Scott Walker, eds., *The Graywolf Annual Five: Multicultural Literacy* (St. Paul, Minn.: Graywolf Press, 1988).

9. Albert Memmi, *The Colonizer and the Colonized* (New York: Beacon, 1967). Further references to Memmi's text will indicate the page number.

10. Deborah K. King, "Multiple Jeopardy, Multiple Consciousness: The Context of a Black Feminist Ideology," *Signs* 14, no. 2 (Autumn 1988):42–72.

11. V.Y. Mudimbe, *The Invention of Africa* (Bloomington: Indiana Univ. Press, 1988), ix.

12. In her review of Mudimbe's text, Renato Rosaldo points out Mudimbe's own lingering francophone fixations and, more importantly, his entrapment within the realm of discourse, reading, and writing as the determinant of African social and political reality. His logocentric emphasis, she argues, de-emphasizes important social institutions and nonverbal cultural practices of everyday life. Renato Rosaldo, "Others of Invention," 28–29.

13. Mudimbe, *Invention of Africa*, xi.

14. These are anthroplogist Clifford Geertz's descriptives. To know a culture, Geertz argues, is to know those common-sense, intimate, shared assumptions by which people represent themselves to one another, the symbolic forms

through which they speak intelligibly. Geertz, "From the Native's Point of View: On the Nature of Anthropological Understanding," in *Meaning in Anthropology*, ed. Keith H. Basso and Henry A. Selby (Albuquerque: Univ. of New Mexico Press, 1976), 228. quoted in Bettina Aptheker, *Tapestries of Life: Women's Work, Women's Consciousness and the Meaning of Daily Experience* (Amherst: Univ. of Massachusetts Press, 1989), 13.

15. Patricia Hill Collins, "The Social Construction of Black Feminist Thought," *Signs* 14, no. 4 (Summer 1989):745–73.

16. Ibid., 746–47.

17. Ibid., 747.

18. See Nancy Hartsock's feminist standpoint formulations in *Money, Sex, and Power: Toward a Feminist Historical Materialism* (New York: Longman, 1983); and Sandra Harding's critiques of standpoint epistemologies, "The Instability of the Analytical Categories of Feminist Theory," *Signs* 11, no. 4 (Summer 1986):645–64, and *The Science Question in Feminism* (Ithaca, N.Y.: Cornell Univ. Press, 1986), 26–27, 164–96. Also see Christine Di Stefano, "Dilemmas of Difference: Feminism, Modernity and Postmodernism," in *Feminism/ Postmodernism*, ed. Linda J. Nicholson (New York: Routledge, 1990), 73–75; and Jane Flax, "Postmodernism and Gender Relations in Feminist Theory," *Signs* 12, no. 4 (Summer 1987):621–43.

19. Hill Collins, "Social Construction," 751.

20. For some idea of the range of the critiques of Western political thought, positivism, liberalism, and epistemology in general, to be found in feminist political theory, see: Sandra Harding and Merrill B. Hintikka, eds., *Discovering Reality: Feminist Perspectives on Epistemology, Metaphysics, Methodology, and Philosophy of Science* (Boston: Reidel, 1983); Alison Jagar, *Feminist Politics and Human Nature* (Totowa, N.J.: Rowman & Allanheld, 1983); Harding, *Science Question in Feminism*; Genevieve Lloyd, *Man of Reason* (Minneapolis: Univ. of Minnesota Press, 1984); Kathy Ferguson, *The Feminist Case Against Bureaucracy* (Philadelphia: Temple Univ. Press, 1984); Marian Millman and R.M. Kanter, eds., *Another Voice: Feminist Perspectives on Social Life and Social Science* (New York: Doubleday, 1975); Susan Griffin, "The Way of All Ideology," in *Feminist Theory*, ed. Nannerl O. Keohane, Michelle Z. Rosaldo, and Barbara C. Gelpi (Chicago: Univ. of Chicago Press, 1981); Hartsock, *Money, Sex, and Power*; Susan Bordo, "The Cartesian Masculinization of Thought," *Signs* 11, no. 3 (Spring 1986):439–56; Mary E. Hawkesworth, "Feminist Rhetoric; Discourses on the Male Monopoly of Thought," *Political Theory* 16, no. 3 (August 1988):444–67; Mary Field Belenky, Blythe McVicker Clinchy, Nancy Rule Goldberger, and Jill Mattuck Tarule, *Women's Ways of Knowing: The Development of Self, Voice, and Mind* (New York: Basic, 1986); Jean Bethke Elshtain, *Public Man, Private Woman* (Princeton,

N.J.: Princeton Univ. Press, 1981); Susan Moller Okin, *Women in Western Political Thought* (Princeton, N.J.: Princeton Univ. Press, 1979); Linda J. Nicholson, *Gender and History* (New York: Columbia Univ. Press, 1986); Christine Di Stefano, "Masculinity as Ideology in Political Theory: Hobbesian Man Considered," *Women's Studies International Forum* 6, no. 6 (1983): 633–44; Zillah Eisenstein, *The Radical Future of Liberal Feminism* (New York: Longman, 1981); Carole Pateman and Elizabeth Gross, eds., *Feminist Challenges: Social and Political Theory* (Boston: Northeastern Univ. Press, 1986); Kathleen B. Jones and Anna G. Jonasdottir, *The Political Interests of Gender* (London: Sage, 1985); Kathy Ferguson, "Male-Ordered Politics: Feminism and Political Science," Dept. of Political Science, Univ. of Hawaii, n.d.; Susan Hekman, *Hermeneutics and the Sociology of Knowledge* (Notre Dame, Ind.: Notre Dame Univ. Press, 1986); Eloise Buker, "Hermeneutics: Problems and Promises for Doing Feminist Theory," paper presented at meeting of the American Political Science Association, New Orleans, La., 1985. See "Feminism and Epistemology," entire issue of *Women & Politics* 7, no. 3 (Fall 1987).

21. See Bill Ashcroft, Gareth Griffiths, and Helen Tiffin, *The Empire Writes Back* (New York: Routledge, 1989), esp. 164–77, for a comprehensive analysis of the impact of postcolonial theory in literary cultural studies. For a range of these interdisciplinary writings, see: "Feminism and the Critique of Colonial Discourse," *Inscriptions* 3–4 (1988), ed. Deborah Gordon (published by the Group for the Critical Study of Colonial Discourse, Board of Studies in History of Consciousness, Univ. of California, Santa Cruz, Santa Cruz, Calif. 95064); *Mapping Colonialism*, proceedings from the 1988 conference "Mapping Colonialism" held Oct. 1987 at the Univ. of California, Berkeley (Berkeley, Calif. 94720); the proceedings of the conference on "Gender and Colonialism," Univ. of California, Berkeley, Oct. 1989; "SHE, THE INAPPROPRIATE/D OTHER," *Discourse* 8 (Fall–Winter 1986–87), ed. Trinh T. Minh-ha (published by the Center for Twentieth Century Studies, Univ. of Wisconsin, P.O. Box 413, Milwaukee, Wisc. 53201); "(Un) Naming Cultures," *Discourse* 11, no. 2 (Spring–Summer 1989), ed. Trinh T. Minh-ha (published by the Center for Twentieth Century Studies); "Traveling Theories, Traveling Theorists," *Inscriptions* 5 (1989), ed. James Clifford and Vivek Dhareshwar (published by the Group for the Critical Study of Colonial Discourse and the Center for Cultural Studies); G. C. Spivak, *In Other Worlds: Essays in Cultural Politics* (London: Methuen, 1987); G.C. Spivak, "Can the Subaltern Speak?", in *Marxism and the Interpretation of Culture*, ed. Lawrence Grossberg and Cary Nelson, 271–313 (Chicago: Univ. of Chicago Press, 1988); Chandra Talpade Mohanty, "Under Western Eyes: Feminist Scholarship and Colonial Discourses," *Feminist Review* 30 (Autumn 1988) 61–88; Edward Said, "Representing the Colonized"; Edward Said, *The World, the Text and*

the Critic (Cambridge, Mass.: Harvard Univ. Press, 1983); S.P. Mohanty, "Us and Them"; West, "Minority Discourse"; and the review essay by Chandra T. Mohanty and Satya P. Mohanty, "Contradictions of Colonialism," *Women's Review of Books* 7, no. 6 (Mar. 1990):19–21; and Gates, *"Race," Writing and Difference.*

22. Hill Collins, "Social Construction," 773.

23. Edward Said, "Traveling Theories," in Said, *World, Text and Critic* 226–47.

24. Elsa Barkley Brown, "Womanist Consciousness: Maggie Lena Walker and the Independent Order of Saint Luke," *Signs* 14, no. 3 (Spring 1989):610–33.

25. The concept of rearticulation is developed in Omi and Winant, *Racial Formation*. These authors' explication of the process of rearticulation is pertinent here to oppositional practices. Rearticulation is the process of producing new subjectivity by "making use of information and knowledge already present in the subject's mind," taking elements and themes of familiar culture and traditions and infusing them with new meaning" (93). Rearticulation involves a "redefinition of political interests and identities, through a process of recombination of familiar ideas and values in hitherto unrecognized ways" (n. 8, p. 146).

26. Barbara Smith, "Introduction," in *Home Girls: A Black Feminist Anthology*, ed. Barbara Smith (New York: Kitchen Table: Women of Color Press, 1983), xxxii.

27. Quoted in bell hooks, "A Call for Militant Resistance," *Z Magazine*, Jan. 1990, p. 52.

28. For a discussion of the politics of genre in emerging feminist and postcolonialist discourse, see "Panel Discussion 1," *Inscriptions* 3/4 (1988):58–69, esp. 63, 64.

29. The fragmented, episodic, often externally controlled terrain of women's daily lives forms the center of Bettina Aptheker's luminous book, *Tapestries of Life: Women's Work, Women's Consciousness, and the Meaning of Daily Experience.*

30. Hill Collins, "Social Construction," 770.

31. Marjorie Pryse and Hortense J. Spillers, eds., *Conjuring: Black Women, Fiction, and Literary Tradition* (Bloomington: Indiana Univ. Press, 1985), 5.

32. Patricia Hill Collins, "Learning from the Outsider Within: The Sociological Significance of Black Feminist Thought," *Social Problems* 33, no. 6 (1986):23.

33. Alice Walker, *The Color Purple* (New York: Washington Square Press, 1982); Alice Walker, *The Temple of My Familiar* (New York: Harcourt Brace Jovanovich, 1989), 169, 287–89. In *In Search of Our Mothers' Gardens* (New York: Harcourt Brace Jovanovich, 1974), Alice Walker again praises Black

female blues singers Billie Holiday and Bessie Smith who, along with Zora Neale Hurston (who she argues belongs in the tradition of Black women singers rather than the literati), form a sort of womanist/feminist "unholy trinity" (91).

34. Michele Russell, "Slave Codes and Liner Notes," in *But Some of Us Are Brave*, ed. Gloria Hull, Patricia Bell Scott, Barbara Smith (Old Westbury, N.Y.: Feminist Press, 1982), 130–31. Feminist rock critic Ellen Willis's interpretation of Janis Joplin's mode of singing Black women's blues points to the more politicized connotations of the blues rendered by Black female blues singers. Willis sees in the styles of Big Mama Thornton and Erma Franklin nuances of resistance, determination, and challenge; Joplin's style evokes a more passive, victimized stance, a sort of "agonized hope for reconciliation with the pain-inflicting male." Ellen Willis, *Beginning to See the Light* (New York: Knopf, 1981), 61–67, esp. 64–65; and Hazel V. Carby's essay, "It Jus Be's Dat Way Sometime: The Sexual Politics of Women's Blues," in *Unequal Sisters*, ed. Ellen Carol Du Bois and Vicki L. Ruiz (New York: Routledge, 1990), 238–49.

35. Other feminist theorists have creatively employed the practices of storytelling and poetry as vital repositories of feminist knowledge and politics, and as paradigms for political theorizing and community-building. See Trinh T. Mihn-ha, *Woman Native Other*, 5–17; and Trinh's "Introduction," in *Discourse* 11, no. 2; Eloise Buker, *Politics Through a Looking Glass: A Structuralist Interpretation of Narratives* (New York: Greenwood, 1987).

36. Paule Marshall quoted in Joyce Howe, "Talking Black," *Village Voice*, 26 Mar. 1985, p. 42.

37. Ibid.

38. Ruby Sales, "In Our Own Words: An Interview with Ruby Sales," *Woman's Review of Books* 7, no. 5 (Feb. 1990), p. 24. For a fascinating study of the postcolonial linguistic politics of intellectuals and writers struggling to speak in indigenous languages and idioms, see Manfred Henningsen, "The Politics of Purity and Exclusion: Literary and Linguistic Movements of Political Empowerment in America, Africa, the South Pacific and Europe," in Björn H. Jernudd and Michael J. Shapiro, eds. *The Politics of Language Purism* (New York: Mouton de Gruyter, 1989), 31–52; and Ashcroft, Griffiths, and Tiffin, *The Empire Writes Back*.

39. Sales, "In Our Own Words," 25.

40. Derrick Bell quoted in Jon Weiner, "Law Profs Fight the Power," *The Nation*, 4–11 Sept. 1989, p. 246.

41. Mari Matsuda quoted in Weiner, "Law Profs," p. 247. For other examples of critical legal scholarship, see: Derrick Bell, *And We Are Not Saved*; Kimberlé Crenshaw, "Race, Reform and Retrenchment: Transformation and

Legitimation in Antidiscrimination Law," *Harvard Law Review* 101 (May 1988):1331–87; Richard Delgado, "The Imperial Scholar: Reflections on a Review of Civil Rights Literature," *University of Pennsylvania Law Review*, 132 (March 1984):561–78; Randall Kennedy, "Racial Critiques of Legal Academic, *Harvard Law Review*, 102, no. 8 (June 1989):1745–1819; Charles Lawrence, "The Id, The Ego and Equal Protection: Reckoning with Unconscious Racism," *Stanford Law Review*, 39, No. 2 (Jan. 1987):317–88; Mari Matsuda, "Affirmative Action and Legal Knowledge," *Harvard Women's Law Journal*, 11 (Spring 1988):1–17; "Minority Critique" issue of *Harvard Civil Rights–Civil Liberties Law Review* 22, no. 2 (Spring 1987), with articles by Richard Delgado, Mari Matsuda, and Patricia Williams; Patricia Williams, "On Being the Object of Property, *Signs* 14, no. 1 (Autumn 1988):5–24.

42. Patricia Williams, quoted in Weiner, "Law Profs," 248.

43. Patricia Williams, "On Being the Object of Property," 5, 11.

44. Richard Delgado, quoted in Weiner, "Law Profs," 248.

45. Barbara Christian, "The Race for Theory," *Feminist Studies* 14, no. 2 (Spring 1988):67–80.

46. Bell hooks, *Talking Back*, 37–8.

47. Michelle Cliff, "Women Warriors: Black Writers Load the Canon," *Village Voice Literary Supplement*, May 1990, p. 20.

48. Ibid.

49. Jeffner Allen and Iris Marion Young, *The Thinking Muse: Feminism and Modern French Philosophy* (Bloomington: Indiana Univ. Press, 1989), 1.

Chapter 2

1. W.E.B. Du Bois, *The Souls of Black Folk* (Chicago: A.S. McClurg, 1903), 16.

2. See the 1924 document from the International Council of Women of the Darker Races, an organization of Black American women to foster knowledge, understanding, and "race pride" of "peoples of color the world over." Eleanor Hinton Hoytt, "International Council of Women of the Darker Races: Historical Notes," *Sage: A Scholarly Journal on Black Women* 3, no. 2 (Fall 1986):54–55.

3. Teresa de Lauretis views this theoretical shift away from the single axis of gender to the interrelated oppressions of race and class as the enabling feature which transformed feminist theory into a *theoretical* project rather than a feminist critique of some other theory. This is the moment when feminist theory developed its own self-consciousness and self-critical ability to contest its own terms, histories, and practices. See her "Displacing Hege-

monic Discourses: Reflections of Feminist Theory in the 1980s," *Inscriptions* 3–4 (1988):127–44, esp. 131–32.

4. One of the most significant publishing events in the history of women's studies was the publication of Henry Louis Gates, Jr., ed., *The Schomburg Library of Nineteenth-Century Black Women Writers* (New York: Oxford Univ. Press, 1988), 30 vols. For reviews of this collection, see: Marilyn E. Mobly, "When and Where They Entered," *Women's Review of Books* 5, no. 10/11 (July 1988):5–6; and "Discovering a Lost Tradition," *Newsweek*, 7 Mar. 1988, p. 70. For a sampling of contemporary Black feminist writers, see Thulani Davis, "Family Plots: Black Women Writers Reclaim Their Past, *Village Voice Literary Supplement*, Mar. 1987, (pp. 14–17; and Michelle Cliff, "Women Warriors," 20–22. Another publishing milestone for Black women's history is the series edited by Darlene Clark Hine, *Black Women in United States History* (New York: Carlson Publishing, 1990), 16 vols. Intriguing reading is the epic media coverage of Black filmmaker Spike Lee's work and of the African street fashions inspired by his films. See his published diaries and screen plays: Spike Lee, *Spike Lee's She's Gotta Have It Inside Guerrilla Filmmaking* (New York: Simon & Schuster, 1987); Spike Lee with Lisa Jones, *Do the Right Thing: A Spike Lee Joint* (New York: Simon & Schuster, 1989). For Black feminist critiques of his films, see: bell hooks, "Whose Pussy Is This? A Feminist Comment," in hooks, *Talking Back*, 134–41; Thulani Davis, "We've Gotta Have It," *Village Voice*, 20 June 1989; pp. 67–78; Michele Wallace, "She's Gotta Have It, School Daze," *The Nation*, 4 June 1988, pp. 800–803. For negative white responses to Lee's "Do the Right Thing," see David Denby, "He's Gotta Have It," *New York*, 26 June 1989, pp. 53–54; Joe Klein, "Spiked?", *New York*, 26 June 1989, pp. 14–15. For critical Black male reviews, see Stanley Crouch, "Do The Right Thing: Spike Lee's Afro-Fascist Chic," *Village Voice*, 20 June 1989, pp. 73–76; Juan Williams, "'Do the Right Thing' Doesn't Say Anything," *Washington Post*, July 2, 1989, p. G1. For a survey of African fashion hairstyles inspired by Lee's films, see "An Old Look Is New Again," *Newsweek*, 16 Oct. 1989, pp. 76–79.

5. This is Thulani Davis's lively phrase. "Don't Worry, Be Buppie," *Village Voice Literary Supplement* May 1990, p. 26.

6. Memmi, *Colonizer and Colonized*, 134.

7. "Fannie Lou Hamer," words and music by Bernice Johnson Reagon, Songtalk Publishing Co., Copyright 1977, recorded by Sweet Honey in the Rock for Flying Fish Records.

8. Alice Walker, *Temple of My Familiar*, 169.

9. Quoted in Jonathan Bradford Brennan, "Words with Walker," *San Francisco Review of Books*, Summer 1989, p. 13.

10. "A Gravestone of Memories," *Newsweek*, 25 Sept. 1987, p. 74.

11. Toni Morrison, *Beloved*, 188, 274.

12. "The Pain of Being Black," *Time*, 22 May 1989, p. 120. Morrison here addresses the issue of the number of slaves who died during slavery. The figure of sixty million, upon which her dedication to *Beloved* is based, has been questioned by critics as an overcalculation of the number of Blacks who died during the Middle Passage.

13. Toni Morrison, *Beloved*, 186.

14. See Roger Wilkins's moving essay (stimulated by this passage in Morrison's *Beloved*) about the need for middle-class Blacks to fulfill their responsibilities to poor Blacks by recementing ties with the growing and dispirited Black underclass: "Black Like Us," *Mother Jones*, May 1988, p. 60.

15. The papers from the 1979 conference are collected in Joseph E. Harris, ed., *Global Dimensions of the African Diaspora* (Washington: Howard Univ. Press, 1982). See the entire issue of *Sage* 3, no. 2 (Fall 1986), for the Diaspora statement and accounts of the 1985 conference on "The Black Woman Writer and the Diaspora; the 1983 conference on "Women in the African Diaspora," sponsored by the Association of Black Women Historians; and other topics.

16. "Return of a Native Daughter: "An Interview with Paule Marshall and Maryse Condé," *Sage* 3, no. 2 (Fall 1986):52–53 (translated by John Williams).

17. Ibid., 53.

18. Filomina Chioma Steady, ed., *The Black Woman Cross-Culturally* (Cambridge, Mass.: Schenkman, 1981), 3.

19. Rosalyn Terborg-Penn, "African Feminism: A Theoretical Approach to the History of Women in the African Diaspora," in *Women in Africa and the African Diaspora*, ed. Rosalyn Terborg-Penn, Sharon Harley, and Andrea Benton Rusing (Washington: Howard Univ. Press, 1987), 45.

20. Ibid., 4.

21. Deborah King, "Multiple Jeopardy," 42–72.

22. Hill Collins, "Social Construction," 755–70. Sandra Harding, in *The Science Question in Feminism*, 172–186, esp. 172, points out the incongruity of generalizations valorizing traits of the oppressed which originated in colonial and patriarchal conceptual schemes: "It reinforces the contrast paradigm that has been so useful in projects of domination."

23. Ibid., 759.

24. Ibid., 760.

25. Michelle Cliff, "Women Warriors," 21.

26. Hill Collins, "Social Construction," 763.

27. Ibid., 768.

28. Renato Rosaldo, "Others of Invention," 27.

29. Nancy Hartsock has critiqued Michel Foucault's metaphor of the "netlike organization of power." She argues that such a diffuse and totalistic conception of power ignores social structures and minimizes the agency of per-

sons. Hartsock resists Foucault's assumption that all social life comes to be a network of power relations. See her essay, "Foucault on Power: A Theory for Women?", in *Feminism/Postmodernism*, ed. Linda Nicholson, 157–75 (New York: Routledge, 1990), esp. 167–70.

30. I have borrowed Sandra Harding's modifier as a criterion for the kind of political actor (demonstrated by Hill Collins's portrait of Black feminism) who is not immobilized by the fragmentations of postmodernism. Harding, *Science Question in Feminism*, 247.

31. Hill Collins, "Social Construction," 771.

32. Deborah King, "Multiple Jeopardy," 49.

33. Ibid., 52.

34. Ibid., 49

35. Susan Bordo marshals this argument to show the impossibility of avoiding ethnocentrism and universalizing constructions:

> We need to guard against the "view from nowhere" supposition that if we employ the right method we can avoid ethnocentrism, totalizing constructions, and false universalizations. No matter how local and circumscribed the object or how attentive the scholar is to the axes that constitute social identity, some of those axes will be ignored and others selected. . . . This selectivity, moreover, is never innocent. We always "see" from points of view that are invested with our social, political, and personal interests, inescapably "centric" in one way or another, even in the desire to do justice to heterogeneity. ("Feminism, Postmodernism, and Gender-Scepticism," in *Feminism/Postmodernism*, 140.)

36. Said, "Representing the Colonized," 205–225.

37. Teresa de Lauretis, *Technologies of Gender* (Bloomington: Indiana Univ. Press, 1987), ix, x.

Chapter 3

1. Kathy Ferguson, however, characterizes two poles of the epistemological debate within feminism as "genealogical" (postmodern) approaches and "interpretative" (subject-centered feminism) models of feminist theory. See her "Interpretation and Genealogy in Feminism," paper presented at the Western Political Science Association, San Francisco, Calif., 10–12 Mar. 1988.

2. Jane Flax, "Postmodernism and Gender Relations," 621–43.

3. John Barth, "The Literature of Replenishment," *Atlantic Monthly*, Jan. 1980, p. 70, quoted in Alice Jardine, *Gynesis: Configurations of Woman and Modernity* (Ithaca, N.Y.: Cornell Univ. Press, 1985), 23.

4. Andrew Ross, *Universal Abandon?*, 10.

5. Negative dialectics arose in the neo-Marxist formulations of the Frankfurt School of Critical Theory, in the work of philosophers Max Horkheimer, Theodore Adorno, and Herbert Marcuse, among others. See Martin Jay's intellectual history of the Frankfurt School, *The Dialectical Imagination* (Boston: Little, Brown, 1973). The term "hermeneutics of suspicion" derives from the genealogical "demystification" practices of Marx, Freud, Nietzsche, Heidegger, Foucault, Derrida. See Allan Megill, *Prophets of Extremity* (Berkeley: Univ. of California Press, 1985).

6. Andrew Ross, *Universal Abandon?*, xi, xv.

7. Michel Foucault, *The Archaeology of Knowledge*, quoted in S.P. Mohanty, "Us and Them," 3.

8. S.P. Mohanty, "Us and Them," ix. In my discussion I have chosen the term *postmodernism*, rather than *poststructuralism*, to define cultural, philosophical, and political attitudes which are in tune with the *zeitgeist* under consideration here.

9. Flax, "Postmodernism and Gender Relations," 624, 626.

10. Donna Haraway, "Cyborgs," 73. For a critique of Haraway's disembodied cyborg metaphor, see Susan Bordo, "Feminism, Postmodernism, and Gender-Scepticism," 141–45.

11. Haraway, "Cyborgs," 73.

12. Ibid., 74.

13. Harding, *Science Question in Feminism*, 164, 28.

14. Ferguson, "Interpretation and Genealogy," 3–4.

15. Hazel V. Carby, quoted in Elliott Butler-Evans, "Beyond Essentialism: Rethinking Afro-American Cultural Theory," *Inscriptions* 5 (1989):126.

16. See the essays by Henry Louis Gates, Jr., "Writing 'Race' and the Difference It Makes," and "'Talkin' That Talk," in *"Race," Writing and Difference*, and Gates, *The Signifying Monkey: A Theory of Afro-American Literary Criticism* (New York: Oxford Univ. Press, 1988), all of which argue the case for a Black literary tradition if not "aesthetic." The following articles comment on the debate about the construction of a "Black aesthetic": Martin Kilson, "Paradoxes of Blackness," *Dissent* (Winter 1986):70–78; Adolph J. Reed, Jr., "Black Particularity Reconsidered," *Telos*, no. 39 (Spring 1979):71–93; Greg Tate, "Cult-Nats Meet Freaky-Deke, *Village Voice Literary Supplement*, Dec. 1986, pp. 5–8; Michele Wallace, "A Race Man and a Scholar," *Emerge*, Feb. 1990, pp. 56–61. For positive accounts of the dimensions of Black culture, see Cornel West, *Prophesy Deliverance!*; Sheila Collins, *The Rainbow Challenge* (New York: Monthly Review Press, 1986); John Langston Gwaltney, *Drylongso: A Self Portrait of Black America* (New York: Vintage, 1981); Carol Stack, *All Our Kin* (New York: Harper, 1974); Sterling Stuckey, *Slave Culture: Nationalist Theory and the Foundations of Black America*

(New York: Oxford Univ. Press, 1987); Harold Cruse, *Plural but Equal* (New York: William Morrow, 1987); Molefi Kete Asante, *The Afrocentric Idea* (Philadelphia: Temple Univ. Press, 1987).

17. Memmi, *Colonizer and Colonized*, 37, xv.

18. Ibid., xi, xii.

19. Lorde, *Burst of Light* 66–67.

20. This is Marx's term, quoted in Roger M. Keesing's controversial essay on the project of indigenous Pacific anticolonial movements' efforts to construct a romanticized, pastoral, often Eurocentric vision of precontact native life, "Creating the Past: Custom and Identity in the Contemporary Pacific," *Contemporary Pacific* 1, nos. 1 and 2 (Spring/Fall 1989):19–42.

21. This is one of the questions James Clifford and Vivek Dhareshwar propose in their consideration of postcolonial discourses. An absolutist anti-essentialist posture forecloses the possibility of resisting any dominant constructions with empowering alternatives. See their preface in Clifford and Dhareshwar, "Traveling Theories, Traveling Theorists," *Inscriptions* 5 (1989):vii.

22. Iris M. Young, "Difference and Policy: Some Reflections in the Context of New Social Movements," *University of Cincinnati Law Review* 56, no. 2 (1987):535–50.

23. Michel Foucault, *Power/Knowledge* (New York: Pantheon, 1980), 99.

24. Harding, "Instability of Analytical Categories" 645–64.

25. Jane Tompkins's essay, "'Indians': Textualism, Morality, and the Problem of History," in *"Race," Writing and Difference*, ed. Henry Louis Gates, Jr., 59–77, (Chicago: Univ. of Chicago Press, 1985), esp. 74–76, concerns the problem of point of view in giving accounts of historical events. The poststructuralist commitment to perspectivism — the idea that all accounts of history are located in selective perceptions of "reality" (Nietzsche, *On the Genealogy of Morals*) — means, she tells us, that one will never know "the" truth. In her effort to understand aspects of Native American history, Tompkins determined that, in order to judge and evaluate differing accounts, she needed to proceed "as she did before poststructuralism." Rather than ending up in a morass of "metastatements about perspectives," Tompkins rightly argues that, in order to get our bearings, we must utilize the evidences, authorities, and analogies traditionally cited by conventional scholarship, being aware that all facts are motivated. Her project to understand the "meaning" of American histories of genocide against Native Americans dramatizes and exposes the paralyzing deadends which anti-foundationalism gets us into when we meet it, as she says, in the road.

26. See the following essays which critique postmodernism's treatment of subjectivity and agency: Hartsock, "Foucault on Power"; Di Stefano, "Dilemmas of Difference"; and Bordo, "Feminism, Postmodernism." Kathy Ferguson's position on postmodernism seems closer to my own. Both of us are willing

to utilize certain of postmodernism's resources as a critical reminder of limits; as Ferguson notes, "[Feminist postmodernism] need not be hostile to the political commitments of its sisters; it can help us to select principles and actions that are worthy of our endorsement even after their ambiguities come to light." Ferguson, "Subject-Centeredness in Feminist Discourse," in *The Political Interests of Gender*, ed. Kathleen B. Jones and Anna G. Jonasdottir, 66–78 (London: Sage, 1985), esp. 77.

27. Leslie Wahl Rabine, "A Feminist Politics of Non-Identity," *Feminist Studies* 14, no. 1 (Spring 1988):11–32.

28. Darlene Clark Hine, "Rape and the Inner Lives of Black Women in the Middle West: Preliminary Thoughts on the Culture of Dissemblance," *Signs* 14, no. 4 (Summer 1989):912–20.

29. Elsa Barkley Brown, "Womanist Consciousness," 618.

30. Rabine, "Feminist Politics of Non-Identity," 26. Iris Young too has warned of the consequences for politics when feminists refuse to engage in mainstream politics and get their hands dirty in male-dominated institutions and arenas of power. Iris Marion Young, "Humanism, Gynocentrism and Feminist Politics," *Women's Studies International Forum* 8, no. 3 (1985):173–83.

31. Barbara Christian, "Race for Theory," 69, 71.

32. Michelle Cliff, "Women Warriors," 20.

33. bell hooks, *Talking Back*, 36–37.

34. Aptheker, *Tapestries of Life*, 10–11. Sandra Harding, "Instability of Analytical Categories," comments on the problems involved in trying to "fit" women's experiences into critical theory, psychoanalysis, functionalism, structuralism, deconstructionism, hermeneutics. Because these frames do not derive from women's experiences, feminists can end up being manipulated and diverted by the structures of nonfeminist frameworks. As Harding argues,

> On the one hand, we have been able to use aspects or components of each of these discourses to illuminiate our subject matters. We have stretched the intended domains of these theories, reinterpreted their central claims, or borrowed their concepts and categories to make visible women's lives and feminist views of gender relations. After our labors, these theories often do not much resemble what their nonfeminist creators and users had in mind, to put the point mildly. . . . Moreover, the very fact that we borrow from these theories often has the unfortunate consequence of diverting our energies into endless disputes with the nonfeminist defenders of these theories: we end up speaking not to other women but to patriarchs.(646)

35. This is Eloise Buker's query regarding recent feminist semiotic theories. Buker, "Sign, Sex and Symbol: Feminist Semiotics and Political Philosophy," paper presented at meeting of the Western Political Science Association, Salt Lake City, Utah, Spring 1989, p. 40.

36. Peter A. Angeles, ed., *Dictionary of Philosophy* (New York: Barnes and Noble, 1981), 212, 265.

37. Quoted in Renato Rosaldo, "Others of Invention," 27; Lillian Robinson, "Are We There Yet?", *Women's Review of Books* 7, no. 3 (Dec. 1989):10.

38. Cornel West, "Postmodernism and Black America," *Z Magazine*, June 1988, p. 27.

39. Ibid., 28.

40. Ibid., 29.

41. Anders Stephanson, "Interview with Cornel West," 277.

42. I think that Nancy Hartsock, "Foucault on Power," 168, underestimates the extent to which feminists can utilize Foucault's theories about power. She is correct in identifying his lack of allegiance to normative political ideals and his purely destabilizing stance toward power, i.e., his view that one can only resist power, since otherwise one risks transforming liberatory projects into merely different forms of domination. But why do we have to take the full dose of his pessimism? I think Foucault's warnings about the "capillary" character of modern power, his references to power's ability to operate at the lowest realms of the social body, provide an important corrective to the notion that power stems only "from above," from established authority (see his essays and interviews in *Power/Knowledge*, esp. 86, 96). The truth of this insight about "local forms of power" should be obvious to any "oppressed" feminist who has attempted to build coalitions of diverse, multiethnic, multiracial women — where embitterment, distrust, and anger present their own economies of power and rancor. I take up the problems of feminist interracial coalition politics in chapter 6. For an excellent treatment of Foucault's analysis of "disciplinary power/knowledge" by a feminist scholar concerned with the exigencies of political practice, see Nancy Fraser's essays "Foucault on Modern Power: Empirical Insights and Normative Confusions," 17–34, and "Michel Foucault: A 'Young Convervative'?", 35–54, in Fraser, *Unruly Practices: Power, Discourse and Gender in Contemporary Social Theory* (Minneapolis: Univ. of Minnesota, 1989). Fraser points out the radical resources of Foucault's work as well as its normative one-dimensionality. His critique, as she notes, is engaged but non-normative, implying serious political limitations.

43. Donna Haraway, "Reading Buchi Emecheta: Contests for Women's Experiences in Women's Studies," *Inscriptions* 3, no. 4 (1988):109.

44. Iris Young, "Difference and Policy," 536–37.

45. The Algerian feminist Marnia Lazreg has emphasized the importance of liberal democracy in Third-World liberation struggles. See her "Feminism and Difference: The Perils of Writing as a Woman on Women in Algeria," *Feminist Studies* 14, no. 4 (Spring 1988):81–107; "Indeed the universalistic

claim to a supracultural human entity embodied in reason provided colonized societies with the tool necessary to regain their freedom. Colonized women and men were willing to give up their lives in order to capture their share of humanity celebrated but denied by colonial powers."

Black Americans will remember David Walker's 1829 treatise as a classical statement of their struggle to become rights-bearing Americans. In the rhetoric of Jeffersonian democracy, Walker laid claim to citizenship and personhood for all African and African-American peoples. *David Walker's Appeal to the Coloured Citizens of the World*, ed. Charles M. Wiltse (New York: Hill and Wang, 1965).

46. Mary Helen Washington, *Invented Lives: Narratives of Black Women, 1860–1960* (New York: Doubleday, 1988), xxi.

47. S.P. Mohanty, "Us and Them," 21.

48. Ibid., 26.

49. This is Nancy Fraser's criterion for an efficacious politics, one which is engaged in a "diagnosis of the times." Fraser, *Unruly Practices*, 6.

50. I have borrowed this formulation from the Black anthropologist John Langston Gwaltney, whose graceful readings of the "core Black culture" of ordinary Black folk ("Drylongso") make clear that Black Americans are no less capable of "abstract thinking" than are those members of other human cultures. Blacks' abstractions, however, are linked to a fully articulated lived reality. Gwaltney, *Drylongso*, xxix.

51. My discussion here has been stimulated greatly by the critiques and analyses offered by feminist political theorists participating in two roundtable discussions, "Roundtable on Postmodernism, Critiques of Cultural Imperialism, and the Identity Crisis for Feminism"; and "How Has Feminist Theory Affected the Field?", at the 85th Annual Meeting of the American Political Science Association, 31 Aug.–3 Sept. 1989, Atlanta, Ga. In particular, I have benefited from Nancy Love's discussions of feminist theory's political and democratic (as opposed to strictly philosophical) imperatives as an "extrafoundationalist" project; and Joan Tronto's insistence that feminist theory must refocus its resources toward the explication of a vision of a "good feminist future." Tronto's comments warn of the pitfalls of an exclusive focus on methodism, a technical focus that deemphasizes our responsibilities to theorize moral and ethical criteria which can "impact on the world." Kathy Ferguson's analyses warn of the simple reversals of the crude essentialist tendency in some strands of feminism which suggest a "low-minded revenge, a transparent effort to elevate the low and depose the high." Her postmodernist sensitivity to the necessity of destabilizing the categories of "praxis" feminism, in order to "agitate into existence a different approach to categoriza-

tion," is a crucial reminder of the dangers of feminism's own potential to naturalize prevailing subjectivities as unproblematical.

52. Patricia Williams, "On Being the Object of Property," 5.

53. Ibid., 11.

54. Donna Haraway, "Situated Knowledges," 575–99.

Chapter 4

1. Michele Russell, "Slave Codes and Liner Notes," 13.

2. White men at a women's rights meeting in Silver Lake, Ind., demanded this of Sojourner Truth, who militantly obliged with the riposte that those black breasts had suckled many a white man — to the detriment of her own children. Truth's experience, as historian Deborah Gray White claims, serves as a metaphor for the slave woman's general experience of being totally unprotected: "Only black women had their womanhood so totally denied." See White, *Ar'n't I a woman: Female Slaves in the Plantation South* (New York: Norton, 1985), 162.

3. Saartjie Baartman, or the Hottentot Venus, was exhibited nude in the capitals of Europe and died in Paris at the age of 25; other African men and women were displayed in zoos. Sander Gilman, "Black Bodies, White Bodies: Toward an Iconography of Female Sexuality in Late Nineteenth-Century Art, Medicine, and Literature," in *"Race," Writing and Difference*, ed. Henry Louis Gates, Jr., 223–61 (Chicago: Univ. of Chicago Press, 1985). Also see Nicholas Penny, "Fraternity," *London Review of Books*, 8 Mar. 1990, p. 22.

4. This is one of the incidents labor organizer Dorothy Bolden related about her exploitation as a domestic worker in white households; she was jailed for "talking back" to her employers. Dorothy Cowser Yancy, "Dorothy Bolden, Organizer of Domestic Workers: She Was Born Poor but She Would Not Bow Down," *Sage* 3, no. 1 (Spring 1986):53–55.

5. This is the remarkable story of the slave Harriet Jacobs. Aware of the sexual calculation which forced her to give her body to one white man in order to escape another, Jacobs forcefully questions the moral probity of whites in her slave narrative. Jacobs's narrative takes full responsibility for her actions, which seemed the only means available to free her children or herself. It was not she who should be blamed for her sexual violation, she argued, but slavery and the moral code which failed to provide protection for Black slave women. Jacobs refused both the role of pathetic victim and the injustice of being held accountable to the same standards of "ladyhood" as applied to free white women:

It seems less degrading to give one's self than to submit to compulsion. There is something akin to freedom in having a lover who has no control over you, except that which he gains by kindness and attachment. . . . Still, in looking back calmly, on the events of my life, I feel that the slave woman ought not to be judged by the same standard as others." (Jean Yellin, "Text and Contexts of Harriet Jacobs's *Incidents in the Life of a Slave Girl: Written by Herself*," in *The Slave's Narrative*, ed. Charles T. Davis and Henry Louis Gates, Jr. [New York: Oxford Univ. Press, 1985], 55–56)

Also see Mary Helen Washington, "Meditations on History: The Slave Woman's Voice," 3–15, and "Harriet Jacobs: The Perils of a Slave Woman's Life," 16–70, in Washington, *Invented Lives*; Hazel Carby, *Reconstructing Womanhood: The Emergence of the Afro-American Woman Novelist* (New York: Oxford Univ. Press, 1987), 40–61; Elizabeth Fox-Genovese, *Within the Plantation Household* (Chapel Hill: Univ. of North Carolina Press, 1988), 372–96.

6. Zora Neale Hurston, *Their Eyes Were Watching God* (Urbana: Univ. of Illinois Press, 1978), 29. Emphasis added.

7. For interpretations of the 19th-century "cult of true womanhood" and the polarized images of 19th-century black and white women, see Elizabeth Fox-Genovese, *Within the Plantation Household*; Deborah Gray White, *Ar'n't I a Woman*; Hazel Carby, *Reconstructing Womanhood*; Beverly Guy-Sheftall, *Daughters of Sorrow: Attitudes Toward Black Women, 1880–1920*, vol. 11 in the series Black Women in United States History, ed. Darlene Clark Hine (New York: Carlson Publishing, 1990); Catherine Clinton, *The Plantation Mistress: Woman's World in the Old South* (New York: Pantheon, 1982); Barbara Welter, *Dimity Convictions: The American Woman in the Nineteenth Century* (Columbus: Univ. of Ohio Press, 1976); Julia Cherry Spruill, *Women's Life and Work in the Southern Colonies* (rptd. 1938; New York: Norton, 1972); Ann Scott, *The Southern Lady: From Pedestal to Politics, 1830–1930* (Chicago: Univ. of Chicago Press, 1970); Barbara Berg, *The Remembered Gate: Origins of American Feminism* (Oxford: Oxford Univ. Press, 1978); Carol Hymowitz and Michaele Weissman, *A History of Women in America* (New York: Bantam, 1978), 40–75; Rosemary Reuther, *New Woman New Earth* (New York: Seabury, 1983), 115–33; Adrienne Rich, "Disloyal to Civilization," in Rich, *On Lies, Secrets and Silence* (New York: Norton, 1979). George Rable's study of 19th-century southern women and nationalism, *Civil Wars: Women and the Crisis of Southern Nationalism* (Urbana: Univ. of Illinois Press, 1989), is a damning indictment of southern white women's lack of gender consciousness during and after the Civil War. The war offered them a respite from their traditional restrictive domestic duties, but, according to Rable, it did not alter them or spur them to challenge their status as women. His reading instead reveals a fervent white female defense both of slavery and the social institutions of female subordination. The classic textual statement of the Con-

federacy's adulation of white womanhood comes from W.J. Cash, *The Mind of the South* (New York: Knopf, 1941). He describes "gyneolatry," the hyperbolic form that glorification took:

> She was the South's Palladium, this Southern woman—the shield-bearing Athena gleaming whitely in the clouds . . . The mystic symbol of its nationality in face of the foe. . . . There was hardly a sermon that did not begin with tributes to her honor . . . the ranks of the Confederacy went rolling into battle in the misty conviction that it was wholly for her that they fought. Woman!!! (83)

8. Adrienne Rich, "Disloyal to Civilization," 283.

9. bell hooks, *Ain't I a Woman? Black Women and Feminism* (Boston: South End Press, 1981). This is the title of hooks's chapter 2, 51–86.

10. "Cookie Jars of Oppression," *Newsweek*, 16 May 1988, pp. 75–76; "Prejudice and Black Sambo," *Time* 15 Aug. 1988, p. 25.

11. hooks, *Ain't I a Woman*, 86.

12. Toni Morrison, *The Bluest Eye* (New York: Washington Square Press Pocket Books, 1970), 97.

13. In his study of antebellum gender conventions among northern Blacks, James Oliver Horton charts the ideological patterns of Black women's socialization to white middle-class norms of acceptability and attractiveness, as well as the implications of these gender exhortations for strengthening Black patriarchy. Horton, "Freedom's Yoke: Gender Conventions among Antebellum Free Blacks," *Feminist Studies* 12, no. 1 (Spring 1986):51–76, esp. 57–58.

14. W.E.B. Du Bois was one of America's strongest advocates of female liberation. His essay, "The Servant in the House," is a powerful attack on the abuse and dishonor of Black women, a condition perpetuated, as he thought, by the performance of manual labor in whites' homes. The essay is collected in Du Bois, *Darkwater: Voices from Within the Veil* (New York: AMS Press, 1969), 115.

15. Anthropologist Jayne Ifekwunigwe, of the University of California, Berkeley, called to my attention this potential for employing a neo-pornographic discourse on Black women's bodies. Although I disagree with her that simply to engage the ideology reinforces its images, how we treat such material analytically is vitally important. My project in speaking to white feminists is both pedagogical and political: to demonstrate the severity and intensity of the racist discourses which have debased Black women, to teach us that history, and to situate us as deconstructors in that legacy. We cannot, however, allow venal characterizations of Black women to remain, as objective, on our pages. How could we be "objective" about material which causes so much pain, both to Black women and to everyone who reads it? Our meta-emotions about the anguish we feel in presenting such discourses need to become a liv-

ing part of our critique and remarked upon. Scholarship ought not mute the horror of these words which killed.

I am also grateful to Lata Mani for conversations about this issue.

16. Reading Beverly Guy-Sheftall's study, *Daughters of Sorrow*, 48–49, is both a depressing and enraging experience, although the pages contain a crucial scholarly compilation. The negative materials the author brings together, particularly her presentation of the brutal animal metaphors used by whites to describe and devalue Black women's bodies and sexuality must be recorded and subjected to critical analysis. But the muted objective tone with which Guy-Sheftall discusses them is disturbing. Masculinist norms of "value-free" scholarship often mean that we do not hear the pain that we feel in reading hateful language. We do not hear of the pain she, as a Black woman, must have felt in reading such descriptions. As I discussed in n. 15, this experience can be overwhelming. I do think that expressions of violent disagreement with such discourses are a necessary methodological caveat. Still, this does not wholly satisfy the fear that, by repeating such words of horror, one is somehow giving them currency.

17. Bonner's work is discussed in Kathy A. Perkins, ed., *Black Female Playwrights: An Anthology of Plays Before 1950* (Bloomington: Indiana Univ. Press, 1989); quoted in Michelle Cliff, "Woman Warriors," 22.

18. Adrienne Rich, "Disloyal to Civilization," 298.

19. Bell hooks, *Ain't I a Woman?*, 7, 55. For an account of white lynching rituals and the inflammatory discourse which developed around the fabrications of Black men "ravishing" white females, what historian Jacqueline Dowd Hall calls "a type of folk pornography," see Hall, *Revolt Against Chivalry: Jessie Daniel Ames and the Women's Campaign Against Lynching* (New York: Columbia Univ. Press, 1979). Also see Trudier Harris's study of incidents of white lynching, burning, castrating, raping, and mutilation of Blacks, as these histories are reflected in the works of Black writers since the mid-19th-century: *Exorcising Blackness: Historical and Literary Lynching and Burning Rituals* (Bloomington: Indiana Univ. Press, 1984).

20. Hortense Spillers, "Interstices: A Small Drama of Words," in *Pleasure and Danger: Exploring Female Sexuality*, ed. Carole S. Vance (Boston: Routledge & Kegan Paul, 1984), 78–79.

21. Darlene Clark Hine, "Rape and the Inner Lives of Black Women," 915.

22. Winthrop D. Jordan, *White Over Black: American Attitudes Toward the Negro, 1550–1812* (Baltimore, Md.: Penguin, 1969), 141.

23. James Oliver Horton, "Freedom's Yoke," 53.

24. Hazel Carby, *Reinventing Womanhood*, 30.

25. Fox-Genovese, *Within the Plantation Household*, 145, 241.

26. Angela Davis, "Reflections on the Black Woman's Role in the Community of Slaves," *Black Scholar* 3 (Dec. 1971):3–15.

27. Sherley Anne Williams' novel *Dessa Rose* (New York: William Morrow, 1986), is one of the few fictive renderings of the erotic lives and sexual pleasures of Black slaves. The traditional slave narratives, stories told by Blacks to unfamilar white interviewers, were warily silent about the sexual agency of slaves. One, after all, did not want to fuel popular perceptions about Black sexual promiscuity, a literally deadly pastime.

28. Barbara Omolade, "Hearts of Darkness," in *Powers of Desire: The Politics of Sexuality*, ed. Ann Snitow, Christine Stansell, and Sharon Thompson (New York: Monthly Review Press, 1983), 355.

29. For this courageous record of Black female slave resistance and sabotage of slavery's institutions, also see Darlene Hine and Kate Wittenstein, "Female Slave Resistance: The Economies of Sex," in *The Black Woman Cross-Culturally*, ed. Filomina Chioma Steady (Cambridge, Mass.: Schenkman, 1981), 289–300.

30. Omolade, "Hearts of Darkness," 364–65.

31. Teresa de Lauretis, *Feminist Studies/Critical Studies* (Bloomington: Indiana Univ. Press, 1986), 13.

32. In speaking about the socially constructed, power-laden character of language, Carby classifies the sign as "an arena of struggle and a construct between socially organized persons in the process of their interactions"; *Reconstructing Womanhood*, 17.

33. Michele Russell, "Slave Codes and Liner Notes," 130.

34. Wendy Chapkis, *Beauty Secrets: Women and the Politics of Appearance* (Boston: South End Press, 1986), 6.

35. Ibid., 140, 5.

36. Gerda Lerner, *Black Women in White America* (New York: Vintage, 1973), 610–11.

37. Ibid., 611.

38. Toni Morrison, *Bluest Eye*, 109.

39. Hortense Spillers, "Interstices: A Small Drama of Words," 79.

40. Orlando Patterson, *Slavery and Social Death* (Cambridge, Mass.: Harvard Univ. Press, 1982):

> . . . The master's authority was derived from his control over symbolic instruments, which effectively persuaded both slave and others that the master was the only mediator between the living community to which he belonged and the living death that his slave experienced. The symbolic instruments may be seen as the cultural counterpart to the physical instruments used to control the slave's body. In much the same way that the literal whips were fashioned from different materials, the symbolic whips of slavery were woven from

many areas of culture. Masters all over the world used special rituals of enslavement upon first acquiring slaves: the symbolism of naming, of clothing, of hairstyle, of language, and of body marks. (8–9)

41. Gerda Lerner, *Black Women in White America*, 163–64.

42. Ibid., 579–80.

43. Abbey Lincoln, "Who Will Revere the Black Woman?", in *The Black Woman: An Anthology*, ed. Toni Cade (New York: New American Library, 1970), 84.

44. Black men were not immune to the idealization of white hair and appearance. Malcolm X related in his autobiography a riveting demonstration of his coming to political consciousness as a Black man after enduring many painful hair-straightening treatments. This torturous process, usually done at home, involved the use of lye which scalded the scalp:

> When Shorty let me stand up and see in the mirror, my hair hung down in limp, damp strings. My scalp still flamed. . . . My first view in the mirror blotted out the hurting. I'd seen some pretty conks, but when it's the first time, on your *own* head, the transformation, after the lifetime of kinks, is staggering . . . on top of my head was this thick, smooth sheen of shining red hair — real red — as straight as any white man's. . . . This was my first really big step towards self-degradation. (Malcolm X, *The Autobiography of Malcolm X* [Harmondsworth, England: Penguin, 1965], 164, 137–8.

45. Alice Walker, "Oppressed Hair Puts a Ceiling on the Brain," *Ms.*, June 1988, p. 53.

46. I'm remembering one such experience within my own feminist community in Hawai'i. One glorious Saturday, a group of us — an Iranian woman, two local *haole* women, and a visiting colleague, an accomplished photographer who had just returned from doing women's support work in Asia — drove to the beautiful seaside village of Kaaawa on Oahu to spend the day catching up on one another's lives with another friend, an African-American feminist poet who lived there. Sitting on her deck, surrounded by mango, papaya, and banana trees and by miscellaneous cats, dogs, and children, we noticed that our host (renowned for her flamboyant sense of style) had bright red toenails. In the midst of expressing our takes on just about every political event, book, or film possible, we decided to engage in, or reclaim, a "feminist ritual." We began painting each other's toenails with the brightest, most vibrant nail polish we could find. Our photographer friend then had us stand with our variously shaped and hued feet in a circle (our own mandala, we called the image) while she took photographs. The result was wonderful, a circle of feet. We later took turns guessing which toes belonged to which woman. In our context of bonding, we did not think of this ritual as capitulat-

ing to male-enforced standards of beauty, but rather as a playfully ironic experience we had shared; soon the black-and-white photographs would go on our respective bulletin boards.

47. Bell hooks, "Straightening Our Hair," *Z Magazine*, Sept. 1988, pp. 33, 35.

48. Ayoka Chenzira's sassy 1984 short film, "Hair Piece: A Film for Nappy-headed People," is a feminist celebration of "natural" African-American beauty and a humorous spoof of those instruments used to "whiten" Blacks — hot combs, hair-straighteners, wigs, gels.

49. Margo Okazawa-Rey, Tracy Robinson, and Janie Victoria Ward, "Black Women and the Politics of Skin Color and Hair," *Women's Studies Quarterly* 14, nos. 1/2 (Spring/Summer 1986):13–14.

50. These are Jeffers's words, quoted in Alice Walker's essay, "If the Present Looks Like the Past," in Alice Walker, *In Search of Our Mothers' Gardens*, 295.

51. Ibid., 310, 307, 311.

52. Quoted in Chapkis, *Beauty Secrets*, 59.

53. Ibid., 193.

54. Alice Walker, *In Search of Our Mothers' Gardens*, 232, 237.

55. When Murray attempted to have the case dismissed on this point, the judge ruled her out of order, denied her motion, found the woman from Harlem guilty, and sentenced her to a prison term. Quoted in Bettina Aptheker, *Woman's Legacy: Essays on Race, Sex, and Class* (Amherst, Mass.: Univ. of Massachusetts Press, 1982), 2–3. Also see Murray's autobiography, *Song in a Weary Throat* (New York: Harper and Row, 1986).

56. Adrienne Rich, "Disloyal to Civilization," 309.

57. All quotes from Brenda Eichelberger, "Voices on Black Feminism," *Quest* 3, no. 4 (Spring 1977):16–28.

58. For an analysis which rejects the notion that poverty is "feminized" equally along racial lines, see Linda Burnham, "Has Poverty Been Feminized in Black America?", *Black Scholar* (March/April 1985):14–24; and Julianne Malveaux, "Current Economic Trends and Black Feminist Consciousness," *Black Scholar* 16, no. 2 (Mar./Apr. 1985): 26–31.

59. See "Slipping Through the Cracks: The Status of Black Women," special issue of *Review of Black Political Economy* 14, nos. 2/3 (Fall–Winter 1985–86). Black women's history in America has been one of steady, albeit brutal, labor force participation in low-paid, unstable work in the service sector. Despite the presence of a small number of Black female professionals, this legacy is and has been harsh and demanding.

60. Jacqueline Jones, *Labor of Love, Labor of Sorrow* (New York: Basic, 1985), 316.

61. This is only one of the many encounters the audacious Alice Childress satirizes in her humorous but hard-hitting novel about the lives of Black female domestics, *Like One of the Family: Conversations from a Domestic's Life* (Boston: Beacon, 1986), 42–43. Consult the excellent introduction and bibliography by Trudier Harris. Childress, a creative writer of Black children's stories as well as a playwright and novelist, charts the racism her fiesty character, Mildred, endures from white families based on true stories told her by her own aunt, a lifelong domestic worker. Childress's Mildred is no long-suffering, defeated workhorse for whites, but at every turn she challenges with humor and will her employer's stereotypes and attempted exploitations. By giving voice to these women, Childress takes the white reader behind the feigned "Yes, Ma'am"s of Black domestics to reveal a savvy, self-determined person with a keen understanding of the privatized patterns of white racism.

Childress's Black characters are meant to pique whites, let them know that Black women won't "be messed with." Childress's spirited portrayal of poor, working Black females affords a compelling contrast to more comforting depictions of Blacks such as that portrayed by the Black chauffeur in the film *Driving Miss Daisy*. Why are white audiences so moved by the Morgan Freeman character? Is it because he appears so servile and unthreatening? The depictions of his white employer's slights and his own pained restraint are disturbing to watch. One keeps waiting for him to assert himself in a more forceful manner. Audre Lorde's point that oppressed folks are expected to walk the extra mile, exert more patience and understanding toward their white oppressors, is surely operative in this film.

62. Judith Rollins, *Between Women: Domestics and Their Employers* (Philadelphia: Temple Univ. Press, 1985), 172.

63. The life of Dorothy Bolden, the Black domestic worker who in 1968 founded the National Domestic Workers Union in Atlanta, is a symbol of courage and political commitment. Having suffered the indignities of poor wages and working conditions for most of her life, Bolden not only gave dignity to the work of poor Black female maids but also, through her organizing skills, lobbied to achieve minimum-wage scales, insurance, Social Security benefits, and other advantages for domestic laborers. See Yancy's account of this admirable woman's life story, "Dorothy Bolden, Organizer of Domestic Workers."

64. This is Alice Childress's term. For other accounts of the domestic-mistress relation, see Trudier Harris, *From Mammies to Militants* (Philadelphia: Temple Univ. Press, 1982). For a white feminist account of the exploitive nature of household labor and the oppressive practices of white housewives with servant women of color (both of whom derive their identities and hier-

archies through domestic service), see Phyllis Palmer, *Domesticity and Dirt: Housewives and Domestic Servants in the United States, 1920–1945* (Philadelphia, Pa.: Temple Univ. Press, 1990). Barbara Brown has analyzed the exploitive relations between white mistresses and Black maids in South Africa. Her analysis shows how white South African women maintain the *status quo* of apartheid through organizations supporting the white government. Brown, "White Women in South Africa," *Sojourner*, Dec. 1985, pp. 12–13. Cynthia Enloe has examined the role of domestic servants and nannies in an international context, examining how the participation of women hired to perform such labor was a vital component of empire-building and the racist projects of Western colonialism. Enloe is especially insightful about the contradictions that arise when progressive feminist women employ domestic help. Hiring domestics recently has been endorsed by the conservative governments of Britain and the U.S. as a "solution" to the career woman's double burdens. See her "'Just Like One of the Family': Domestic Servants in World Politics," in Enloe, *Bananas, Beaches and Bases: Making Feminist Sense of International Politics* (Berkeley: Univ. of California Press, 1990), 177–201.

The 1980 documentary film, *Yes Ma'am*, produced by the Louisiana Committee on the Humanities, is a revealing depiction of the two worlds at play in "white lady–Black maid" relationships. White families are shown as patronizing and smug, sometimes lavishing "affection" on their elderly Black female servants and giving them gifts and birthday cakes as "one of their own," while ignoring the structural inequities of their separate lives. This film intercuts images of Black servants in their white workplaces with scenes of them in their own homes and cultural settings. The contrast is jolting, as maids in their own communities express anger, self-confidence, and determination to organize to improve their working conditions.

65. These are the words of Pauline Breedlove in Toni Morrison's *Bluest Eye*, 97, 100. One of the most despairing portraits of Black maids in literature, Pauline comes to detest her own shabby surroundings and fantasizes about privileged white portrayals in movies: "white men taking such good care of they women, and they all dressed up in big clean houses with the bathtubs right in the same room with the toilet." Pauline, basking in the luxury of her white mistress's home, "became the ideal servant." When she bathed the little white girl instead of her own children, she reveled in the comfort of fluffy white towels, combed silky blonde hair, and despised her own dreary life. Morrison's description of such a dynamic makes us feel the agony of material denials and understand how the very institution of servanthood rubbed Black maids' noses in luxuries denied their own families:

> No zinc tub, no buckets of stove-heated water, no flaky, stiff, grayish towels washed in a kitchen sink, dried in a dusty backyard, no tangled black puffs of

rough wool to comb. Soon she stopped trying to keep her own house. The things she could afford to buy did not last, had no beauty or style, and were absorbed by the dingy storefront. More and more she neglected her house, her children, her man — they were like the afterthoughts one had just before sleep . . . the dark edges that made the daily life with the Fishers lighter, more delicate, more lovely . . . Here her foot flopped around on deep pile carpets. . . . She reigned over cupboards stacked high with food that would not be eaten for weeks, even months; she was queen of canned vegetables bought by the case. . . . The creditors and service people who humiliated her when she went to them on her own behalf respected her, were even intimidated by her, when she spoke for the Fishers. . . . Power, praise, and luxury were hers in this household.

66. See Elaine Bell Kaplan's review of Judith Rollins, *Between Women*, in which Kaplan discusses these burdens in her own life growing up the child of a Black maid. "Oppression Begins at Home," *Women's Review of Books* 3, no. 5 (Feb. 1986):7.

67. Quoted in Yancy, "Dorothy Bolden, Organizer of Domestic Workers," 53. One of the most memorable moments in Jesse Jackson's speech at the 1988 Democratic party convention was his recounting of his youth as a poor "illegitimate" son of a single mother who labored in the homes of whites as a maid. He spoke of the many idle holidays he and his siblings spent in Columbia, South Carolina, waiting alone all day for their mother to return home late in the evening with leftovers, so that they could begin their own celebrations.

That white America generally is oblivious to the emotional toll such absences take on so many Black and immigrant families in service jobs is startlingly illustrated in Woody Allen's film, *Hannah and Her Sisters*. A paean to New York City bourgeois family life, Allen's camera literally glows with warmth in the many scenes of the white families' sumptuous Thanksgiving fetes, with clinking glasses, gourmet food, friends and family singing around the piano. As the camera repeatedly pans these tableaux, a peripheral, shadowy figure can be seen in the background ministering to the revelers present: the smiling Black female maid in crisp black uniform and starched white collar. Her own absent family (celebrating at home alone?) becomes a cinematic absence, a lack. The invisible Black family offscreen voices (at least in the minds of some viewers) a silent protest against this racist scene.

68. This is Elizabeth Fox-Genovese's characterization, in *Within the Plantation Household*, of female relationships in the plantation household of southern white slaveholding mistresses. Her interpretation of these complex relationships between white mistress and Black female slave is surprisingly biased in favor of white women, enamored as she is of the white mistresses' metaphor, "my family, black and white." Fox-Genovese's affection for the

articulate, emotional, dutiful (with respect to her "white family," that is) white women leaps off the page; she is generously sympathetic to the self-described lives recorded in their diaries. She ultimately minimizes the horror and brute power visited on Black slave women, whose pain and victimization are never felt in Fox-Genovese's prose. At one point, Fox-Genovese concludes haughtily, "The inherent injustice and inevitable atrocities [of white mistresses] need not be belabored" (132). And her equanimity with respect to the exercise of the white woman's privilege and power leads her to comment admiringly on their lack of "neurotic inhibition," (240). These white women are characterized as "remarkably attractive people who loved their children, their husbands, their families . . ." (243). One is left to ponder to what extent these white women brought such "decent" qualities to bear against the economic and social system of slavery, an institution which provided for their own sense of "largesse." We ought to ask, as did Fox-Genovese's reviewer Christine Stansell, what a more critical feminist analysis of the "collective psychology of female niceness and its place in the slave regime" would have revealed about failed sisterhood (Stansell, "Explosive Intimacy," *The Nation*, 27 Mar. 1989, pp. 417–22, esp. 420). With her usage of the phrase "white lady and Black servant," Fox-Genovese adopts the slaveholding women's point of view in many discussions. It is doubtful that Black female slaves in bondage thought of themselves as "servants" or found their often brutal "superiors" as being in any way repositories of gentility. Although she records the voices of Black slave women as they tell of often barbaric beatings, physical assaults, and deaths at the hands of white slaveholding women, she minimizes the depth of their pain. In a particularly shocking formulation, Fox-Genovese writes as if the institution and prerogatives of "motherhood" were shared equally by Black slaves and their mistresses: "Slaveholders and slaves both acknowledged the special pain of separating mothers and children by sale" (322). But surely not to the same degree! As Jacqueline Jones, in "One Big Happy Family?", *Women's Review of Books* 6, no. 5 (Feb. 1989):4, rightly asserts of Fox-Genovese's work, the bottom line is missing from this book.

69. Minrose C. Gwin, *Black and White Women of the Old South* (Knoxville: Univ. of Tennesee Press, 1985), 5.

70. Judith Rollins, *Between Women*, 183.

71. Ibid., 184.

72. Hazel Carby, *Reconstructing Womanhood*, 26.

73. Maya Angelou writes in her autobiography, *I Know Why the Caged Bird Sings* (New York: Bantam, 1969), 90–92, esp. 91, of the arrogant manner in which her white employer changed her name from Margaret to Mary. Margaret, the white woman asserted, was "too long." Angelou tells us how vital the possession of one's name is to African Americans:

> Every person I knew had a hellish horror of being "called out of his name." It was a dangerous practice to call a Negro anything that could be loosely construed as insulting because of the centuries of their having been called niggers, jigs, dinges,blackbirds, crows, boots and spooks" (91).

74. Rollins, *Between Women*, 200.

75. Historian Gerda Lerner's description of the existence of urban street-corner labor markets in the 1940s in the Bronx and Brooklyn gives us another example of Black women's exploitation as "day maids." To these modern versions of slavery's auction blocks, white women came each morning to pick over and bargain for the services of Black women, some of them as young as 15. Lerner, *Black Women in White America*, 229–30.

76. Kathy Dobie's revealing article, "Black Women, White Kids, A Tale of Two Worlds," *Village Voice*, 12 Jan. 1988, pp. 20–27, chronicles the working lives of contemporary women of color, many of them immigrants, as they labor as maids in New York City. Her interviews with such women tell us that the demands made of them and their own families replicate, systemically and emotionally, longstanding patterns of economic and racial exploitation.

77. Childress, *Like One of the Family*, xxxii.

78. June Jordan, "Report from the Bahamas," in Jordan, *On Call: Political Essays* (Boston: South End Press, 1985), 46, 41.

79. Ibid., 41.

80. Ibid., 46.

81. Lorraine Bethel, "What Chou Mean *We* White Girl?", in *Conditions: Five The Black Woman's Issue* 2, no. 2 (1979):86.

82. Mary Helen Washington, *Black-Eyed Susans* (Garden City, N.J.: Anchor, 1975), xviii.

83. Ibid., xix–xx.

84. Adrienne Rich, "Disloyal to Civilization," 307.

85. Carolyn Di Palma reminds me that these issues are a part of some lesbian discourse as well. In carving out an oppositional identity, lesbians pay close attention to the signifiers of lesbian identity. Who carries a purse, who wears a dress, who has long hair, who wears makeup?

Shane Phelan offers an insightful reading of the dynamics of lesbian community and identity building, while critically assessing the essentializing tendencies which lead to dogmatic, "politically correct" strictures. Shane Phelan, *Identity Politics: Lesbian Feminism and the Limits of Community* (Philadelphia: Temple Univ. Press, 1989), passim, but esp. 37–134.

86. See Wendy Chapkis's compelling analyses of these issues in her discussion of lesbian styles of dressing and eroticism, *Beauty Secrets*, 133–40.

Also refer to Elizabeth Wilson's provocative detailing of the cultural politics of fashion, esp. the chapter "Oppositional Dress," in *Adorned in Dreams: Fashion and Modernity* (Berkeley: Univ. of California Press, 1985), 179–206.

87. One of Chinua Achebe's characters in his novel, *Anthills of the Savannah* (New York: Anchor/Doubleday, 1987), 131, exposes the hypocrisy of elite cheerleaders for the oppressed. In Achebe's story, a high-ranking official adopts a downward-mobility lifestyle, deliberately below his "rank," in order to identity with the African masses. Ikem, the elite journalist, recognizes his condescending attitude and learns that the poor *can* tell the difference: "the oppressor must not be allowed to camouflage his appearance or confuse the poor by stealing and masquerading in their clothes. . . . [the poor insist] that your badge of privilege must never leave your breast."

88. Surely it matters whether we purchase "folk items" from multinational department stores which plunder these treasures at criminally low prices on buying sweeps to Third-World countries, or from indigenous producers, street vendors, neighborhood fairs, or institutions such as the nonprofit organization "Pueblo to People" (PTP), 1616 Montrose #3900, Houston TX 77006. This mail-order marketing cooperative markets Central American goods whose conditions of production are amply described in the group's brochures. PTP supports local Central and South American grassroots craft and agricultural collectives, often underwriting such community-based enterprises. Its catalogs contain essays on the working conditions, problems, and needs of indigenous laborers, as well as information about support organizations and small-scale development projects to which buyers can contribute.

We ought not to be naive, however about the "feel-good" marketing techniques of multinational capital. Any cultural theme (including antiracism) is grist for the profit mill. The trendy Italian clothing manufacturer, Benetton, rocked the advertising world with its innovative "multicultural" advertising campaign using photographs of young Asian, African-American, Hispanic, white, and Arab models, often entwined in one another's arms or hugging and kissing (one ad released in Europe dared to image a Black female with a white infant nursing her breast). Some of these ads can appear socially progressive and joyful; I have even used them in my classes to discuss the politics of race, class, and gender, pointing out that the interracial conviviality expressed by the young models might not be so "naturalized" without the gorgeous clothing on their backs.

The hypocrisy of Benetton's racial commitments is exposed by the experience of University of Wisconsin law professor Patricia Williams. A light-skinned Black woman in her thirties, Williams attempted to enter a Benetton shop in New York City, where most trendy boutiques employ locked doors and buzzer systems to keep out "undesirables" (read "youth of color"). She buzzed several times, saw white customers inside, and made eye contact with the salesclerk, only to be ignored and refused entry into the shop.

Williams is arch and ironic telling the saga of the legal machinations that aimed to thwart her ability to write about, discuss at legal conferences and politicize such issues. She submitted an article to a law review about Benetton's apartheid; the review *deleted* the name of the corporation; she resisted the excision; the review declined her article. She was warned by the review's editor that she (a respected legal scholar) could face legal action if she persisted in her remarks against Benetton. Her Kafkaesque tale was related at the seminar on "Rethinking Rights: Law, Social Movements, and Institutional Reform," at New York University, 25 June 1990.

89. "Are My Hands Clean?" Words and music by Bernice Johnson Reagon, Songtalk Publishing Co., copyright, 1987, recorded by Sweet Honey in the Rock for Flying Fish Records. The song chronicles the economic journey of multinational textile manufacturing. A blouse is produced by the exploited labor of a Central American female textile worker, "a Third World Sister," toiling doing piecework for American retail corporations; the fabric is made from cotton "from the blood-soaked fields of El Salvador," in a province "soaked in blood, [where] pesticide-sprayed workers toil in a broiling sun, pulling cotton for two dollars a day." Finally the garment is "wrapped in plastic" and sold to the American female customer at Sears for a "20% discount." Reagon's lyrics hit hard, forcing us to acknowledge global marketing networks which impoverish Third World workers and infuse Western consuming practices. Reagon's lyrics are quoted in Cynthia Enloe's book, *Bananas, Beaches, and Bases: Making Feminist Sense of International Politics*, 158. Enloe weaves female material and psychic labor into analyses which reveal international linkages, proving that "the personal is international."

90. Sara Suleri, *Meatless Days* (Chicago: Univ. of Chicago Press, 1989).

91. bell hooks, "Stylish Nihilism at the Movies," 27.

92. Trinh T. Mihn-ha, *Woman Native Other*, 88.

93. Quoted in Adele Jones and Group, "Ebony Minds and Black Voices, in *The Black Woman*, ed. Cade, 181.

94. This phrase is from Jo Carrillo's poem, "And When You Leave, Take Your Pictures with You," in ed. Moraga and Anzaldúa, *This Bridge Called My Back*, 63–64. This poem rejects the romanticized images of Third-World women held by some white feminists, who, when they "see us in the flesh . . . are not quite as sure if they like us as much. We're not as happy as we look on their wall." I want to borrow Carrillo's imagery here to suggest that we all occasionally hold erroneous "pictures" of one another in our minds, and

to suggest that we go slow in our deliberations about what those pictures really tell us.

95. Walter Benjamin is discussing the artistic manifestos of Marinetti and the Italian Futurists in the conclusion to his essay, "The Work of Art in the Age of Mechanical Reproduction," in Benjamin, *Illuminations* (New York: Schocken, 1969), 241–42.

96. In a series of interviews given at the time her autobiography, *I Tina* (New York: Avon, 1986), was published, Tina Turner confided her dissatisfaction with her "big, raunchy, body and sexy image," her desire for public acceptability as a "lady" with "class": "But society doesn't look [at me] as class, that type of woman . . . it was the high-class black people I wanted respect from. . . . I am raunchy. But I know I'm a lady and that deep inside me there's a craving for class. . . . what I always wanted was the principal's daughters' world." See Nancy Collins, "The Rolling Stones Interview: Tina Turner," *Rolling Stone*, 23 Oct. 1986, p. 108. Turner's courageous publicizing of her years of sexual and physical abuse by Ike Turner, however, is an indication of her fierce determination to survive and of her solidarity with countless other women who have endured battering. She had spoken for them.

97. Chapkis, *Beauty Secrets*, 174–75.

Chapter 5

1. Two groundbreaking essays by Rosalyn Terborg-Penn document these historical errors: "Discrimination Against Afro-American Women in the Woman's Movement, 1830–1920," in *The Afro-American Woman*, ed. Sharon Harley and Rosalyn Terborg-Penn, 17–27 (Port Washington, N.Y.: Kennikat, 1978); Rosalyn Terborg-Penn, "Discontented Black Feminists: Prelude and Postscript to the Passage of the Nineteenth Amendment," in *Decades of Discontent: The Woman's Movement, 1920–1940*, ed. Lois Scharf and Joan M. Jensen (Westport, Conn.: Greenwood, 1983), 261–78.

2. This is a radicalization of Gerda Lerner's phrase that, since men have defined their experience as history and omitted women, for women, all history is "prehistory." It follows that, since white women have defined their history as feminist history, for Black women, all history is similarly prehistory. Gerda Lerner, *The Majority Finds Its Past: Placing Women in History* (Oxford, Eng.: Oxford Univ. Press, 1979), xxxi.

3. Hymowitz and Weissman, *A History of Women in America*, 96; Lerner, *Majority Finds Its Past*, 111.

4. Lerner, *Majority Finds Its Past*, 73–74.

5. Barbara Omolade, "Black Women and Feminism," in *The Future of*

Difference, ed. Hester Eisenstein and Alice Jardine, 247–57 (Boston: G.K. Hall, 1980); bell hooks, *Ain't I a Woman*; Hazel Carby, "'On the Threshold of Woman's Era': Lynching, Empire, and Sexuality in Black Feminist Theory," *Critical Inquiry 12* (Autumn 1985):262–77; Hazel Carby, *Reconstructing Womanhood*; Angela Davis, *Women, Race and Class* (New York: Random House, 1983); Angela Davis, "Reflections on the Black Woman's Role," 3–15; Paula Giddings, *When and Where I Enter: The Impact of Black Women on Race and Sex in America* (New York: William Morrow, 1984). In addition, Terborg-Penn, "To Find A Place in History," *Women's Review of Books* 2, no. 10 (July 1985):10–11, provides a theoretical survey of epistemological approaches to the study of Black women historically—racial integrationist, black nationalist, socialist-feminist, Marxist-feminist.

6. Paula Giddings, "Black Feminism Takes Its Rightful Place," *Ms.* Oct. 1985, pp. 25–26.

7. hooks, *Ain't I a Woman?*, 124.

8. Angela Davis, *Women, Race and Class*, 148.

9. Harley and Terborg-Penn, *Afro-American Woman*, 27.

10. Hymowitz and Weissman, *A History of Women in America*, 159. In this text, the authors devote three and one-half pages to "Black Women," in which they discuss the Black "matriarchy," SES data, and Rosa Parks (336–40).

11. All Harper quotes from Dorothy Sterling, *We Are Your Sisters: Black Women in the Nineteenth Century* (New York: Norton, 1984), 405.

12. hooks, *Ain't I a Woman?*, 161.

13. Quoted in Lerner, *Black Women in White America*, 574, 573.

14. Cooper's poem quoted in Sharon Harley, "Anna J. Cooper: A Voice for Black Women," in Harley and Terborg-Penn, *Afro-American Woman*, 91.

15. Quoted in Lerner, *Black Women in White America*, 575.

16. Carby, "On the Threshold of Woman's Era," 266.

17. Giddings, "Black Feminism," 30.

18. Omolade, "Black Women and Feminism," 251.

19. Gloria T. Hull, Patricia Bell Scott, and Barbara Smith, *But Some of Us Are Brave*, xxi.

20. Omolade, "Black Women and Feminism," 252. For a survey of early Black political resistance, see Philip Foner, ed., *Life and Writings of Frederick Douglass* (New York: International Publishers, 1975), vol. 1.

21. Linda Perkins, "Black Women and Racial 'Uplift' Prior to Emancipation," in *The Black Woman Cross-Culturally*, ed. Filomina Chioma Steady (Cambridge, Mass.: Schenkman, 1981), 319–20.

22. Robert Allen, with the collaboration of Pamela P. Allen, *Reluctant Reformers, Racism and Social Reform Movements in the United States* (Washington, D.C.: Howard Univ. Press, 1983), 6.

23. Ellen Carol DuBois, *Feminism and Suffrage: The Emergence of an Independent Woman's Movement in America, 1848–1869* (Ithaca, N.Y.: Cornell Univ. Press, 1978). Ellen Carol DuBois, ed., *Elizabeth Cady Stanton–Susan B. Anthony Correspondence, Writings, Speeches* (New York: Schocken, 1981). Alma Lutz, *Created Equal: A Biography of Elizabeth Cady Stanton* (New York: Octagon Books, 1974). Blanche Glassman Hersh, *The Slavery of Sex: Feminist-Abolitionists in America* (Urbana: Univ. of Illinois Press, 1978); of the 51 women in this study, none is Black. Aileen S. Kraditor, *Means and Ends in American Abolitionism: Garrison and His Critics on Strategy and Tactics, 1834–1850* (New York: Vintage, 1969). Aileen S. Kraditor, *The Ideas of the Woman Suffrage Movement, 1890–1920* (Garden City, N.Y.: Anchor Books, 1971); June Sochen, *Herstory: A Woman's View of American History* (Sherman Oaks, Calif.: Alfred Publishing, 1981). Barbara Deckard, *The Women's Movement* (New York: Harper & Row, 1975), 248–84. Judith Hole and Ellen Levine, eds., *Rebirth of Feminism* (New York: Quadrangle/New York Times Book Co., 1971), 1–14. Barbara Berg, *The Remembered Gate.* Jennie C. Croly, *History of the General Federation of Women's Clubs* (New York, 1898); this 1,100-page narrative omits any record of Black women's organizing and provides no reference to the national organization of Negro women's clubs begun in Boston in 1895.

As a nonhistorian, I do not intend to enter the stream of historiographical debates; as Bettina Aptheker rightly reminds me, it is problematical to divide historians along racial lines. Nevertheless, the extent to which the contributions of the 19th-century Black female activists have been ignored by so many white "feminist" historians is striking. The excellent research of Aptheker herself and of other white feminist scholars, such as Gerda Lerner, Jacqueline Dowd Hall, Jacqeuline Jones, Pamela Allen, Dorothy Sterling, Minrose Gwin, Barbara Hilkert Andolsen, and Adrienne Rich, has helped to bring early Black feminists alive. Part of our contemporary political project involves a struggle over this historical terrain.

24. Hymowitz and Weissman, *A History of Women in America*, 98, 152, 223. Many popular white feminist accounts neglect the career of Black feminist, suffragist, educator, and journalist Mary Ann Shadd. An outstanding exception is Dorothy Sterling, *We Are Your Sisters*, 164–75, 165, 223, 227, 231–32, 257–58, 168–72; and Harley and Terborg-Penn, *Afro-American Woman*, 26–27.

25. hooks, *Ain't I a Woman?*, 163.

26. Alice S. Rossi, ed., *The Feminist Papers: From Adams to de Beauvoir* (New York: Bantam, 1973). The only contribution by a Black woman in this volume is a three-page speech by Sojourner Truth, 426–29.

27. Quoted in Lerner, *Black Women in White America*, 553.

28. Mary Church Terrell, *A Colored Woman in a White World* (Wash-

ington, D.C.: Ransdell, 1940), first page of the introduction. Also see Beverly Washington Jones, *Quest for Equality: The Life and Writings of Mary Eliza Church Terrell*, vol. 13, Black Women in United States History, ed. Darlene Clark Hine (New York: Carlson Publishing, 1990). The Jones volume contains an excellent overview of the Black women's club movement.

29. Quoted in Sharon Harley, "Anna J. Cooper: A Voice for Black Women," 88, 96, 89.

30. Quoted in Sterling, *We Are Your Sisters*, 435–36.

31. Quoted in Lerner, *Black Women in White America*, 578–79.

32. Lerner, *Black Women in White America*, 83.

33. Giddings, *When and Where I Enter*, 50, 52, 53, 52. Also see the new collection of Stewart's essays and speeches: Marilyn Richardson, ed., *Maria Stewart, America's First Black Woman Political Writer* (Bloomington: Indiana Univ. Press, 1989).

34. Giddings, *When And Where I Enter*, 55.

35. Lerner, *Black Women in White America*, 564–65.

36. Giddings, *When and Where I Enter*, 52.

37. Lerner, *Black Women in White America*, 530.

38. Quoted in Sterling, *We Are Your Sisters*, 154–55.

39. Ibid., 156.

40. Phyllis Palmer, "White Women/Black Women: The Dualism of Female Identity and Experience in the United States," *Feminist Studies* 9, no. 1 (Spring 1983):152.

41. Quoted in Rossi, *Feminist Papers*, 426, 428.

42. Lerner, *Majority Finds Its Past*, 95.

43. Rossi, *Feminist Papers*, 427.

44. Angela Davis, *Women, Race and Class*, 63.

45. Quoted in ibid., 64.

46. Quoted in Giddings, *When and Where I Enter*, 172.

47. Frederick Douglass, *The Life and Times of Frederick Douglass* (1892; rptd. New York: Macmillan, Collier Books, 1962), 469.

48. Bettina Aptheker, *Woman's Legacy*; 13.

49. For accounts of racism in the abolitionist movement and the exclusion of Black female antislavery activists, see Lerner, *Black Women in White America*, 361–70, esp. 368, for expressions from Black female abolitionist leaders Sarah M. Douglass and Charlotte Forten Grimké. Blacks were routinely segregated from white "Christians" at abolitionist meetings and forced to sit alone on church benches reserved for Blacks. Lerner also reprints Clarissa Lawrence's poignant statement to the Anti-Slavery Convention of American Women in Philadelphia in 1838. Lawrence's words speak to the great struggle of Blacks who desperately sought white allies to end slavery: "We meet the

monster prejudice everywhere. We have not power to contend with it, we are so down-trodden. We cannot elevate ourselves. . . . We want light; we ask it; and it is denied us. Why are we thus treated? Prejudice is the cause." (Quoted in Lerner, *Black Women in White America*, 359.) Omolade's interpretation of white abolitionist work, "Black Women and Feminism," 252, stresses the exclusion of Black women. Lerner, in contrast, claims that "antislavery women showed a greater awareness of the implications of prejudice than their contemporaries; their meetings were integrated"; further, Lerner argues that white female antislavery reformers maintained interracial meetings. As proof of this, she cites one instance in 1835 when the Boston and the Philadelphia Female Anti-Slavery Societies were faced with mob actions because of that policy. In Boston, "Negro" and white women linked arms as they marched out in pairs through the exercised mob. Lerner, *Majority Finds Its Past*, 98. Historian Eleanor Flexner recounts this incident—where Garrison was dragged through the streets at the end of a rope—as follows: "At the direction of Maria Weston Chapman, each white lady present took a colored 'sister' by the hand, and two by two, they walked calmly down the stairs and out the building, . . . their eyes busily identifying the genteel leaders of the mob." Flexner, *Century of Struggle: The Woman's Rights Movement in the United States* (Cambridge, Mass.: Harvard University Press, Belknap Press, 1950), 43. This one example is not taken as representative of interracial practice by Black feminist scholars such as Omolade, hooks, Perkins, Giddings, and Harley and Terborg-Penn, however.

Consult also Giddings, *Where and Where I Enter*, 55; and Perkins, "Black Women and 'Racial Uplift,'" 318, 322, 323. Perkins stresses Black self-reliance and initiative in protesting slavery through coordinated boycotts of slave-made products, and other strategies such as violence and legal petitioning. It is interesting to note, in relation to the racial dynamics of the abolitionist movement, that most white female abolitionists preferred to have Black males rather than Black females in their organizations. This suggests the extent to which white women had internalized the idea of male superiority and demonstrates the distance which conflicting ideals of "womanhood" created between Black and white women. Harley and Terborg-Penn note that Frederick Douglass, William C. Nell, and Charles Lenox Remond, all feminist supporters as well as abolitionists, recorded the support of white female abolitionists. Historian Louis Filler has written that in the mid-19th-century the best-known women's rights advocates were Black men: Frederick Douglass; Charles Remond; James Forten, Sr.; James Forten, Jr.; Robert Purvis; Charles Purvis; William Whiper; William J. Whiper; C. Nell; James McCune Smith; Jermain Loguen; Henry Highland Garnet; and George T. Downing. Harley and Terborg-Penn, *Afro-American Woman*, 19, and esp. Terborg-Penn's essay,

"Black Male Perspectives on the 19th-Century Woman," 28–42. Bettina Aptheker recounts the story of white abolitionist Lucretia Mott, who, when founding the Philadelphia Female Anti-Slavery Society, had to call on James McCrummell, "a colored man," to conduct the meeting for her. Aptheker, *Woman's Legacy,* 18–19.

A recent work by Jean Fagan Yellin, *Women and Sisters: Antislavery Feminists in American Culture* (New Haven, Conn.: Yale Univ. Press, 1990), provides an important reading of interracial feminist solidarity among Angelina Grimké, L. Maria Child, Sojourner Truth, and Harriet Jacobs — all female activists committed to the double crusade to liberate all women as well as all slaves.

50. hooks, *Ain't I a Woman?,* 125.

51. Robert Allen, *Reluctant Reformers,* 35:

> Few whites, however, deigned to mingle with their black co-workers as social peers. Such conduct was both unpopular and uncommon. Racists asserted that social intermingling led to interracial marriages and thus defiled the "pure" blood of the white race. White abolitionists accepted this argument and went to great lengths to deny that they were amalgamationists. "We do not encourage intermarriage between the whites and blacks," said the New Hampshire Anti-Slavery Society in a notice to the public. . . . Lydia Maria Child, an advocate of racial equality, termed the race mixing issue "a false charge . . . " yet she could not resist adding that "by universal emancipation we want to *stop* amalgamation." Even Garrison found it expedient to admit that "at the present time mixed marriages would be in bad taste."

52. Davis, *Women, Race and Class,* 32–33; also see Davis, "Black Women and Feminism," 252.

53. hooks, *Ain't I a Woman?,* 126. hooks's criticism may be correct in a general sense, but Abby Kelly, Lucretia Mott, and Charlotte and Angelina Grimké all practiced social equality with Blacks in their personal lives. Sterling, *We Are Your Sisters,* 130, contains the intimate letters of the Black abolitionist-feminist, Sarah M. Douglass, to her close friend and political ally, Abby Kelly.

54. Lerner, *Majority Finds Its Past,* 103, 111.

55. Hymowitz and Weissman, *A History of Women in America,* 81.

56. Sara Evans, *Personal Politics: The Roots of Women's Liberation in the Civil Rights Movement and the New Left* (New York: Vintage, 1980), 26, 25.

57. Angelina Grimké, *Letters to Catherine E. Beecher,* (Arno Press and the New York Times, 1969), quoted in Adrienne Rich, "Disloyal to Civilization," 277; Gerda Lerner, *The Grimké Sisters from South Carolina: Pioneers for Women's Rights and Abolition* (New York: Schocken, 1971); Yellin, *Women and Sisters*; Aptheker, *Woman's Legacy,* 23.

58. Davis, *Women, Race and Class*, 39.

59. Lerner, *Grimké Sisters*, 353.

60. Ellen Carol DuBois, *Stanton-Anthony Correspondence*, 78.

61. Aptheker, *Woman's Legacy*, 40.

62. Ellen Carol DuBois, *Stanton-Anthony Correspondence*, 90.

63. Elizabeth Cady Stanton, Susan B. Anthony, and Matilda Joslyn Gage, eds., *History of Woman Suffrage*, vol. 2 (1861–76) (Rochester, N.Y.: Charles Mann, 1887), 172.

64. Aptheker, *Woman's Legacy*, 42.

65. Stanton, Anthony, and Gage, *History of Woman Suffrage*, 2:220.

66. Flexner, *Century of Struggle*, 110–11.

67. For the full text of these amendments, see Robert Allen, *Reluctant Reformers*, 139–40, 144.

68. For accounts of this traumatic period from the white perspective, see Ellen Carol DuBois, *Feminism and Suffrage*, and Flexner, *Century of Struggle*, ch. 10.

69. Flexner, *Century of Struggle*, 147.

70. Quoted in Giddings, *When and Where I Enter*, 67–68.

71. Quoted in Flexner, *Century of Struggle*, 147.

72. Quoted in Hymowitz and Weissman, *A History of Women in America*, 158.

73. Ellen Carol DuBois, *Stanton-Anthony Correspondence*, 92.

74. Quoted in Ida Husted Harper, *History of Woman Suffrage*, vol. 5 (New York: J.J. Little and Ives, 1922), 77.

75. In her discussion of Simone de Beauvoir, Mary Lowenthal Felstiner points to this contradiction: "Seeing *The Second Sex* through the Second Wave," *Feminist Studies* 6, no. 2 (Summer 1980):247–76.

76. Robert Allen, *Reluctant Reformers*, 147.

77. Ibid., 141.

78. Flexner, *Century of Struggle*, 148.

79. All quotations from Aptheker, *Woman's Legacy*, 46–47.

80. All quotations from Giddings, *When and Where I Enter*, 65. Vis-à-vis the sexist proclivities of 19th-century Black males, see James Oliver Horton, "Freedom's Yoke," 51–76.

81. Giddings, *Where and Where I Enter*, 67.

82. Robert Allen, *Reluctant Reformers*, 147. Allen makes the further point that Anthony's legalistic conception of citizenship blinded her to the survival struggle of Blacks. In May 1866, at the first woman's rights convention held after the Civil War, Anthony proposed that "by the act of emancipation and the Civil Rights Bills, the Negro and woman now had the same civil and political status, alike needing only the ballot." (143–44). Anthony seems to

have believed that these abstract declarations automatically led to material advancement, a premise the ex-slaves knew to be grievously wrong.

Susan A. Mann's study of changes in production and economic practices in the antebellum southern transition from slavery to sharecropping reveals few freedoms, especially for Black female workers. Males generally controlled their earnings in the patriarchally organized sharecropping households. Mann, "Slavery, Sharecropping, and Sexual Inequality," *Signs* 14, no. 4 (Summer 1989):774–98.

83. Robert Allen, *Reluctant Reformers*, 147.

84. Giddings, *When and Where I Enter*. 68.

85. Quoted in Aptheker, *Woman's Legacy*, 48.

86. This is Adrienne Rich's assessment, in "Disloyal to Civilization," 286.

87. Barbara Hilkert Andolsen, *"Daughters of Jefferson, Daughters of Bootblacks": Racism and American Feminism* (Macon, Ga.: Mercer Univ. Press, 1986), 7.

88. Ibid., 8–9.

89. Aptheker, *Woman's Legacy*, 49.

90. Ibid., 48–50.

91. Giddings, *When and Where I Enter*, 68.

92. Ellen Carol DuBois, *Stanton-Anthony Correspondence*, 92. Gerda Lerner, too, ascribes historical inevitability to white feminist abandonment of Black freedom: "They followed the spirit of the times," she writes, "in turning away from the race issue." Lerner, *Majority Finds Its Past*, 104.

93. Quoted in Eileen Borris, "Wordwatch" (review of *Feminism and Suffrage*), *Quest* 5, no. 4 (1982): 86.

94. E. Frances White, "Listening to the Voices of Black Feminism," *Radical America* 8, nos. 2–3 (Mar.-June 1984):7–24.

95. All quotes from Ellen Carol DuBois, *Stanton-Anthony Correspondence*, 93–94, 92, 98. Also see Aptheker's judgment, in *Woman's Legacy*, 12: "Indeed DuBois poses the break with abolitionism as the prerequisite for the emergence of an authentic, i.e., independent, women's movement in the United States."

96. Lerner, *Majority Finds Its Past*, 104.

97. DuBois, *Stanton-Anthony Correspondence*, 176; Flexner, *Century of Struggle*, 222.

98. Giddings, *When and Where I Enter*, 123.

99. Kraditor, *Ideas of the Woman Suffrage Movement*.

100. Quoted in Giddings, *When and Where I Enter*, 124.

101. Quoted in Hymowitz and Weissman, *A History of Women in America*, 276.

102. Ibid., 277.

103. Andolsen, *Daughters of Jefferson*, 13; Harley and Terborg-Penn, *Afro-American Woman*, 91. Ralph Ellison's biting essay on the southern Jim Crow bus system reflects the trauma, for African Americans, associated with the idea of "traveling":

> A Southern bus was a contraption contrived by laying the South's social pyramid on its side, knocking out a few strategic holes, and rendering it vehicular through the addition of engine, windows, and wheels . . . For blacks and whites alike, Southern buses were places of hallucination, but especially for Negroes. Because once inside, their journey ended even before the engine fired and the wheels got rolling. (Ellison, *Going to the Territory* (New York: Random House, 1986], quoted in Louis Menard, "Literature and Liberation," *New Republic*, 4 Aug. 1986, p. 40)

104. Lerone Bennett, Jr., *Before the Mayflower: A History of Black America*, 5th ed. (New York: Penquin, 1982), 274.

105. Davis, *Woman, Race and Class*, 117. See also C. Vann Woodward, *The Strange Career of Jim Crow*, 3d ed. (New York: Oxford Univ. Press, 1974).

106. All Cooper quotes from Carby, *Reconstructing Womanhood*, 106.

107. Ibid., 107.

108. Ibid.

109. Quoted in Hymowitz and Weissman, *A History of Women in America*, 276.

110. Quoted in Harper, *History of Woman Suffrage*, 5.

111. Andolsen, *Daughters of Jefferson*, 14; emphasis added.

112. Ibid., 15.

113. Carby, *Reconstructing Womanhood*, 105.

114. Harley and Terborg-Penn, *African-American Woman*, 24.

115. Ida B. Wells, *Crusade for Justice: The Auto-Biography of Ida B. Wells*, ed. Alfreda M. Duster (Chicago: Univ. of Chicago Press, 1970), 228–29.

116. Ibid., 230.

117. For a more thorough account of the racist practices in 20th century suffragist politics, see Andolsen, *Daughters of Jefferson*; and Terborg-Penn, "Discontented Black Feminists," 262: "It is a wonder that Afro-American women dared to dream a white man's dream — the right to enfranchisement — especially at a time when white women attempted to exclude them from that dream." Following Anthony as the leaders of NAWSA, Carrie Catt and Alice Paul displayed ugly racial attitudes toward Black women, excluding them from public parades and meetings and even supporting congressional provisions which would have barred Black women from suffrage. Also see Harley and Terborg-Penn, *African-American Woman*, 25.

In 1919, the Black educator, feminist, and activist Mary Church Terrell told the NAACP about white suffrage leader Alice Paul. Terrell admitted that she was highly skeptical of Paul's loyalty to Black women, concluding that "if she and other white suffragist leaders could get the amendment through without enfranchising black women they would." Giddings gives a detailed account of the machinations behind the anti-Black female suffrage amendments, in *When and Where I Enter*, 159–62. See also bell hooks, *Ain't I a Woman?*, 172. Hooks argues that the women's movement of the 1920s and the Woman's Party were both racist and classist, quoting historian June Sochen: "When suffragists suggested to Alice Paul that the voting rights of black women would be a continuing vital issue, she replied that the year 1920 was not the time to discuss that question" (*Herstory: A Record of the American Woman's Past* [Sherman Oaks, Calif.: Alfred Publishing, 1981], 253).

118. Robert Allen, *Reluctant Reformers*, 155.

119. Aptheker, *Woman's Legacy*, 51–52.

120. Darlene Clark Hine, *Black Women in White: Racial Conflict and Cooperation in the Nursing Profession, 1890–1950* (Bloomington: Indiana Univ. Press, 1990).

121. Carby, *Reconstructing Womanhood*.

122. Beverly Washington Jones, *Quest for Equality*.

123. Mildred I. Thompson, *Ida B. Wells-Barnett: An Exploratory Study of an American Black Woman, 1893–1930* (Brooklyn, N.Y.: Carlson Publishing, 1990), vol. 15 of the series Black Women in United States History, ser. ed. Darlene Clark Hine.

124. Beverly Washington Jones, *Quest for Equality*, ch. 2, pp. 17–29; Flexner, *Century of Struggle*, 195; Sterling, *We Are Your Sisters*, xiii.

125. Carby, *Reconstructing Womanhood*, 70–71.

126. Aptheker, *Woman's Legacy*, 65.

127. All quotes from Giddings, *When and Where I Enter*, 12.

128. Quoted in Sterling, *We Are Your Sisters*, 416–17.

129. Carby, *Reconstructing Womanhood*, 70.

130. Thompson, *Ida B. Wells-Barnett*, 127.

131. All three pamphlets, "A Red Record: Tabulated Statistics and Alleged Causes of Lynching in the United States, 1892–1894," "Southern Horrors," and "Mob Rule in New Orleans," are published in Ida B. Wells, *On Lynchings* (New York: Arno Press and the New York Times, 1969).

132. For accounts of Wells's personal bravery and political mobilization in resisting the lynchings, see Thompson, *Ida B. Wells-Barnett*; Wells, *Crusade for Justice*; Aptheker, *Woman's Legacy*, 60–61; Carby, *Reconstructing Womanhood*, 109–10.

133. Quoted in Thompson, *Ida B. Wells-Barnett*, 267.

134. Wells, *Crusade for Justice*, 64.

135. Wells, "Red Record," in Wells, *On Lynchings*, 9.

136. See Wells's essay, "How Enfranchisement Stops Lynching," in Thompson, *Ida B. Wells-Barnett*, 267–76.

137. Carby, *Reconstructing Womanhood*, 109–10.

138. Ibid., 111.

139. Aptheker, *Woman's Legacy*, 62–63.

140. Jean Fagan Yellin's interpretation of 19th-century feminist antislavery activists employs an ambiguous visual metaphor. The emblem was a common one used in abolitionist pamphlets. It depicts a Black woman kneeling, chained like an animal, while a white woman stands before her with extended hand. The white woman carries the scales of justice. A motto encircling the image reads, "Am I Not A Woman And A Sister?" Yellin traces the efforts of Angelina Grimké, L. Maria Child, Sojourner Truth, and Harriet Jacobs (the latter two were former slaves) to appropriate this emblem of the female supplicant to redefine their condition. I read this image as hypocritical, given the systematic abandonment of Black females by a great majority of white women in both North and South. Further, it depicts a relationship of hierarchy, with the white female the embodiment of justice and compassion, a dubious construction.

141. Quoted in Lerner, *Black Women in White America*, 575.

142. Quoted in Lorde, *Sister Outsider*, 130.

143. Quoted in hooks, *Ain't I a Woman?*, 169–70. For a historical-psychological analysis of lynching, see Jacqueline Dowd Hall, "'The Mind That Burns in Each Body': Women, Rape, and Racial Violence," in *Powers of Desire*, ed. Ann Snitow, Christine Stansel, and Sharon Thompson (New York: Monthly Review Press, 1983), 330–31. White southern women did briefly organize to combat lynching and mob violence in the 1930s, under the rubric of the Association of Southern Women for the Prevention of Lynching (ASWPL), led by Jessie Daniel Ames of Texas. These women, who briefly engaged in interracial efforts with Black women, deconstructed the fiction that such atrocities were done to protect white women against the rape of Black men; they also challenged the right of white men to claim "possession" of their honor. See Jacquelyn Dowd Hall, *Revolt Against Chivalry*; Aptheker, *Woman's Legacy*, 63–64; Lerner, *Black Women in White America*, 472–77. Black feminist historian Paula Giddings faults the ASWPL and its leaders for exhibiting a patronizing attitude toward Blacks, whom they expected to be passive participants in the interracial efforts. Giddings also points out the grievous position taken by the organization in 1931, when it failed to come to the aid of the nine innocent Black men accused, in the Scottsboro trial, of raping white women. See Giddings, *When and Where I Enter*, 208–9.

144. Quoted in Lerner, *Black Women in White America*, 470; Andolsen, *Daughters of Jefferson*, 59–60.

145. Quoted in hooks, *Ain't I a Woman?*, 193.

146. Ibid., 164.

147. Carby, *Reconstructing Womanhood*, 115.

148. This is Woodward's thesis in *Thinking Back: The Perils of Writing History* (Baton Rouge: Louisiana State Univ. Press, 1986). In this work, he took the position that to view the the American apartheid system (which he had interpreted in *The Strange Career of Jim Crow*) statically would immobilize popular efforts to enact social change. The structures of white supremacy and desegregation had to be viewed historically, Woodward advised; to avoid historical despair, one must have an appreciation of change. Bertram Wyatt-Brown, "The Sound and the Fury," *New York Review of Books*, 13 Mar. 1986, p. 15.

Chapter 6

1. Iris M. Young, "The Ideal of Community," 301.

2. Michelle Cliff, "The Making of Americans: Maxine Hong Kingston's Crossover Dreams," *Village Voice Literary Supplement*, May 1989, 11. It was Cliff's ingenious phrase which inspired the title of this chapter.

3. Spelman, *Inessential Woman*, 13.

4. Luce Irigaray, *This Sex Which Is Not One*, tr. Catherine Porter with Carolyn Burke (Ithaca, N.Y.: Cornell Univ. Press), 161.

5. Lorde, *Sister Outsider*, 116.

6. My understanding of Sandoval's theory is filtered through Donna Haraway's reading in "Cyborgs," 197–98.

The self-identification of women of color is sometimes contested by other women of color on the grounds of "inauthentic" locations, as in the case of the British-exiled Nigerian feminist writer Buche Emecheta. The Nigerian "womanist" (not Alice Walker's articulation of this term, but Ogunyemi's own) literary critic, Chikwenye Okonjo Ogunyemi, has challenged Emecheta's Western-oriented "feminism" and the novelist's legitimacy as a salutary model of African womanhood, because of Emecheta's criticism of African traditional patriarchal marriage customs. Ogunyemi questioned Emecheta's authority to speak about Nigerian gender relations in her fiction, because of Emecheta's hybrid status as an "exiled" Nigerian involved with international feminist theories and activism. See Ogunyemi, "The Dynamics of the Contemporary Black Female Novel in English," *Signs* 11, no. 1 (Autumn 1985): 63–80; Donna Haraway points out Ogunyemi's contestation of Emecheta's legitimacy in Haraway, "Reading Buchi Emecheta," 107–24.

Another example of the difficulties and contested nature of "women of color" concerns criteria of acceptable skin color. A white-skinned Chicana, Cherríe Moraga expressed her trauma and ambivalence over inclusion in texts written "exclusively" by Third-World women: "I have had to look critically at my claim to color," she explains, "at a time when, among white feminist ranks, it is a 'politically correct' [and sometimes peripherally advantageous] assertion to make. I must acknowledge the fact that, physically, I have had a *choice* about making that claim, in contrast to women who have not had such a choice, and have been abused for their color." See Moraga's essay "La Güera" in Moraga and Anzaldúa, *This Bridge Called My Back*, 33–34.

7. Elly Bulkin, "Hard Ground: Jewish Identity, Racism, and Anti-Semitism," in Bulkin, Pratt, and Smith, *Yours in Struggle*, 89–203.

8. Quoted in Alice Wexler, *Emma Goldman in Exile: From the Russian Revolution to the Spanish Civil War* (Boston: Beacon, 1989), p. 95.

9. These are the words of the French filmmaker and novelist Marguerite Duras. Ever attuned to political contradictions, Duras has written about her attempt to deprogram herself of the romanticized attitudes she held toward "the proletariat" during her years as a member of the French Communist party. As an intellectual member of the *avant-garde*, Duras adopted the quiescent approval demanded of her class toward the insular and often dogmatic practices of workers with whom she associated in party activities. "When I was a secretary in the cell, I would never have dared to attack an immigrant worker straight-on," Duras remarked. The iconoclastic politics of May 1968, however, freed her both to struggle in solidarity with and to contest the oppressed other: "Before '68 I would hot have been able, would not have dared [criticize workers' conformism]. Now I can see a worker and talk to him like an equal." Marguerite Duras, *Marguerite Duras* (San Francisco, Calif.: City Lights Books, 1987), 117.

10. William E. Connolly theorizes a useful neo-Nietzchean analytic which includes both genealogies and problematics. The aim of such methodological attitudes can be to scramble "the network through which thought has been organized." "A problematic sets a frame within which questions are posed and a range of possible responses are opened to reflection and debate." Connolly, *Political Theory and Modernity* (New York: Basil Blackwell, 1988), 140.

11. I've borrowed the alchemical strategy from Patricia Williams, "Alchemical Notes: Reconstructing Ideals from Deconstructed Rights," *Harvard Civil Rights–Civil Liberties Law Review* 22 (1987):401.

12. Combahee River Collective, "A Black Feminist Statement," in Moraga and Anzaldúa, in *This Bridge Called My Back*, 213–14.

13. The fascinating concept of picture thoughts is Jane Bennett's, from her *Unthinking Faith and Enlightenment: Nature and the State in a Post-*

Hegelian Era (New York: New York Univ. Press, 1987), which came to me via Kathy Ferguson's interpretation in her manuscript, *The Man Question: Reversals and Their Discontents in Feminist Theory* (Berkeley: Univ. of California Press, forthcoming), 92.

14. I'm tripping a bit here the deconstructive analyses of "woman" of Denise Riley, *"Am I That Name?": Feminism and the Category of "Women" in History* (Minneapolis: Univ. of Minnesota, 1988), 6, 4–5.

15. Julia Kristeva, "Woman, Can Never Be Defined," in *New French Feminisms*, ed. Elaine Marks and Isabelle de Courtivron, (New York: Schocken, 1981), 137.

16. Ferguson, *The Man Question: Reversals and Their Discontents*, 32.

17. "Inspired by Gospel and African Rhythms, Sweet Honey in the Rock Delivers Political Punch A Cappella," *People* (1990).

18. Bernice Johnson Reagon, "Coalition Politics: Turning the Century," in *Home Girls: A Black Feminist Anthology*, ed. Barbara Smith (New York: Kitchen Table Women of Color Press, 1983), 365.

19. Ibid., 364, 362.

20. Ibid, 364, 366.

21. I owe the analytical model of the script to Joan Cocks, who employs it in a discussion of desire and the "meaning" of the female body: *The Oppositional Imagination: Feminism, Critique and Political Theory* (New York: Routledge, 1989), 167–68.

22. Donna Haraway, "Cyborgs," 218.

23. bell hooks, *Feminist Theory from Margin to Center* (Boston: South End Press, 1984), preface, n.p.

24. Ibid, 14.

25. Flax, "Postmodernism and Gender Relations," 642.

26. Terry Eagleton, "Use of Criticism," *New York Times Book Review*, 9 Dec. 1984, p. 45.

27. Lorde, *Sister Outsider*, 123, 132.

28. Ibid., 151, 153.

29. bell hooks, *Talking Back*, 181–82. This volume also contains hooks's essay, "Homophobia in Black Communities," 120–26.

30. Ibid, 181–82, 180, 178–79.

31. Mirtha Quintanales, "I Paid Very Hard for My Immigrant Ignorance," in Moraga and Anzaldúa, *This Bridge Called My Back*, 151.

32. Ibid., 152, 154.

33. Michele Russell, "Slave Codes and Liner Notes," 138–39.

34. Combahee River Collective, "A Black Feminist Statement," in Moraga and Anzaldúa, *This Bridge Called My Back*, 17.

35. These maxims are from Albert Camus. Quoted in Norman Jacobson, *Pride and Solace* (Berkeley: Univ. of California Press, 1978), 149, 154.

36. Camus, *The Rebel*, quoted in ibid., 149.

37. Maxine Hong Kingston, *Tripmaster Monkey* 307–8.

38. Joan Cocks, *Oppositional Imagination*, 181.

39. Ibid., 181–83.

40. Nancy Fraser here restates Foucault's conception of capillary modern power, in "Foucault on Modern Power," 28.

41. Chandra T. Mohanty, "Under Western Eyes," 64–65.

42. Gloria Anzaldúa, "Tlilli, Tlapalli: The Path of the Red and Black Ink," in *Graywolf Annual Five: Multi-Cultural Literarcy*. ed. Rick Simonson and Scott Walker (St. Paul, Minn.: Graywolf Press, 1988), 33.

43. Alice Walker, *Meridian* (New York: Harcourt, Brace, Jovanovich, 1967), 103–4.

44. Françoise Lionnet, *Autobiographical Voices*, 6.

45. Barbara Cameron, "'Gee, You Don't Seem Like an Indian from the Reservation,'" in Moraga and Anzaldúa, *This Bridge Called My Back*, 46.

46. JanMohamed, "Economy of Manichean Allegory," 78–106, esp. 86.

47. Thanks to Christine Di Stefano for persuasively arguing this point to me.

48. Bordo, "Feminism, Postmodernism," 138 and n. 5, p. 154. "This, of course, is the way we learn; it is not a process that should be freighted (as it often is nowadays) with the constant anxiety of 'exposure' and political discreditation."

49. Aptheker, *Tapestries of Life*, 12.

50. Elsa Barkley Brown, "African-American Women's Quilting: A Framework for Conceptualizing and Teaching African-American Women's History," *Signs* 14, no. 4 (Summer 1989):921–22. Brown borrows Luisah Teish's intriguing "gumbo ya ya" talk-story methodology as a creole practice derived from Teish's New Orleans family. Teish describes this family mode of talk (which she admits is difficult to reenter after being steeped in Western styles of communication) in her book *Jambalaya: The Natural Woman's Book of Personal Charms and Practical Rituals* (San Francisco: Harper & Row, 1985), 139–40.

51. Bernice Johnson Reagon, "Coalition Politics," 363, 365.

52. Edward Said, "Orientalism Reconsidered," *Race and Class* 27, no. 2 (1985):15.

53. Donna Haraway, "Reading Buchi Emecheta," 108–9, esp. 10.

54. Ibid., 109.

55. The breakdown of interracial alliances in the National Women's Studies Association (NWSA) over the termination of Black feminist Ruby Sales from the national NWSA staff is a case in point. For a detailed account of the events of the NWSA 1990 annual conference, in which the Women of Color

Caucus resigned in solidarity with Sales, see the coverage in *off our backs* 20, no. 8 (Aug./Sept. 1990).

Bell hooks has recently recounted an aggressive encounter which transpired between herself and a white feminist theorist working on issues of race. Hooks writes that her efforts to confront the white feminist about practices which control Black women's speech were met with repeated screams from the white feminist: "I could care less about what black women think about my work. I don't owe black women anything." Bell hooks, "Feminism and Racism: The Struggle Continues," Z Magazine (July/Aug. 1990): 41–43, esp. 41.

Efforts to organize a Women's Center at the University of Hawaii–Manoa resulted in tensions and polarizations between the predominantly white Women's Studies Program and other feminist women of color on campus. Although rancorous and sometimes divisive, subsequent debates have highlighted the need for diversity and for leadership by women of color around our shared desire to empower and provide needed resources for all women in our community, particularly Native Hawaiian women.

56. Chantal Mouffe, "Hegemony and New Political Subjects: Toward a New Concept of Democracy," in *Marxism and the Interpretation of Culture*, ed. Cary Nelson and Lawrence Grossberg (Urbana: Univ. of Illinois Press, 1988), 100.

57. Critical legal race theorist Patricia Williams is among those scholars redefining the discourse of rights. She writes:

> To say that blacks never fully believed in rights is true; yet it is also true that blacks believed in them so much and so hard that we gave them life where there was none before. . . . The making of something out of nothing took immense alchemical fire: the fusion of a whole nation and the kindling of several generations. . . . it is true that the constitutional foreground of "rights" was shaped by whites, parcelled out to blacks in pieces, ordained in small favors as random insulting gratuities. . . . "Rights" feels so new in the mouths of most black people. It is still so deliciously empowering to say. It is a sign for and a gift of selfhood that is very hard to contemplate reconstructing (deconstruction is too awful to think about!). . . . In discarding rights altogether, one discards a symbol too deeply enmeshed in the psyche of the oppressed to lose without trauma and much resistance. ("Alchemical Notes," 430–31, 433.)

The provocative seminar, "Rethinking Rights: Law, Social Movements, and Institutional Reform," sponsored by the Faculty Resources Network of New York University and conducted by Dr. Christine Harrington in June 1990, stimulated my own rethinking about the theoretical and practical application of rights.

58. Chantal Mouffe, "Radical Democracy: Modern of Postmodern?", in *Universal Abandon?* ed. Andrew Ross (Minneapolis: University of Minnesota Press, 1988), 42.

59. See Kathleen B. Jones's critical discussion of the problematic of defin-

ing feminist citizenship as politics among friends/sisters, in "Citizenship in a Woman-Friendly Polity," *Signs* 15, no. 4 (Summer 1990):781–812.

60. Mouffe, "Radical Democracy," 44.

61. This is Seyla Benhabib's term, from her *Critique, Norm, Utopia* (New York: Columbia Univ. Press, 1986), 344.

62. Spelman, *Inessential Woman*, 178. Further references to this text are indicated by page number.

63. Lorde, *Sister Outsider*, 113.

64. Hannah Arendt argued in favor of a theory of political life based on artificial civic equality, rather than any "natural" equality between persons. Through her reflections on the political experiences of ancient Greece, she formulated her own ideas around the concept of *isonomy*, a conventional equality contrived specifically for the purposes of enjoying political freedom *in the company of one's peers*. In *On Revolution*, Arendt notes: "Isonomy guaranteed equality, but not because all men [*sic*] were born or created equal, but, on the contrary, because men [*sic*] were by nature not equal, and needed an artificial institution, the polis, which . . . would make them equal." Hannah Arendt, *On Revolution* (New York: Viking, 1963), 22–23, esp. 23. Arendt was skeptical of the notion that individuals could be free and relate as equals in the private sphere; it was only through the political artifice of the *polis* realm of citizenship that persons might experience freedom. It is this notion which I find important to matters of multicultural feminism. It is not via any conception of authentic experience or "identity" that we might found feminist collectivity, but on a specifically "artificial" notion of coalition (or isonomic citizenship) grounded in principles of democratic equivalences and inclusion.

65. Iris Marion Young, "The Ideal of Community and the Politics of Difference," in Nicholson, *Feminism/Postmodernism*, 308.

66. Ibid., 311.

67. Hannah Arendt, *The Human Condition* (Garden City, N.J.: Doubleday, Anchor, 1958), 47–48.

68. Ibid., 303.

69. Shane Phelan, *Identity Politics*, 170.

70. Bernice Johnson Reagon, "My Black Mothers and Sisters, or, On Beginning a Cultural Autobiography," *Feminist Studies* 8, no. 1 (Spring 1982), 96.

71. Mary King, *Freedom Song: A Personal Story of the 1960s Civil Rights Movement* (New York: Wiliam Morrow, 1987), 472.

72. Ruth Frankenberg's work on the social construction of whiteness is an excellent and urgent development in this respect. "Social geography of racism" is one of her conceptual innovations. Frankenberg's essay will appear

in her text *White Women, Race Matters: The Social Construction of Whiteness* (Berkeley: Univ. of California Press, forthcoming). Minne Bruce Pratt's compelling narrative, "Identity: Skin Blood Heart," is also a pathbreaking expression of deep feminist self-reflection on whiteness and the potential psychic paralysis to which racism can lead.

73. Sarah Schulman, *People in Trouble* (New York: Dutton, 1990), 45.

74. Aptheker, *Tapestries of Life*, 20. To assume the integrity of one's "opponent," and to approach conflict and debate without bitterness seem to have been ethical markers of Nelson Mandela's politics. On his tour of the USA in summer 1990, Mandela told a reporter: "Firstly, you do not negotiate with anybody unless you accept his integrity. That is the general principle irrespective of with whom you discuss." "Excerpts from Remarks by Mandela to Newspaper Editors and Writers," *New York Times*, 22 June 1990, p. A20. In another press account, Mandela demonstrated that he had not survived 27 years in prison to live as a man of hate; he reiterated his decision not to criticize those who imprisoned him. They were caught up in an oppressive system, he said, and it is the system that has to be changed. "You look at what can be done today, and you forget the past quite easily," he said. "It would be unfair to think in terms of any measures of revenge. It would be absolutely unfair." Quoted in Anthony Lewis, "Abroad At Home," *New York Times*, 22 June, 1990, p. A27.

75. Surely Václav Havel is among the foremost contemporary exemplars of both humility and paradox. Radiating good will, intelligence, charm, and a deliberate embrace of the absurd, Havel's introspective writings—plays, prison journals, and letters—contain depths of political and psychological insight which he constantly turns back on himself. He is the "anti-President" Czech president who declares:

> For many people I'm a constant source of hope, and yet I'm always succumbing to depressions, uncertainties, and doubts, and I'm constantly having to look hard for my own inner hope and revive it, win it back from myself with great difficulty, so that I scarcely seem to have any to give away. So I'm not really comfortable in the role of a distributor of hope and encouragement to those around me. . . . And there are times when I have to laugh at my reputation. The fact is, I'm always afraid of something, and even my alleged courage and stamina spring from fear: fear of my own conscience, which delights in tormenting me for real and imaginary failures.

See the excerpts of Havel's interviews with Karel Hvizdala in Václav Havel, "Reflections on a Paradoxical Life, *New York Review of Books*, 14 June 1990, p. 38.

76. Alice Walker, *Temple of My Familiar*, 315.

References

Achebe, Chinua. *Anthills of the Savannah*. New York: Doubleday, Anchor, 1987.

Alder, Jerry, with Frank S. Washington. "Cookie Jars of Oppression." *Newsweek*, 16 May 1988.

Allen, Jeffner, and Iris Marion Young. *The Thinking Muse: Feminism and Modern French Philosophy*. Bloomington: Indiana University Press, 1989.

Allen, Robert, with the collaboration of Pamela P. Allen. *Reluctant Reformers: Racism and Social Reform Movements in the United States*. Washington, D.C.: Howard University Press, 1983.

Andolsen, Barbara Hilkert. *"Daughters of Jefferson, Daughters of Bootblacks": Racism and American Feminism*. Macon, Ga.: Mercer University Press, 1986.

Angeles, Peter A., ed. *Dictionary of Philosophy*. New York: Barnes and Noble, 1981.

Angelou, Maya. *I Know Why the Caged Bird Sings*. New York: Bantam, 1969.

Anzaldúa, Gloria. "Tlilli, Tlapalli: The Path of the Red and Black Ink." In *The Graywolf Annual Five: Multi-Cultural Literacy*, edited by Rick Simonson and Scott Walker. St. Paul, Minn.: Graywolf Press, 1988.

Aptheker, Bettina. *Tapestries of Life: Women's Work, Women's Consciousness and the Meaning of Daily Experience*. Amherst: University of Massachusetts Press, 1989.

———. *Woman's Legacy: Essays on Race, Sex, and Class*. Amherst: University of Massachusetts Press, 1982.

Arendt, Hannah. *On Revolution*. New York: Viking, 1963.

————. *The Human Condition*. Garden City, N.Y.: Doubleday, Anchor Books, 1958.

Asante, Molefi Kete. *The Afrocentric Idea*. Philadelphia, Penn.: Temple University Press, 1987.

Ashcroft, Bill; Gareth Griffiths; and Helen Tiffin. *The Empire Writes Back*. London: Routledge, 1989.

Barth, John. "The Literature of Replenishment." *Atlantic Monthly*, Jan. 1980.

Belenky, Mary Field; Blythe McVicker Clinchy; Nancy Rule Goldberger; and Jill Mattuck Tarule. *Women's Ways of Knowing: The Development of Self, Voice, and Mind*. New York: Basic, 1986.

Bell, Derrick. *And We Are Not Saved: The Elusive Quest for Racial Justice*. New York: Basic, 1987.

Benhabib, Selya. *Critique, Norm, Utopia*. New York: Columbia University Press, 1986.

Benjamin, Walter. "The Work of Art in the Age of Mechanical Reproduction." In Benjamin, *Illuminations*. New York: Schocken, 1969.

Bennett, Jane. *Unthinking Faith and Enlightenment: Nature and the State in a Post-Hegelian Era*. New York: New York University Press, 1987.

Bennett, Lerone, Jr. *Before the Mayflower: A History of Black America*. 5th ed. New York: Penguin, 1982.

Berg, Barbara. *The Remembered Gate: Origins of American Feminism*. Oxford, Eng.: Oxford University Press, 1978.

Bernstein, Richard. "In Dispute on Bias, Stanford Is Likely to Alter Western Culture Program." *New York Times*, 19 Jan. 1988.

Bethel, Lorraine. "What Chou Mean *We*, White Girl?" *Conditions: Five the Black Woman's Issue* 2, no. 2 (1979), edited by Lorraine Bethel and Barbara Smith, pp. 1–187. P.O. Box 56, Van Brunt Station, Brooklyn, N.Y. 11215.

Bordo, Susan. "Feminism, Postmodernism, and Gender-Skepticism." In *Feminism/Postmodernism*, edited by Linda Nicholson. New York: Routledge, 1990.

————. "The Cartesian Masculination of Thought." *Signs* 11, no. 3 (1986): 439–56.

Borris, Eileen. "Word Watch." Review of *Feminism and Suffrage* by Ellen Carol Du Bois (Ithaca, N.Y.: Cornell University Press, 1980) in *Quest* 5, no. 4 (1982):85–94.

Brennan, Johnathan Bradford. "Words with Walker." *San Franciso Review of Books*, Summer (1989):13.

Breytenbach, Breyten. "The South African Wasteland." *New Republic*, 4 Nov. 1985.

Brown, Barbara. "White Women in South Africa." *Sojourner* 14, no. 11 (Dec. 1985).

Brown, Elsa Barkley. "African-American Women's Quilting: A Framework for Conceptualizing and Teaching African-American Women's History." *Signs* 13, no. 4 (1989):921–29.

―――. "Womanist Consciousness: Maggie Lena Walker and the Independent Order of Saint Luke." *Signs* 14, no. 3 (1989):610–33.

Buker, Eloise. "Foreword." In *A Time for Sharing: Women's Stories from the Waianae Coast*, 1982.

―――. "Hermeneutics: Problems and Promises for Doing Feminist Theory." Paper presented at annual meeting of the American Political Science Association, New Orleans, La., 1985.

―――. *Politics Through a Looking Glass: A Structualist Interpretation of Narratives*. New York: Greenwood, 1987.

―――. "Sign, Sex and Symbol: Feminist Semiotics and Political Philosophy." Paper presented at annual meeting of the Western Political Science Association, Salt Lake City, Utah, 1989.

Bulkin, Elly. "Hard Ground: Jewish Identity, Racism and Anti-Semitism." In *Yours in Struggle: Three Feminist Perspectives on Anti-Semitism." and Racism*, by Elly Bulkin, Minne Bruce Pratt, and Barbara Smith. Brooklyn, N.Y.: Long Haul Press, 1984.

Bulkin, Elly; Minnie Bruce Pratt; and Barbara Smith. *Yours in Struggle: Three Feminist Perspectives on Anti-Semitism and Racism*. Brooklyn, N.Y.: Long Haul Press, 1984.

Burnham, Linda. "Has Poverty Been Feminized in Black America?" *Black Scholar* 16, no. 2 (Mar.-Apr. 1985):14–24.

Butler, Johnella. "Women's Studies in the 90s: Achieving Transformation." *NWSAction* 2, no. 4 (1989):1–4.

Butler-Evans, Elliott. "Beyond Essentialism: Rethinking Afro-American Cultural Theory." *Inscriptions* 5 (1989), edited by James Clifford and Vivek Dhareshwar, Group for the Critical Study of Colonial Discourse and the Center for Cultural Studies, University of California at Santa Cruz, Santa Cruz, Ca. 95064. pp. 121–34.

Cade, Toni, ed. *The Black Woman*. New York: New American Library, 1970.

Cameron, Barbara. "'Gee, You Don't Seem Like an Indian from the Reservation.'" In *This Bridge Called My Back: Writings by Radical Women of Color*, edited by Cherríe Moraga and Gloria Anzaldúa. Watertown, Mass.: Persephone Press, 1981.

"Cannons under Fire." *Time*, 11 Apr. 1988.

Carby, Hazel V. "It Just Be's Dat Way Sometime: The Sexual Politics of Women's Blues." In *Unequal Sisters*, edited by DuBois and Vicki L. Ruiz. New York: Routledge, 1990.

————. "'On the Threshold of Woman's Era': Lynching, Empire, and Sexuality in Black Feminist Theory." *Critical Inquiry* 12 (Autumn 1985):262–77.

————. *Reconstructing Womanhood: The Emergence of the Afro-American Woman Novelist.* Oxford, Eng.: Oxford University Press, 1987.

Carrillo, Jo. "And When You Leave Take Your Pictures with You." In *This Bridge Called My Back: Writings by Radical Women of Color*, edited by Cherríe Moraga and Gloria Anzaldúa. Watertown, Mass.: Persephone Press, 1981.

Cash, W. J. *The Mind of the South.* New York: Knopf, 1941.

Castellano, Olivia. "Canto, locura y poesia." *Women's Review of Books.* 7, n. 5 (1990):18–20.

Chapkis, Wendy. *Beauty Secrets: Women and the Politics of Appearance.* Boston: South End Press, 1986.

Chenzira, Ayoka. *Hair Piece: A Film for Nappyheaded People.* Film, 1984. Ayoka Chenzira, 265 Bainbridge St., Brooklyn, N.Y. 11233, (718) 773-6571.

Childress, Alice. *Like One of the Family: Conversations from a Domestic's Life.* Boston: Beacon, 1986.

Christian Barbara. "The Race for Theory." *Feminist Studies* 14, no. 1 (1988): 67–80.

Clemons, Walter. "A Gravestone of Memories." *Newsweek*, 28 Sept. 1987.

Cliff, Michelle. "A Journey into Speech." In *Graywolf Annual Five: Multicultural Literacy*, edited by Rick Simonson and Scott Walker. St. Paul, Minn.: Graywolf Press, 1988.

————. "The Making of Americans: Maxine Hong Kingston's Crossover Dreams." *Village Voice Literary Supplement*, May 1989.

————. "Women Warriors: Black Writers Load the Canon." *Village Voice Literary Supplement*, May 1990.

Clinton, Catherine. *The Plantation Mistress: Woman's World in the Old South.* New York: Pantheon, 1982.

Cocks, Joan. *The Oppositional Imagination: Feminism, Critique and Political Theory.* New York: Routledge, 1989.

Collins, Nancy. "The Rolling Stones Interview: Tina Turner." *Rolling Stone*, 23 Oct. 1986.

Collins, Patricia Hill. "Learning from the Outsider Within: The Sociological Significance of Black Feminist Thought." *Social Problems* 33, no. 6 (1986): 14–32.

————. "The Social Construction of Black Feminist Thought." *Signs* 14, no. 4 (1989):745–73.

Collins, Sheila. *The Rainbow Challenge.* New York: Monthly Review Press, 1986.

Combahee River Collective. "A Black Feminist Statement." In *This Bridge*

Called My Back: Writings by Radical Women of Color, edited by Cherríe Moraga and Gloria Anzaldúa. Watertown, Mass.: Persephone Press, 1981.

Connolly, William E. *Political Theory and Modernity.* Oxford, Eng.: Basil Blackwell, 1988.

Crenshaw, Kimberlé. "Race, Reform and Retrenchment: Transformation and Legitimation in Antidiscrimination Law." *Harvard Law Review* 101, no. 7 (1988):1331–87.

Croly, Jennie C. *History of the General Federation of Women's Clubs.* New York: N.p., 1898.

Crouch, Stanley. "Do the Right Thing: Spike Lee's Afro-Fascist Chic." *Village Voice,* 20 June 1989, pp. 73–76.

Cruse, Harold. *Plural but Equal.* New York: William Morrow, 1987.

Darnton, Nina; with Sonya Vann; Howard Manly; and Shawn Doherty. "An Old Look Is New Again." *Newsweek,* 16 Oct. 1989.

Davis, Angela. "Reflections on the Black Woman's Role in the Community of Slaves." *Black Scholar* 3 (Dec. 1971):3–15.

———. *Women, Race and Class.* New York: Random House, Vintage Books, 1983.

Davis, Thulani. "Don't Worry, Be Buppie." *Village Voice Literary Supplement,* May 1990.

———. "Family Plots: Black Women Writers Reclaim Their Past" *Village Voice Literary Supplement,* Mar. 1987, pp. 14–17.

———. "We've Gotta Have It." *Village Voice,* 20 June 1989, pp. 67–78.

Deckard, Barbara. *The Women's Movement.* New York: Harper & Row, 1975.

de Lauretis, Teresa. "Displacing Hegemonic Discourses: Reflections on Feminist Theory in the 1980s." *Inscriptions* 3–4 (1988), edited by Deborah Gordon, Group for the Critical Study of Colonial Discourse, Board of Studies in History of Consciousness, University of California at Santa Cruz, Santa Cruz, California 95064. pp. 127–44.

———, ed. *Feminist Studies/Critical Studies.* Bloomington: Indiana University Press, 1986.

———. *Technologies of Gender.* Bloomington: Indiana University Press, 1987.

Delgado, Richard. "The Imperial Scholar: Reflections on a Review of Civil Rights Literature." *University of Pennsylvania Law Review* 132, no. 3 (1984):561–78.

Denby, David. "He's Gotta Have It." *New York Magazine,* 26 June 1989.

Di Prima, Dominque. "Beat the Rap Queen Latifah." *Mother Jones,* Sept.–Oct. 1990.

"Discovering a Lost Tradition." *Newsweek,* 7 March 1988.

Di Stefano, Christine. "Dilemmas of Difference: Feminism, Modernity and

Postmodernism." In *Feminism/Postmodernism*, edited by Linda Nicholson. New York: Routledge, 1990.

————. "Masculinity as Ideology in Political Theory: Hobbesian Man Considered." *Women's Studies International Forum* 6, no. 6 (1983):633–44.

Dobie, Kathy. "Black Women, White Kids: A Tale of Two Worlds." *Village
Voice*, 12 Jan. 1988, pp. 20–27.

Douglass, Frederick. *Life and Times of Frederick Douglass* (1892). Reprint
ed. New York: Macmillan, Collier Books, 1962.

DuBois, Ellen Carol. *Feminism and Suffrage: The Emergence of an Independent Woman's Movement in America, 1848–1869*. Ithaca, N.Y.: Cornell
University Press, 1978.

————, ed. *Elizabeth Cady Stanton, Susan B. Anthony: Correspondence,
Writings, Speeches*. New York: Schocken, 1981.

Du Bois, W.E.B. *Darkwater: Voices from Within the Veil*. New York: Schocken,
1969.

————. *The Souls of Black Folk*. Chicago: A. S. McClurg, 1903.

Duras, Marguerite. *Marguerite Duras*. San Francisco, Calif.: City Lights
Books, 1987.

Eagleton, Terry. "Uses of Criticism." *New York Times Book Review*, 9 Dec.
1984.

Eichelberger, Brenda. "Voices on Black Feminism. *Quest* 3, no. 4 (1977):16–28.

Eisenstein, Zillah. *The Radical Future of Liberal Feminism*. New York: Longman, 1981.

Ellison, Ralph. *Going to the Territory*. New York: Random House, 1986.

Elshtain, Jean Bethke. *Public Man, Private Woman*. Princeton, N.J.: Princeton University Press, 1981.

Enloe, Cynthia. *Bananas, Beaches, and Bases: Making Feminist Sense of
International Politics*. Berkeley: University of California Press, 1990.

————. "'Just like one of the family'– Domestic Servants in World Politics."
In Enloe, *Bananas, Beaches, and Bases*. Berkeley: University of California
Press, 1990.

Evans, Sara. *Personal Politics: The Roots of Women's Liberation in the Civil
Rights Movement and the New Left*. New York: Random House, Vintage
Books, 1980.

Felstiner, Mary Lowenthal. "Seeing *The Second Sex* Through the Second
Wave." *Feminist Studies* 6 (Summer 1980):247–76.

"Feminism and Epistemology." *Women and Politics* 7, no. 3 (1987): entire
issue.

"Feminism and the Critique of Colonial Discourse." *Inscriptions* 3–4 (1988),
edited by Deborah Gordon, Group for the Critical Study of Colonial Dis-

course, Board of Studies in History of Consciousness, University of California at Santa Cruz, Santa Cruz, California 95064. Entire issue.

Ferguson, Kathy. "Interpretation and Genealogy in Feminism." Paper presented at annual meeting of Western Political Science Association, San Francisco, Calif., 10–12 March, 1988.

———. "Knowledge, Politics, and Persons in Feminist Theory." *Political Theory* 17, no. 2 (1989):302–13.

———. "Male-Ordered Politics: Feminism and Political Science." Department of Political Science, University of Hawaii, Honolulu, Hawaii, n.d.

———. *The Feminist Case Against Bureaucracy.* Philadelphia, Penn.: Temple University Press, 1984.

———. *The Man Question: Reversals and Their Discontents in Feminist Theory.* Berkeley: University of California Press, forthcoming.

Flax, Jane. "Postmodernism and Gender Relations in Feminist Theory." *Signs* 12, no. 4 (1987):621–43.

Flexner, Eleanor. *Century of Struggle: The Woman's Rights Movement in the United States.* Cambridge, Mass.: Harvard University Press, Belknap Press, 1950.

Foner, Philip, ed. *Life and Writings of Frederick Douglass,* vol. 1. New York: International Publishers, 1975.

Foucault, Michel. *Power/Knowledge.* New York: Pantheon, 1980.

Fox-Genovese, Elizabeth. *Within the Plantation Household.* Chapel Hill: University of North Carolina Press, 1988.

Frankenberg, Ruth. "Feminism, Racism and the Social Geography of Childhood." In Frankenberg, *White Women, Race Matters: The Social Construction of Whiteness.* Berkeley: University of California, forthcoming.

Fraser, Nancy. "Foucault on Modern Power: Empirical Insights and Normative Confusions." In Fraser's *Unruly Practices: Power, Discourse and Gender in Contemporary Social Theory.* Minneapolis: University of Minnesota Press, 1989.

———. "Michel Foucault: A 'Young Conservative'?" In Fraser's *Unruly Practices: Power, Discourse and Gender in Contemporary Social Theory.* Minneapolis: University of Minnesota Press, 1989.

Gates, Henry Louis, Jr. "Talkin' That Talk." In *"Race," Writing and Difference,* edited by Henry Louis Gates, Jr. Chicago: University of Chicago Press, 1985.

———. *The Signifying Monkey: A Theory of Afro-American Literary Criticism.* New York: Oxford University Press, 1988.

———. "Writing 'Race' and the Difference It Makes." In *"Race," Writing and Difference,* edited by Henry Louis Gates, Jr. Chicago: University of Chicago Press, 1985.

————, ed. *"Race," Writing and Difference.* Chicago: University of Chicago Press, 1985.

————, ed. *The Schomburg Library of Nineteenth-Century Black Women Writers.* 30 vols. New York: Oxford University Press, 1988.

Geertz, Clifford. "From the Native's Point of View: On the Nature of Anthropological Understanding." In *Meaning in Anthropology,* edited by Keith H. Basso and Henry A. Selby. Albuquerque: University of New Mexico Press, 1976.

Gender and Colonialism. Conference Proceedings. Berkeley: University of California, Oct. 1989.

Giddings, Paula. "Black Feminism Takes Its Rightful Place." *Ms.,* October 1985.

————. *When and Where I Enter: The Impact of Black Women on Race and Sex in America.* New York: William Morrow, 1984.

Gilman, Sander L. "Black Bodies, White Bodies: Toward an Iconography of Female Sexuality in Late-Nineteenth-Century Art, Medicine, and Literature." In *"Race," Writing and Difference,* edited by Henry Louis Gates, Jr. Chicago: University of Chicago Press, 1985.

Goldberg, David Theo, ed. *The Anatomy of Racism.* Minneapolis: University of Minnesota Press, 1990.

Griffin, Susan. "The Way of All Ideology." In *Feminist Theory,* edited by Nannerl O. Keokane, Michelle Z. Rosaldo, and Barbara C. Gelpi. Chicago: University of Chicago Press, 1981.

Grimké, Angelina E. *Letters to Catherine E. Beecher.* New York: Arno Press and the *New York Times,* 1969.

Guy-Sheftall, Beverly. *Daughters of Sorrow: Attitudes Toward Black Women, 1880–1990.* Vol. 11, Black Women in United States History, series, edited by Darlene Clark Hine. New York: Carlson Publishing, 1990.

Gwaltney, John Langston. *Drylongso: A Self-Portrait of Black America.* New York: Vintage Books, 1981.

Gwin, Minrose C. "A Theory of Black Women's Texts and White Women's Readings, or the Necessity of Being Other." *NWSA Journal* 1, no. 1 (1988): 21–31.

————. *Black and White Women of the Old South.* Knoxville: University of Tennessee Press, 1985.

Hall, Jacqueline Dowd. *Revolt Against Chivalry: Jessie Daniel Ames and the Women's Campaign Against Lynching.* New York: Columbia University Press, 1979.

Haraway, Donna. "A Manifesto for Cyborgs: Science, Technology, and Socialist Feminism in the 1980s." *Socialist Review* 15, no. 2 (1985):65–107.

————. "Reading Buchi Emecheta: Contexts for Women's Experience in

Women's Studies." *Inscriptions* 3–4 (1988), edited by Deborah Gordon, Group for the Critical Study of Colonial Discourse, Board of Studies in History of Consciousness, University of California at Santa Cruz, Santa Cruz, California 95064. Pp. 107–24.

———. "Situated Knowledges: The Science Question in Feminism and the Privilege of Partial Perspective." *Feminist Studies* 14, no. 3 (1988):575–99.

———. "Spirits of Resistance and Capitalist Discipline: Factory Women in Malaysia." *Signs* 14, no. 4 (1989):945–47.

Harding, Sandra. The Instability of the Analytical Categories of Feminist Theory." *Signs* 11, no. 4 (1986):645–64.

———. *The Science Question in Feminism*. Ithaca, N.Y.: Cornell University Press, 1986.

Harding, Sandra, and Merrill B. Hintikka, eds. *Discovering Reality: Feminist Perspectives on Epistemology, Metaphysics, Methodology, and Philosophy of Science*. Boston: D. Reidel, 1983.

Harley, Sharon. "Anna J. Cooper: A Voice for Black Women." In *The Afro-American Woman*, edited by Sharon Harley and Rosalyn Terborg-Penn. Port Washington, N.Y.: Kennikat, 1978.

Harley, Sharon, and Rosalyn Terborg-Penn, eds. *The Afro-American Woman*, Port Washington, N.Y.: Kennikat, 1978.

Harris, Joseph E., ed. *Global Dimensions of the African Diaspora*. Washington, D.C.: Howard University Press, 1982.

Harris, Trudier. *Exorcising Blackness: Historical and Literary Lynching and Burning Rituals*. Bloomington: Indiana University Press, 1984.

———. *From Mammies to Militants*. Philadelphia, Penn.: Temple University Press, 1982.

Hartsock, Nancy. "Foucault on Power: A Theory for Women?" In *Feminism/Postmodernism*, edited by Linda Nicholson. New York: Routledge, 1990.

———. *Money, Sex and Power: Toward a Feminist Historical Materialism*. Boston: Northeastern University Press, 1985.

Hawkesworth, Mary E. "Feminist Rhetoric: Discourses on the Male Monopoly of Thought." *Political Theory* 16, no. 3 (1988):444–67.

Hekman, Susan. *Hermeneutics and the Sociology of Knowledge*. Notre Dame, Ind.: Notre Dame University Press, 1986.

Henningsen, Manfred. "The Politics of Purity and Exclusion: Literary and Linguistic Movements of Political Empowerment in America, Africa, the south Pacific, and Europe." In *The Politics of Language Purism*, edited by Björn H. Jernudd and Michael J. Shapiro. Berlin: Mouton de Gruyter, 1989.

Hersh, Blanche Glassman. *The Slavery of Sex: Feminist-Abolitionists in America*. Urbana: University of Illinois Press, 1978.

Hine, Darlene Clark. "Rape and the Inner Lives of Black Women in the Middle West: Preliminary Thoughts on the Culture of Dissemblance." *Signs* 14, no. 4 (1989):912–20.

Hine, Darlene Clark, ser. ed. Black Women in United States History. 16 vols. New York: Carlson Publishing, 1990.

Hine, Darlene, and Kate Wittenstein. "Female Slave Resistance: The Economies of Sex." In *The Black Woman Cross-Culturally*, edited by Filomina Chioma Steady. Cambridge, Mass.: Schenkman, 1981.

Hole, Judith, and Ellen Levine, eds. *Rebirth of Feminism*. New York: Quadrangle/New York Times Book Co., 1971.

hooks, bell. "A Call for Militant Resistance." *Z Magazine*, Jan. 1990.

———. *Ain't I a Woman?: Black Women and Feminism*. Boston: South End Press, 1981.

———. "Feminism and Racism: The Struggle Continues." *Z Magazine*, July–Aug. 1990, pp. 41–43.

———. *Feminist Theory: From Margin to Center*. Boston: South End Press, 1984.

———. "Homophobia in Black Communities." In hooks, *Talking Back*. Boston: Beacon, 1989.

———. "Straightening Our Hair." *Z Magazine*, Sept. 1988.

———. "Stylish Nihilism at the Movies." *Z Magazine*, May 1988.

———. *Talking Back*. Boston: South End Press, 1989.

———. "Whose Pussy Is This?: A Feminist Comment." In hooks, *Talking Back*. Boston: Beacon, 1989.

Horton, James Oliver. "Freedom's Yoke: Gender Conventions Among Antebellum Free Blacks." *Feminist Studies* 12, no. 1 (1986):51–76.

Howe, Joyce. "Talking Black." *Village Voice*, 26 March 1985.

Hoytt, Eleanor Hinton. "International Council of Women of the Darker Races: Historical Notes." *Sage: A Scholarly Journal on Black Women* 3, no. 2 (1986):54–55.

Hull, Gloria T.; Patricia Bell Scott; and Barbara Smith, eds. *All the Women Are White, All the Blacks Are Men, but Some of Us Are Brave*. Old Westbury, N.Y.: Feminist Press, 1982.

Hurston, Zora Neal. *Their Eyes Were Watching God*. Urbana: University of Illinois Press, 1978.

Huyssen, Andreas. "Mapping the Postmodern." In *Feminism/Postmodernism*, edited by Linda Nicholson. New York: Routledge, 1990.

Hymowitz, Carole, and Michaele Weissman. *A History of Women in America*. New York: Bantam, 1978.

"Inspired by Gospel and African Rhythms, Sweet Honey in the Rock Delivers Political Punch A Cappella." *People*, Spring–Summer 1990.

Irigaray, Luce. *This Sex Which Is Not One.* Translated by Catherine Porter with Carolyn Burke. Ithaca, N.Y.: Cornell University Press, 1985.

Jacobson, Norman. *Pride and Solace.* Berkeley: University of California Press, 1978.

Jagar, Allison. *Feminist Politics and Human Nature.* Totowa, N.J.: Rowman and Allanheld, 1983.

JanMohamed, Abdul R. "The Economy of Manichean Allegory: The Function of Racial Difference in Colonialist Literature." In *"Race," Writing and Difference,* edited by Henry Louis Gates, Jr. Chicago: University of Chicago Press, 1985.

Jardine, Alice. *Gynesis: Configurations of Woman and Modernity.* Ithaca, N.Y.: Cornell University Press, 1985.

Jay, Martin. *The Dialectical Imagination.* Boston: Little, Brown, 1973.

John, Mary E. "Postcolonial Feminists in the Western Intellectual Field: Anthropologists and Native Informants?" *Inscriptions* 5, edited by James Clifford and Vivek Dhareshwar, Group for the Critical Study of Colonial Discourse and the Center for Cultural Studies, University of California at Santa Cruz, Santa Cruz, California 95064. Pp. 49–74.

Jones, Adele and Group. "Ebony Minds and Black Voices." In *The Black Woman,* edited by Toni Cade. New York: New American Library, 1970.

Jones, Beverly Washington. *Quest for Equality: The Life and Writings of Mary Eliza Church Terrell.* Vol. 13, Black Women in United States History, edited by Darlene Clark Hine. New York: Carlson Publishing, 1990.

Jones, Jacqueline. *Labor of Love, Labor of Sorrow: Black Women, Work, and the Family from Slavery to the Present.* New York: Basic, 1985.

———. "One Big Happy Family?" *Women's Review of Books* 6, no. 5 (1989).

Jones, Kathleen. "Citizenship in a Woman-Friendly Polity." *Signs* 15, no. 4 (1990):781–812.

Jones, Kathleen B., and Anna G. Jonasdöttir. *The Political Interests of Gender.* London: Sage, 1985.

Jordan, June. "Report from the Bahamas." *On Call:*Political Essays Boston: South End Press, 1985.

Jordan, Winthrop. *White Over Black: American Attitudes Toward the Negro, 1550–1812.* Baltimore, Md.: Penguin, 1969.

Kaplan, Elaine Bell. "Oppression Begins at Home." *Women's Review of Books* 3, no. 5 (1986).

Keesing, Roger M. "Creating the Past: Custom and Identity in the Contemporary Pacific." *Contemporary Pacific* 1, nos. 1 and 2 (1989):19–42.

Kennedy, Randall. "Racial Critiques of Legal Academia." *Harvard Law Review* 102, no. 8 (1989):1745–1819.

Kilson, Martin. "Paradoxes of Blackness." *Dissent* 33, no. 1 (Winter 1986): 70–78.

King, Deborah. "Multiple Jeopardy, Multiple Consciousness: The Context of a Black Feminist Ideology." *Signs* 14, no. 2 (1988):42–72.

King, Mary. *Freedom Song: A Personal Story of the 1960s Civil Rights Movement.* New York: William Morrow, 1987.

Kingston, Maxine Hong. *Tripmaster Monkey.* New York: Knopf, 1989.

Klein, Joe. "Spiked?" *New York Magazine,* 26 June 1989.

Kraditor, Aileen S. *Means and Ends in American Abolitionism: Garrison and His Critics on Strategy and Tactics, 1834–1850.* New York: Vintage, 1969.

———. *The Ideas of the Woman Suffrage Movement, 1899–1929.* Garden City, N.Y.: Anchor Books, 1971.

Kristeva, Julia. "Woman Can Never Be Defined." In *New French Feminisms,* edited by Elaine Marks and Isabelle de Courtivron. New York: Schocken, 1981.

Lawrence, Charles. "the Id, the Ego and Equal Protection: Reckoning with Unconscious Racism." *Stanford Law Review* 39, no. 2 (1987):317–88.

Lawrence, Clarissa. "Statement by Clarissa Lawrence." Proceedings of the Anti-Slavery Convention of American Women held in Philadelphia May 15, 16, 17, 28 of 1838. Philadelphia: Merrirew and Gun, 1838. Quoted in Gerda Lerner, *Black Women in White America: A Documentary History.* New York: Random House, Vintage Books, 1973, p. 359.

Lazreg. Marnia. "Feminism and Difference: The Perils of Writing as a Woman on Women in Algeria." *Feminist Studies* 14, no. 1 (1988):81–107.

Lee, Spike. *Spike Lee's* She's Gotta Have It: *Inside Guerrilla Filmmaking.* New York: Simon and Schuster, 1987.

Lee, Spike. with Lisa Jones. *Do the Right Thing.* New York: Simon and Schuster, 1989.

Lerner, Gerda. *Black Women in White America: A Documentary History.* New York: Random House, Vintage Books, 1973.

———. *The Grimké Sisters from South Carolina: Pioneers for Women's Rights and Abolition.* New York: Schoken, 1971.

———. *The Majority Finds Its Past: Placing Women in History.* Oxford, Eng.: Oxford University Press, 1979.

Lewis, Anthony. "Abroad at Home." *New York Times,* 22 June 1990, p. A27.

Lincoln, Abbey. "Who Will Revere the Black Woman?" In *The Black Woman,* edited by Toni Cade. New York: New American Library, 1970.

Lionnett, Françoise. *Autobiographical Voices: Race, Gender, Self-Portraiture.* Ithaca, N.Y.: Cornell University Press, 1989.

Lloyd, Genevieve. *Man of Reason.* Minneapolis: University of Minnesota Press, 1984.

Lorde, Audre. *A Burst of Light*. Ithaca, N.Y.: Firebrand Books, 1988.

————. *Sister Outsider*. Trumansburg, N.Y.: Crossing Press, 1984.

Louisiana Committee on the Humanities. *Yes Ma'am*. Documentary film. 1980.

Lutz, Alma. *Created Equal: A Biography of Elizabeth Cady Stanton*. New York: Octagon Books, 1974.

Malcolm X. *The Autobiography of Malcolm X*. Harmondsworth, Eng.: Penguin, 1965.

Malveaux, Julianne. "Current Economic Trends and Black Feminist Consciousness." *Black Scholar* vol. 16, no. 2 (Mar.-Apr. 1985):26–31.

Mandela, Nelson. Excerpts from remarks to newspaper editors and writers. *New York Times*, 11 June 1990, p. A20.

Mann, Susan A. "Slavery, Sharecropping, and Sexual Inequality." *Signs* 14, no. 4 (1989):774–98.

Mapping Colonialism. Conference Proceedings. Group for the Critical Study of Colonialism. University of California, Berkeley, Oct. 1987. Berkeley, California 94720. Pp. 1–89.

Matsuda, Mari. "Affirmative Action and Legal Knowledge." *Harvard Women's Law Journal* 11 (Spring 1988):1–17.

Megill, Allan. *Prophets of Extremity*. Berkeley: University of California Press, 1985.

Memmi, Albert. *The Colonizer and the Colonized*. Boston: Beacon, 1967.

Menard, Louis. "Literature and Liberation." *New Republic*, 4 Aug. 1986.

Millman, Marian, and R. M. Kanter, eds. *Another Voice: Feminist Perspectives on Social Life and Social Science*. New York: Doubleday, 1975.

Mobly, Marilyn E. "When and Where They Entered." *Women's Review of Books* 5, nos. 10 and 11 (1988).

Mohanty, Chandra T. "Under Western Eyes: Feminist Scholarship and Colonial Discourses." *Feminist Review* 30 (August 1988):61–88.

Mohanty, Chandra T., and Satya P. Mohanty. "Contradictions of Colonialism." *Women's Review of Books* 7, no. 6 (1990):19–21.

Mohanty, S. P. "Us and Them: On the Philosophical Bases of Political Criticism." *Yale Journal of Criticism* 2, no. 2 (1989):1–31.

Moraga, Cherríe. "La Güera." In *This Bridge Called My Back: Writings By Radical Women of Color*, edited by Cherríe Moraga and Gloria Anzaldúa. Watertown, Mass. Persephone Press, 1981.

Moraga, Cherríe, and Gloria Anzaldúa, eds. *This Bridge Called My Back: Writings by Radical Women of Colour*. Watertown, Mass.: Persephone Press, 1981.

Morales, Rosario. "We're All in the Same Boat." In *This Bridge Called My*

Back: Writings by Radical Women of Color, edited by Cherríe Moraga and Gloria Anzaldúa. Watertown, Mass.: Persephone Press, 1981.

Morrison, Toni. *Beloved.* New York: Knopf, 1987.

———. *The Bluest Eye.* New York: Washington Square Press/Pocket Books, 1970.

Mouffe, Chantal. "Hegemony and New Political Subjects: Toward a New Concept of Democracy." In *Marxism and the Interpretation of Culture,* edited by Cary Nelson and Lawrence Grossberg. Urbana: University of Illinois Press, 1988.

———. "Radical Democracy: Modern or Postmodern?" In *Universal Abandon? The Politics of Postmodernism,* edited by Andrew Ross. Minneapolis: University of Minnesota Press, 1988.

Mudimbe, V. Y. *The Invention of Africa.* Bloomington: Indiana University Press, 1988.

Murray, Pauli. *Song in a Weary Throat.* New York: Harper & Row, 1986.

Nicholson, Linda. *Gender and History.* New York: Columbia University Press, 1986.

———, ed. *Feminism/Postmodernism.* New York: Routledge, 1990.

"NWSA: Troubles Surface at Conference." *Off Our Backs* 20, no. 8 (Aug.–Sept. 1990):1–16.

Okin, Susan Moller. *Women in Western Political Thought.* Princeton, N.J.: Princeton University Press, 1979.

Ogunyemi, Chikwenye Okonjo. "The Dynamics of the Contemporary Black Female Novel in English." *Signs* 11, no. 1 (1985):63–80.

Okazawa-Rey, Margo; Tracy Robinson; and Janie Victoria Ward. "Black Women and the Politics of Skin Color and Hair." *Women's Studies Quarterly* 14, nos. 1 and 2 (1986):13–14.

Omi, Michael, and Howard Winant. *Racial Formation in the United States.* New York: Routledge, 1986.

Omolade, Barbara. "Black Women and Feminism." In *The Future of Difference,* edited by Hester Eisenstein and Alice Jardine. Boston: G. K. Hall, 1980.

———. "Hearts of Darkness." In *Powers of Desire: The Politics of Sexuality,* edited by Ann Snitow, Christine Stansell, and Sharon Thompson. New York: Monthly Review Press, 1983.

"Pain of Being Black." *Time,* 22 May 1989.

Palmer, Phyllis. *Domesticity and Dirt: Housewives and Domestic Servants in the United States, 1920–1945.* Philadephia, Penn.: Temple University Press, 1990.

———. "White Women/Black Women: The Dualism of Female Identity and

Experience in the United States." *Feminist Studies* 9, no. 1 (Spring 1983): 151–70.

"Panel Discussion 1." *Inscriptions* 3–4 (1988), edited by Deborah Gordon, Group for the Critical Study of Colonial Discourse, Board of Studies in History of Consciousness, University of California at Santa Cruz, Santa Cruz, California 95064. Pp. 58–59.

Pateman, Carole, and Elizabeth Gross, eds. *Feminist Challenges: Social and Political Theory.* Boston: Northeastern University Press, 1986.

Patterson, Orlando. *Slavery and Social Death.* Cambridge, Mass.: Harvard University Press, 1982.

Penny, Nicholas. "Fraternity." *London Review of Books,* 8 Mar. 1990, p. 22.

Perkins, Kathy A. *Black Female Playwrights: An Anthology of Plays Before 1950.* Bloomington: Indiana University Press, 1989.

Perkins, Linda. "Black Women and Racial 'Uplift' Prior to Emancipation." In *The Black Woman Cross-Culturally,* edited by Filomina Chioma Steady. Cambridge, Mass.: Schenkman, 1981.

Phelan, Shane. *Identity Politics: Lesbian Feminism and the Limits of Community.* Philadelphia, Penn.: Temple University Press, 1989.

Pratt, Minnie Bruce. "Identity: Skin Blood and Heart." In *Yours in Struggle: Three Feminist Perspectives on Anti-Semitism and Racism,* Elly Bulkin, Minnie Bruce Pratt, and Barbara Smith. Brooklyn, N.Y.: Long Haul Press, 1984.

"Prejudice and Black Sambo." *Time,* 15 Aug. 1988.

Pryse, Marjorie, and Hortense J. Spillers, eds. *Conjuring: Black Women, Fiction, and Literary Tradition.* Bloomington: Indiana University Press, 1985.

Quintanales, Mirtha. "I Paid Very Hard for My Immigrant Ignorance." In *This Bridge Called My Back: Writings by Radical Women of Color,* edited by Cherríe Moraga and Gloria Anzaldúa. Watertown, Mass.: Persephone Press, 1981.

Rabine, Leslie Wahl. "A Feminist Politics of Non-Identity." *Feminist Studies* 14, no. 1 (1988):11–32.

Rable, George. *Civil Wars: Women and the Crisis of Southern Nationalism.* Urbana: University of Illinois Press, 1989.

Reagon, Bernice Johnson. "Coalition Politics: Turning the Century." In *Home Girls: A Black Feminist Anthology,* edited by Barbara Smith. New York: Kitchen Table Women of Color Press, 1983.

———. "My Black Mothers and Sisters, or On Beginning a Cultural Autobiography." *Feminist Studies* 8, no. 1 (1982):81–96.

Reed, Adolph J., Jr. "Black Particularity Reconsidered." *Telos* 39 (Spring 1979): 71–93.

"Return of a Native Daughter: An Interview with Paule Marshall and Maryse Condé." *Sage: A Scholarly Journal on Black Women* 3, no. 2:52–53.

Reuther, Rosemary. *New Woman New Earth*. New York: Seabury Press, 1983.

Rich, Adrienne. "Disloyal to Civilization: Feminism, Racism, Gynophobia." In Rich, *On Lies, Secrets and Silence*. New York: Norton, 1979.

Richardson, Marilyn, ed. *Maria Stewart, America's First Black Woman Political Writer*. Bloomington: Indiana University Press, 1989.

Riley, Denise. *Am I That Name?": Feminism and the Category of "Women" in History*. Minneapolis: University of Minnesota Press, 1988.

Robinson, Lillian. "What Culture Should Mean." *The Nation*, 25 Sept. 1989, pp. 319–21.

Robinson, Lillian. "Are We There Yet?" *Women's Review of Books* 7, no. 3 (Dec. 1989).

Rollins, Judith. *Between Women: Domestics and Their Employers*. Philadelphia, Penn.: Temple University Press, 1985.

Rorty, Richard. "The Old-Time Philosophy." *New Republic*, 4 Apr. 1988.

Rosaldo, Renato. "Others of Invention: Ethnicity and Its Discontents." *Village Voice Literary Supplement*, Feb. 1990.

Ross, Andrew, ed. *Universal Abandon? The Politics of Postmodernism*. Minneapolis: University of Minnesota Press, 1988.

Rossi, Alice S., ed. *The Feminist Papers: From Adams to de Beauvoir*. New York: Bantam, 1973.

Russell, Michele. "Slave Codes and Liner Notes." In *All the Women Are White, All the Blacks Are Men, But Some of Us Are Brave*, edited by Gloria Hull, Patricia Bell Scott, and Barbara Smith. Old Westbury, N.Y.: Feminist Press, 1982.

Said, Edward. "Orientalism Reconsidered." *Race and Class* 27, no. 2 (1985): 1–15.

———. "Representing the Colonized: Anthropology's Interlocutors." *Critical Inquiry* 15 (Winter 1989):205–25.

———. *The World, the Text and the Critic*. Cambridge, Mass.: Harvard University Press, 1983.

Sales, Ruby. "In Our Own Words." Interview. *Women's Review of Books* 7, no. 5 (Feb. 1990):24–25.

Schulman, Sarah. *People in Trouble*. New York: Dutton, 1990.

Scott, Ann Firor. *The Southern Lady: From Pedestal to Politics, 1830–1930*. Chicago: University of Chicago Press, 1970.

"SHE, THE INAPPROPRIATE/D OTHER." *Discourse* 8 (Fall–Winter 1986–87), edited by Trinh T. Minh-ha, Center for Twentieth Century Studies, University of Wisconsin, P.O. Box 413, Milwaukee, Wisconsin 53201. Pp. 3–128.

Simonson, Rick, and Scott Walker, eds. *The Graywolf Annual Five: Multi-cultural Literacy.* St. Paul, Minn.: Graywolf Press, 1988.

"Slipping Through the Cracks: The Status of Black Women." *Review of Black Political Economy* 14, nos. 2 and 3 (1985–86). Special issue.

Smith, Barbara. "Introduction." In *Home Girls: A Black Feminist Anthology,* edited by Barbara Smith. New York: Kitchen Table Women of Color Press, 1983.

———, ed. *Home Girls: A Black Feminist Anthology.* New York: Kitchen Table Women of Color Press.

Sochen, June. *Herstory: A Record of the American Woman's Past.* 2nd ed. Sherman Oaks, Calif.: Alfred Publishing, 1981.

Spelman, Elizabeth. *Inessential Woman: Problems of Exclusion in Feminist Thought.* Boston: Beacon, 1988.

Spillers, Hortense J. "Interstices: A Small Drama of Worlds." In *Pleasure and Danger: Exploring Female Sexuality,* edited by Carole S. Vance. Boston: Routledge, 1984.

Spivak, G. C. "Can the Subaltern Speak?" In *Marxism and the Interpretation of Culture,* edited by Lawrence Grossberg and Cary Nelson. Chicago: University of Illinois Press, 1988.

———. *In Other Worlds: Essays in Cultural Politics.* London: Methuen, 1987.

Spruill, Julia Cherry. *Women's Life and Work in the Southern Colonies.* 1938. Reprint ed., New York: Norton, 1972.

Stack, Carol. *All Our Kin.* New York: Harper, 1974.

Stansell, Christine. "Explosive Intimacy." *The Nation,* 27 Mar. 1989, pp. 417–22.

Stanton, Elizabeth Cady; Susan B. Anthony; and Matilda Joslyn Gage, eds. *History of Women's Suffrage, vol. 2, 1861–1876.* New York: Fowler and Wells, 1881–1922.

Steady, Filomina Chioma, ed. *The Black Woman Cross-Culturally.* Cambridge, Mass.: Schenkman, 1981.

Stephanson, Anders. "Interview with Cornel West." In *Universal Abandon?: The Politics of Postmodernism,* edited by Andrew Ross. Minneapolis: University of Minnesota Press, 1988.

Sterling, Dorothy, ed. *We Are Your Sisters: Black Women in the Nineteenth Century.* New York: Norton, 1984.

Stuckey, Sterling. *Slave Culture: Nationalist Theory and the Foundations of Black America.* New York: Oxford University Press, 1987.

Suleri, Sara. *Meatless Days.* Chicago: University of Chicago Press, 1989.

Tate, Greg. "Cult-Nats Meet Freaky-Deke." *Village Voice Literary Supplement,* Dec. 1986, pp. 5–8.

Teish, Luisah. *Jambalaya: The Natural Woman's Book of Personal Charms and Practical Rituals*. San Francisco, Calif.: Harper & Row, 1985.

Terborg-Penn, Rosalyn. "African Feminism: A Theoretical Approach to the History of Women in the African Diaspora." In *Women in Africa and the African Diaspora*, edited by Rosalyn Terborg-Penn, Sharon Harley, and Andrea Benton Rushing. Washington, D.C.: Howard University Press, 1987.

———. "Discontented Black Feminists: Prelude and Postscript to the Passage of the Nineteenth Amendment." In *Decades of Discontent: The Woman's Movement, 1920–1940*, edited by Lois Scharf and Joan M. Jensen. Westport, Conn.: Greenwood, 1983.

———. "Discrimination Against Afro-American Women in the Woman's Movement, 1830–1920." In *The Afro-American Woman*, edited by Sharon Harley and Rosalyn Terborg-Penn. Port Washington, N.Y.: Kennikat, 1978.

———. "To Find a Place in History." *Women's Review of Books* 2, no. 10 (1985):10–11.

Terrell, Mary Church. *A Colored Woman in a White World*. Washington, D.C.: Ransdell, 1940.

Thompson, Mildred I. *Ida B. Wells-Barnett: An Exploratory Study of an American Black Woman, 1893–1930*. Vol. 15 in Black Women in United States History, edited by Darlene Clark Hine. New York: Carlson Publishing, 1990.

Todorov, Tzvetan. "Stalled Thinkers." *New Republic*, 13 Apr. 1987.

———. "The Philosopher and Everyday." *New Republic*, 14 and 21 Sept. 1987.

Tompkins, Jane. "'Indians': Textualism, Morality, and the Problem of History." In *"Race," Writing and Difference*, edited by Henry Louis Gates, Jr. Chicago: University of Chicago Press, 1985.

"Traveling Theories, Traveling Theorists." *Inscriptions* 5 (1989), edited by James Clifford and Vivek Dhareshwar, Group for the Critical Study of Colonial Discourse and the Center for Cultural Studies, University of California at Santa Cruz, Santa Cruz, California 95064.

Trinh T. Minh-ha. "Introduction." *Discourse* 11, no. 2 (1989), edited by Trinh T. Minh-ha, Center for Twentieth Century Studies, University of Wisconsin, P.O. Box 413, Milwaukee, Wisconsin 53201. Pp. 5–17.

———. *Woman Native Other*. Bloomington: Indiana University Press, 1989.

Turner, Tina. *I Tina*. New York: Avon Books, 1986.

"(Un)Naming Cultures." *Discourse* 11, no. 2 (1989), edited by Trinh T. Minh-ha, Center for Twentieth Century Studies, University of Wisconsin, P.O. Box 413, Milwaukee, Wisconsin 53201. Pp. 5–179.

Vergès, Françoise, letter to author, 1 June 1990.

Walker, Alice. "If the Present Looks Like the Past." In Walker, *In Search of*

Our Mothers' Gardens. San Diego, Calif.: Harcourt Brace Jovanovich, 1984.

———. *In Search of Our Mothers' Gardens.* San Diego, Calif.: Harcourt Brace Jovanovich, 1984.

———. *Meridian.* New York: Harcourt Brace Jovanovich, 1976.

———. "Oppressed Hair Puts a Celing on the Brain." *Ms.,* June 1988.

———. *The Color Purple.* New York: Pocket Books, 1982.

———. *The Temple of My Familiar.* San Diego, Calif.: Harcourt Brace Jovanovich, 1989.

Walker, David. *David Walker's Appeal to the Coloured Citizens of the World,* edited by Charles M. Wiltse. New York: Hill and Wang, 1965.

Wallace, Michele. "A Race Man and a Scholar." *Emerge,* Feb. 1990, pp. 56–61.

———. "She's Gotta Have It, School Daze." *The Nation,* 4 June 1988, pp. 800–803.

———. "When Black Feminism Faces the Music, and the Music is Rap." *New York Times,* 29 July 1990, p. 20H.

Washington, Mary Helen. *Black-Eyed Susans.* Garden City, N.Y.: Anchor Press, 1975.

———. "Harriet Jacobs: The Perils of a Slave Woman's Life." In Mary Helen Washington, *Invented Lives: Narratives of Black Women, 1860–1960.* New York: Doubleday, 1988.

———. *Invented Lives: Narratives of Black Women, 1860–1960.* New York: Doubleday, 1988.

———. "Meditations on History: The Slave Woman's Voice." In Mary Helen Washington, *Invented Lives: Narratives of Black Women, 1860–1960.* New York: Doubleday, 1988.

Weiner, Jon. "Law Profs Fight the Power." *The Nation,* 4 and 11 Sept. 1989.

Wells, Ida B. *Crusade for Justice: The Auto-Biography of Ida B. Wells,* edited by Alfreda M. Duster. Chicago: University of Chicago Press, 1970.

———. *On Lynchings.* New York: Arno Press and New York Times, 1969.

Welter, Barbara. *Dimity Convictions: The American Woman in the Nineteenth Century.* Columbus: University of Ohio Press, 1976.

West, Cornel. "Minority Discourse and the Pitfalls of Canon Formation." *Yale Journal of Criticism* 1, no. 1 (Fall 1987):193–201.

———. "Postmodernism and Black America." *Z Magazine,* June 1988.

———. *Prophesy Deliverance!: An Afro-American Revolutionary Christianity.* Philadelphia, Penn.: Westminster Press, 1982.

———. "Race and Social Theory: Toward a Genealogical Materialist Analysis. In *The Year Left 2.* London: Verso, 1987.

———. "The Crisis of Black Leadership." *Z Magazine,* Feb. 1988.

Wexler, Alice. *Emma Goldman in Exile: From the Russian Revolution to the Spanish Civil War*. Boston: Beacon, 1989.

White, Deborah Gray. *Ar'n't I a Woman?" Female Slaves in the Plantation South*. New York: Norton, 1985.

White, E. Frances. "Listening to the Voices of Black Feminism." *Radical America* 8, nos. 2–3 (1984):7–24.

Wilkins, Roger. "Black Like Us." *Mother Jones*, May 1988.

Williams, Juan. *"Do the Right Thing* Doesn't Say Anything." *Washington Post*, 2 July 1989, p. G1.

Williams, Patricia. "Alchemical Notes: Reconstructing Ideals from Deconstructed Rights." *Harvard Civil Rights-Civil Liberties Law Review* 22 (1987), 401–33.

———. "On Being the Object of Property." *Signs* 14, no. 1 (1988):5–24.

Williams, Sherley Anne. *Dessa Rose*. New York: William Morrow, 1986.

Willis, Ellen. *Beginning to See the Light*. New York: Knopf, 1981.

Wilson, Elizabeth. "Oppositional Dress." In Wilson, *Adorned in Dreams: Fashion and Modernity*. Berkeley: University of California Press, 1985.

Woodward, C. Vann. *The Strange Career of Jim Crow*. 3d ed. New York: Oxford University Press, 1974.

———. *Thinking Back: The Perils of Writing History*. Baton Rouge: Louisiana State University Press, 1986.

Wyatt-Brown, Bertram. "The Sound and the Fury." *New York Review of Books*, 13 March 1986.

Yancy, Dorothy Cowser. "Dorothy Bolden, Organizer of Domestic Workers: She Was Born Poor but She Would Not Bow Down." *Sage: A Scholarly Journal on Black Women* 3, no. 1 (1986):53–55.

Yellin, Jean. "Text and Contexts of Harriet Jacobs's *Incidents in the Life of a Slave Girl: Written by Herself*." In *The Slave's Narrative*, edited by Charles T. Davis and Henry Louis Gates, Jr. New York: Oxford University Press, 1985.

———. *Women and Sisters: Antislavery Feminists in American Culture*. New Haven, Conn.: Yale University Press, 1990.

Young, Iris M. "Difference and Policy: Some Reflections in the Context of New Social Movement." *University of Cincinnati Law Review* 56, no. 2 (1987):535–50.

———. "Humanism, Gynocentrism and Feminist Politics." *Women's Studies International Forum* 8, no. 3 (1985):173–83.

———. "The Ideal of Community and the Politics of Difference." In *Feminism/Postmodernism*, edited by Linda J. Nicholson. New York: Routledge, 1990.

Index

abolitionist movement: impact of on the women's movement, 134–42; racism in, 240–42*n.49*

Achebe, Chinua, 235*n.87*

Adorno, Theodore, 218*n.5*

African-American culture: biblical images in, 49–50. *See also* Black feminist theory; women, Black

African Diaspora, 45–48

Afrocentrism: as element of Black feminist theory, 33, 42–53, 61–62, 68, 72, 175–79, 181–82

Ain't I a Woman? (hooks), 82

Allen, Pamela, 126, 135

Allen, Robert, 126, 135, 141, 144, 243*n.82*

Allen, Woody, 232*n.67*

amendments, constitutional. *See* Constitution, U.S.: amendments to

America: racism in, 248*n.148*

American Anti-Slavery Society, 138

American Women's Suffrage Association (AWSA), 147

Ames, Jessie Daniel, 247*n.143*

Andolsen, Barbara Hilkert, 145–46, 150

Angelou, Maya, 233–34*n.73*

Anthills of the Savannah (Achebe), 235*n.87*

Anthony, Susan B., 117, 138–39, 140–41, 143, 144, 145, 153, 243–44*n.82*; racism of, 147–48, 150, 154–55, 156–57

anti-essentialism, 61, 219*n.21*

Anti-Slavery Convention of American Women, 240*n.49*

Anzaldúa, Gloria, 6, 7, 205*n.2*

appearance. *See* beauty

Appiah, Anthony, 10

Aptheker, Bettina, 4, 66, 134, 138, 146–47, 156, 191, 203, 239*n.23*, 242*n.49*

Arendt, Hannah, 200, 253*n.64*

Association of Southern Women for the Prevention of Lynching, 247*n.143*

Baartman, Saartjie, 223*n.3*

Baker, Augusta, 36

Baldwin, James, 182

Barth, John, 55–56

beauty: ideals of, 11, 12, 78, 81, 88–89, 93–96, 111

Beauty Secrets: Women and the Politics of Appearance (Chapkis), 88–89, 234–35*n.86*

Bell, Derrick, 9

Beloved (Morrison), 44–45, 206*n.13*

Benetton, 235–36*n.88*

Benhabib, Seyla, 70, 199

Benjamin, Walter, 115, 237*n.95*

Bennett, Lerone, 151

Bethel, Lorraine, 107

Bethune, Mary McLeod, 92–93

Between Women (Rollins), 104

biblical images: in African-American
culture, 49–50

Black feminist theory, 1–2, 69–70; and
Afrocentric traditions, 33, 42–53, 62,
68, 72, 175–79, 181–82; analytic skills
of, 8; contribution of to feminist
discourse, 10–11, 53–54; and critics of
postmodern theoretical analysis,
64–69; and dynamics of oppression,
180–82; epistemological concerns of,
31–34; expansions of, 34–41; and
feminist postmodernism, 7, 8–10,
57–60, 62–63, 71–72; from a
historical perspective, 12, 205–6*n.9*;
and legal scholarship, 38–39; Marxist
perspective on, 32, 181; in the nineteenth century, 117–24, 209*n.6*,
239*n.23*; and postcolonial discourse,
26–27, 28–31, 43, 53–54, 176; as
distinguished from white feminism,
5–6, 9, 25–27, 78; white scholar as
interpreter of, 14–22. *See also*
women, Black

Black feminists: biased interpretations
of, 118–24; first wave of, 157–65; lack
of acknowledgment for, 127–34;
methodological critiques by, 125–26.
See also women, Black

The Black Woman Cross-Culturally
(Steady), 47

blues singers, 35–36, 213*n.34*

The Bluest Eye (Morrison), 90, 101,
231*n.65*

Bolden, Dorothy, 102, 223*n.4*, 230*n.63*

Bonner, Marita, 80

Bordo, Susan, 217*n.35*

Breytenbach, Breyton, 16

Brown, Barbara, 231*n.64*

Brown, Charlotte Hawkins, 163

Brown, Elsa Barkley, 33–34, 62, 191,
251*n.50*

Bulkin, Elly, 174–75, 181

Burroughs, Nannie Rice, 128

bus system, Jim Crow, 245*n.103*

Butler, Johnella, 22, 208*n.41*

Carby, Hazel, 60, 87, 124, 152, 157, 159,
161, 227*n.32*

Carillo, Jo, 236–37*n.94*

Cash, W. J., 225*n.7*

Catt, Carrie, 245*n.117*

Chapkis, Wendy, 88–89, 116,
234–35*n.86*

Chapman, Maria Weston, 241*n.49*

Chenzira, Ayoka, 229*n.48*

Chicago Women's Federation, 92

Childress, Alice, 105, 230*nn.61, 64*

Chinese Americans, 20–21

Christian, Barbara, 21, 39, 65, 68

Civil Rights Act of 1875, 151

Cliff, Michelle, 5, 40, 50, 55, 65, 68,
172, 183

Clifford, James, 219*n.21*

"Coalition Politics: Turning the Century" (Reagon), 178

Coalitions. *See* crossover politics

Cocks, Joan, 186–87, 250*n.21*

Collins, Patricia Hill, 31–33, 35, 48–51,
60, 62, 66

colonialism: and self-perceptions of colonized peoples, 28–31, 213*n.38*. *See
also* postcolonial discourse

The Colonizer and the Colonized
(Memmi), 28

The Color Purple (Walker), 35

Combahee River Collective, 176, 185

Connolly, William E., 249*n.10*

Constitution, U.S.: amendments to,
139–40, 142–46, 148

Cooper, Anna Julia, 123, 128–29,
151–54, 164

crossover politics, 171; and multicultural feminism, 172–75, 178–79, 181–82, 193–95, 197, 199–203
Crusade for Justice (Wells), 154

Daughters of Sorrow (Guy-Sheftall), 226n.16
Davis, Angela, 84, 121, 132–33, 137–38
deconstruction. *See* postmodernism
de Lauretis, Teresa, 86, 88, 214n.3
Delgado, Richard, 39
Dessa Rose (Williams), 227n.27
Dhareshwar, Vivek, 219n.21
Dialogue on Woman's Rights (Harper), 158
Diaspora, African. *See* African Diaspora
Di Palma, Carolyn, 234n.85
"Disloyal to Civilization: Feminism, Racism, Gynephobia" (Rich), 81
domestic labor: black women as, 76, 79, 89
Douglass, Frederick, 134, 139, 152, 154; as advocate of universal suffrage, 143–44
Driving Miss Daisy, 230n.61
DuBois, Ellen Carol, 148
Du Bois, W. E. B., 42, 79, 96, 117, 225n.14
Duras, Marguerite, 249n.9

Eagleton, Terry, 181
Elaw, Zilpha, 50–51
Ellison, Ralph, 245n.103
Emancipation Proclamation, 139
Emecheta, Buche, 248n.6
Enloe, Cynthia, 231n.64
Equal Rights Association (ERA), 139, 141, 143, 144, 147
ethnocentrism, 13; and feminist theory, 173–75
Evans, Sarah, 136

Fanon, Frantz Omar, 17
Female Anti-Slavery Society, 125–26, 241n.49, 242n.49

femininity: concepts of, 86–87
feminism, multicultural, 114, 126–27; and crossover politics, 172–75, 178–79, 181–82; in practice, 187–88, 192–93, 195–203; theoretical basis for, 3–4, 193–94
feminism, white. *See* white feminist theory
The Feminist Papers: From Adams to de Beauvoir (Rossi), 128
femnist solidarity. *See* solidarity, feminist
feminist theory: and analytical categories, 220n.34; development of, 214–15n.3; diversity within, 190–93, 195–203, 252n.55; epistemological debate within, 217n.1; ethnocentrism in, 173–75, 217n.35; in the flesh, 3, 171–75; heterogeneity in, 200–201; redefinition of, 124; as a type of postmodern theory, 8–10, 55–57, 219–20n.26, 222–23n.51; white racism in, 1, 120–21, 125–34. *See also* Black feminist theory; women's rights
Feminist Theory: From Margin to Center (hooks), 180
feminist theory, Black. *See* Black feminist theory
feminists, crossover, 12–14, 187–88. *See also* crossover politics
feminists, Third World. *See* Third World feminists
Ferguson, Kathy, 59, 60, 177–78, 208n.35, 217n.1, 219–20n.26, 222–23n.51
Fifteenth Amendment, 140, 142–46, 148, 149
Filler, Louis, 241n.49
Flax, Jane, 55, 57, 181
Flexner, Eleanor, 140, 241n.49
Fortune, Thomas, 159
Foucault, Michel, 8, 30, 62, 69, 216–17n.29, 221n.42

Fourteenth Amendment, 139, 146, 148
Fox-Genovese, Elizabeth, 232–33n.68
Frankenberg, Ruth, 253–54n.72
Frankfurt School of Critical Theory, 218n.5
Fraser, Nancy, 221n.42, 222n.49

Gage, Frances, 132
Garner, Margaret, 44
Garrison, William Lloyd, 117, 125–26, 241n.49
Garvey, Amy Jacques, 129
Geertz, Clifford, 209–10n.14
gender tyrannies, 11; suffered by Black women, 81–86. *See also* women, Black
Giddings, Paula, 120, 129–30, 143, 144–45, 158, 246n.117, 247n.143
Goldman, Emma, 175
Greenlee, Sam, 208n.39
Grimké, Angelina, 117, 136–38
Grimké, Sarah, 117, 130, 136–38
"gumbo ya ya" conversations, 191, 251n.50
Guy-Sheftall, Beverly, 226n.16
Gwaltney, John Langston, 222n.50
Gwin, Minrose, 102, 208n.37

hair: significance of, 93–95, 228n.44, 229n.48
Hall, Jacqueline Dowd, 226n.19
Hamer, Fannie Lou, 43, 89–90, 116, 202
Hannah and Her Sisters, 232n.67
Hansberry, Lorraine, 34, 52
Haraway, Donna, 2, 8, 9, 57–59, 71, 192–93, 248n.6
Harding, Sandra, 57–59, 62–63, 216n.22, 217n.30, 220n.34
Harper, Frances Ellen Watkins, 12, 120, 122–23, 127, 139, 144–45, 149, 152, 157, 158, 159, 162, 167
Harrington, Christine, 252n.57
Harris, Trudier, 100, 226n.19, 230n.61

Hartsock, Nancy, 69, 216–17n.29, 221n.42
Havel, Václav, 254n.75
"Hearts of Darkness" (Omolade), 84–85
hermeneutics of suspicion, 56, 218n.5
Hine, Darlene Clark, 83
A History of Women in America (Hymowitz and Weissman), 122
homophobic attitudes: in the Black community, 183
hooks, bell, 14, 22, 25, 26, 40, 65–66, 77–78, 82, 87, 93–95, 112, 120, 127, 134–35, 180–81, 182, 183–84, 246n.117, 252n.55
Horkheimer, Max, 218n.5
Horton, James Oliver, 225n.13
humanism: feminist posture toward, 69–70
Hurston, Zora Neale, 76–77, 79, 98
Hvizdala, Karel, 254n.75
Hymowitz, Carol, 127, 136

I Know Why the Caged Bird Sings (Angelou), 233–34n.73
Ifekwunigwe, Jayne, 225n.15
Indians, American. *See* Native Americans
Inessential Woman: Problems of Exclusion in Feminist Thought (Spelman), 173, 208n.38
The Invention of Africa (Mudimbe), 30
Irigaray, Luce, 19–20, 173
"isonomy," 253n.64

Jackson, Jesse, 232n.67
Jackson, Lottie Wilson, 150
Jacobs, Harriet, 223–24n.5
JanMohamed, Abdul, 190
Jeffers, Trellie, 96
Jim Crow laws, 150–51, 245n.103
Jones, Jacqueline, 233n.68
Joplin, Janis, 213n.34
Jordan, June, 105–7

Keesing, Roger M., 219*n.20*
Kelly, Abby, 127, 135–36, 146
Kerney, Belle, 153
King, Deborah, 29, 30, 48, 52–53, 63,
 177
King, Mary, 202
Kingston, Maxine Hong, 20–21, 186
kitsch, 177–78, 180
Kraditor, Aileen, 149
Kristeva, Julia, 177
Ku Klux Klan, 151
Kundera, Milan, 177

Lawrence, Clarissa, 240*n.49*
Lazreg, Marnia, 221–22*n.45*
Lee, Spike, 95
legal scholarship: nontraditional approaches to, 38–39
Lerner, Gerda, 91, 132, 234*n.75*, 237*n.2*,
 241*n.49*
lesbian discourse, 234*n.85*
Lincoln, Abbey, 93, 97
Lorde, Audre, 5, 13, 14–15, 25–26, 29,
 54, 60–61, 63, 182–83, 199, 230*n.61*
Love, Nancy, 71, 222*n.51*
Lugones, Maria, 197–98
lynchings, 226*n.19*; political resistance
 to, 159–61, 162–63, 247*n.143*

McCrummell, James, 242*n.49*
Malcolm X, 2, 228*n.44*
Mandela, Nelson, 254*n.74*
Mani, Lata, 226*n.15*
Mann, Susan A., 244*n.82*
Marcuse, Herbert, 218*n.5*
Marshall, Paule, 36, 46
Marxist theory: as perspective on
 feminism, 32, 181
Memmi, Albert, 28–29, 43, 60, 61
men, Black: as advocates of women's
 rights, 241*n.49*; passivity of, 131; sex-
 uality of, 160; suffrage for, 140,
 142–47, 160
Meridian (Walker), 19

mettisage, 208*n.40*
The Mind of the South (Cash), 225*n.7*
Mohanty, Chandra, 188
Mohanty, Satya P., 26, 69–70
Moraga, Cherríe, 6, 7, 171, 205*n.1*,
 249*n.6*
Morrison, Toni, 44–45, 78, 90–91, 101,
 206*n.13*, 216*n.12*, 231*n.65*
Mott, Lucretia, 117, 242*n.49*
Mouffe, Chantal, 193–95
Mudimbe, V. Y., 30, 43, 61, 209*n.12*
multicultural feminism. *See* feminism,
 multicultural
Murray, Pauli, 98, 229*n.55*

National Alliance of Black Feminists, 99
National American Women's Suffrage
 Association (NAWSA), 149–50, 153,
 154, 156, 158
National Woman Suffrage Association
 (NWSA), 147
National Women's Studies Association
 (NWSA), 251–52*n.55*
Native Americans, 151–52, 219*n.25*
NAWSA. *See* National American
 Women's Suffrage Association
negative dialects, 56, 218*n.5*
Nietzsche, Friedrich, 199
The North Star, 144

Ogunyemi, Chikwenye Okonjo, 248*n.6*
Omi, Michael, 16–17, 212*n.25*
Omolade, Barbara, 84–85, 117, 118, 125
"On Being the Object of Property"
 (Williams), 38
oppressed people: perceptions of,
 180–82, 216*n.22*
otherness: politics of, 61–62, 63–64, 182
"others of invention," 3, 205*n.3*

Patterson, Orlando, 91
Paul, Alice, 245–46*n.117*
People, 178
People in Trouble (Schulman), 202

Perkins, Linda, 241*n.49*
perspectivism, 219*n.25*
Phelan, Shane, 201, 234*n.85*
Plessy v. Ferguson, 151
postcolonial discourse, 219*n.21*; and
    Black feminist theory, 26–27, 28–31,
    43, 53–54, 176
postmodernism, 55–72, 218*n.8*; and
    Black feminist theory, 7, 8–10, 57–63,
    64–69, 71–72; and feminist theory,
    55–57, 59
poverty: feminization of, 229*n.58*
power: Foucault's theories about,
    221*n.42*
Pratt, Minnie Bruce, 17, 18
Pryse, Marjorie, 35

Quintanales, Mirtha, 184–85

Rabine, Leslie Wahl, 64
Rable, George, 224–25*n.7*
racism, white, 248*n.148*, 253–54*n.72*;
    impact of on American feminism,
    3–4, 18. *See also* abolitionist move-
    ment; ethnocentrism; suffrage move-
    ment; white feminists
Reagon, Bernice Johnson, 12, 14, 20,
    175, 178–79, 185, 192, 199, 201,
    236*n.89*
rearticulation: process of, 34, 212*n.25*
Reconstruction: political climate of,
    138–39
Red Record (Wells), 160
*Reluctant Reformers: Racism and Social
    Reform Movements in the United
    States* (Allen and Allen), 126
The Revolution, 148
Rich, Adrienne, 75, 81, 88, 99
rights: conceptions of, 194, 252*n.57*
Riley, Denise, 177
Rollins, Judith, 101, 103, 104
Rosaldo, Renato, 51, 205*n.3*, 209*n.12*
Ross, Andrew, 56–57
Rossi, Alice, 128

Ruffin, Josephine St. Pierre, 127, 164
Russell, Michele, 36, 75, 87, 185

*Sage: A Scholarly Journal on Black
    Women*, 45–46
Said, Edward, 27, 33, 53–54, 192
Salem Colored Female Religious and
    Moral Society, 126
Sales, Ruby, 37, 251–52*n.55*
Sammy and Rosie Get Laid, 112
Sandoval, Chela, 58, 174, 248*n.6*
School Daze, 95
Schulman, Sara, 202
The Science Question in Feminism
    (Harding), 216
"The Servant in the House" (Du Bois),
    225*n.14*
sexism. *See* gender tyrannies
sexual abuse: of black women, 76
sexuality: of black men, 160; of black
    women, 82–85, 160
Shange, Ntozake, 36, 37
sharecropping households, 244*n.82*
signs: importance of, 87, 227*n.32*
sisterhood. *See* solidarity, feminist
skin color: significance of, 95–96
"Slave Codes and Liner Notes" (Russell),
    36, 185
slaves: black women as, 76–77, 83–85,
    223*nn.2, 5*; symbolism used against,
    227–28*n.40*. *See also* abolitionist
    movement
Smart-Grosvenor, Vertamae, 36–37
Smith, Barbara, 34
Sochen, June, 246*n.117*
"The Social Construction of Black
    Feminist Thought" (Collins), 31
solidarity, Black, 61, 62, 96
solidarity, feminist, 2–3, 87–88, 106–7,
    193–94, 242*n.49*. *See also* feminism,
    multicultural
The Souls of Black Folks (Du Bois), 42
Southern Horrors (Wells), 160

Spelman, Elizabeth, 173, 195–99, 208*n.38*

Spillers, Hortense, 63, 82–83, 91

Stansell, Christine, 233*n.68*

Stanton, Elizabeth Cady, 117, 138–39, 140–41, 144, 145, 156; racism of, 147–48, 156–57

Steady, Filomina Chioma, 47

Stewart, Maria, 120, 129–31, 136

Stone, Lucy, 127, 145, 147

storytelling, 36–37, 66, 213*n.35*

Stuckey, Sterling, 42

suffrage movement, 12; as divisive issue for white feminists, 134–42; racist tone of, 142–57, 245–46*n.117*

Suleri, Sara, 112

Sweet Honey in the Rock, 43, 175–76, 178, 236*n.89*

Talking Back (hooks), 26

Tapestries of Life (Aptheker), 66, 203

Tarango, Yolanda, 1

Teish, Luisah, 251*n.50*

The Temple of My Familiar (Walker), 35, 44

Terborg-Penn, Rosalyn, 47–48, 121, 154, 158

Terrell, Mary Church, 120, 128, 158, 162, 245–46*n.117*

Their Eyes Were Watching God (Hurston), 76

Third World feminists, 184–85, 208*n.40*, 249*n.6*

Third World people: cultural artifacts of, 111–12, 235–36*n.88*; exploitation of, 236*n.89*; liberation struggles of, 221–22*n.45*; perceptions of, 236–37*n.94*

Thirteenth Amendment, 139

This Bridge Called My Back: Writings by Radical Women of Color (Moraga and Andaldúa), 205*n.2*

Tompkins, Jane, 219*n.25*

Train, George, 148

Trinh T. Minh-ha, 1, 15–16, 112–13, 186

Tripmaster Monkey (Kingston), 20, 186

Tronto, Joan, 222*n.51*

Truth, Sojourner, 118, 125, 131–33, 143, 223*n.2*

Tubman, Harriet, 118, 125, 176

Turner, Ike, 237*n.96*

Turner, Tina, 116, 237*n.96*

The Unbearable Lightness of Being (Kundera), 177–78

Vergès, Françoise, 208*n.40*

A Voice from the South by a Black Woman of the South (Cooper), 123

voting rights. *See* Fifteenth Amendment; suffrage movement

Waianaie Women's Support Group, 15

Walker, Alice, 19, 35, 44, 68, 72, 93–94, 98, 183, 203

Walker, David, 222*n.45*

Walker, Maggie Lena, 64

Washington, Mary Helen, 69, 107, 108

Weissman, Michaele, 127, 136

Wells, Ida B., 154–55, 159–61

West, Cornel, 6, 27, 67–68, 205–6*n.9*, 208*n.39*

"What Would I Do White?" (Jordan), 107

When and Where I Enter: The Impact of Black Women on Race and Sex in America (Giddings), 129–30

White, Deborah Gray, 223*n.2*

White, Frances, 148

white culture: perceptions of, 189–90

white feminist theory: as distinguished from Black feminist theory, 5–6; homogenizing tendencies of, 188

white feminists: as advocates of universal suffrage, 139; as interpreters of Black feminist theory, 14–22, 25–27, 78; as opponents of slavery, 134–38, 139, 142; perceptions of, 110; racism

white feminists (*continued*)
of, 140–41, 142–48, 150, 152–53,
154–55, 156–57, 195, 202, 244*n.92*;
Spelman's perceptions of, 195–99;
and victimization of Black women,
80, 87–88, 108–9, 165–66. *See also*
women, white
Wilkins, Roger, 216*n.14*
Williams, Fannie Barrier, 124, 158, 162
Williams, Patricia, 9, 38, 42, 71,
235–36*n.88*, 249*n.11*, 252*n.57*
Williams, Sherley Anne, 227*n.27*
Willis, Ellen, 213*n.34*
Winant, Howard, 16–17, 212*n.25*
Within the Plantation Household (Fox-
Genovese), 232–33*n.68*
Woman Native Other (Trinh), 15
women: communication among, 15–16;
nineteenth century perceptions of,
224–25*n.7*
women, Black: activism of, 157–65; as
blues singers, 35–36, 213*n.34*; as
domestic labor, 76, 79, 89, 99–109,
225*n.14*, 230–31*n.64*, 231–32*n.65*,
234*nn.75, 76*; early feminism of,
125–34, 166–67, 239*n.23*; empowerment of, 29, 80, 97, 113; exclusionary
practices of, 13; images projected by,
109–16; lack of commonality among,
183–84; misperceptions of, 81–86,
91–92, 109; self-image of, 91–98; sexuality of, 82–85, 160; as slaves,
76–77, 83–85, 223*nn.2, 5*; socialization of to white norms, 225*n.13*;

status of, 229*n.59*; as storytellers,
36–37, 213*n.35*; subordination of, 11,
75–81, 225–26*n.15*, 226*n.16*,
247*n.140*; white women's indifference to, 162–66. *See also* Black
feminist theory; suffrage movement
women, white: as abolitionists,
240–42*n.49*, 247*n.140*; culpability of,
90, 100, 116, 162–66; elevation of, 77;
images of, 114; perceptions of,
189–90, 224–25*n.7*; relationships of
with Black women, 86, 102–3,
104–5, 232–33*n.68*; stereotypes of,
18–19, 107–8. *See also* white feminist
theory; white feminists
women of color: identification of,
173–75, 248–49*n.6*. *See also* women,
Black
Women's Loyalty League, 139
women's movement: and abolitionist
movement, 134–42, 240–42*n.49*;
early history of, 117–24; and slavery
issue, 134–42. *See also* suffrage
movement
Woodward, C. Vann, 166
Woolf, Virginia, 130
World's Congress of Representative
Women, 159

Yellin, Jean Fagan, 247*n.140*
Yes Ma'am, 231*n.64*
Young, Iris, 61, 69, 199–201, 207*n.22*,
220*n.30*